Modern Critical Views

Edward Albee

African American
   Poets Volume I

American and
   Canadian Women
   Poets, 1930–present

American Women
   Poets, 1650–1950

Maya Angelou

Asian-American
   Writers

Margaret Atwood

Jane Austen

James Baldwin

Samuel Beckett

Saul Bellow

The Bible

William Blake

Jorge Luis Borges

Ray Bradbury

The Brontës

Gwendolyn Brooks

Elizabeth Barrett
   Browning

Robert Browning

Italo Calvino

Albert Camus

Lewis Carroll

Willa Cather

Cervantes

Geoffrey Chaucer

Anton Chekhov

Kate Chopin

Agatha Christie

Samuel Taylor
   Coleridge

Joseph Conrad

Contemporary Poets

Stephen Crane

Dante

Daniel Defoe

Charles Dickens

Emily Dickinson

John Donne and the
   17th-Century Poets

Fyodor Dostoevsky

W.E.B. Du Bois

George Eliot

T. S. Eliot

Ralph Ellison

Ralph Waldo Emerson

William Faulkner

F. Scott Fitzgerald

Sigmund Freud

Robert Frost

George Gordon, Lord
   Byron

Graham Greene

Thomas Hardy

Nathaniel Hawthorne

Ernest Hemingway

Hispanic-American
   Writers

Homer

Langston Hughes

Zora Neale Hurston

Henrik Ibsen

John Irving

Henry James

James Joyce

Franz Kafka

John Keats

Jamaica Kincaid

Stephen King

Rudyard Kipling

D. H. Lawrence

Ursula K. Le Guin

Sinclair Lewis

Bernard Malamud

Christopher Marlowe

Gabriel García
   Márquez

Cormac McCarthy

Carson McCullers

Herman Melville

Molière

Arthur Miller

John Milton

Molière

Toni Morrison

Native-American
   Writers

Joyce Carol Oates

Flannery O'Connor

Eugene O'Neill

George Orwell

Octavio Paz

Sylvia Plath

Edgar Allan Poe

Katherine Anne
   Porter

J. D. Salinger

Jean-Paul Sartre

William Shakespeare:
   Histories and
   Poems

William Shakespeare:
   Romances

William Shakespeare:
   The Comedies

William Shakespeare:
   The Tragedies

George Bernard Shaw

Mary Wollstonecraft
   Shelley

Percy Bysshe Shelley

Alexander
   Solzhenitsyn

Sophocles

John Steinbeck

Tom Stoppard

Jonathan Swift

Amy Tan

Alfred, Lord Tennyson

Henry David Thoreau

J. R. R. Tolkien

Leo Tolstoy

Mark Twain

John Updike

Modern Critical Views

Modern Critical Views

AMERICAN WOMEN POETS
1650–1950

Edited and with an introduction by

Harold Bloom

Sterling Professor of the Humanities
Yale University

CHELSEA HOUSE PUBLISHERS
Philadelphia

©2002 by Chelsea House Publishers,
a subsidiary of Haights Cross Communications.

Introduction © 2001 by Harold Bloom.

Printed and bound in the United States of America

10 9 8 7 6 5 4 3 2

Library of Congress Cataloging-in-Publication Data
applied for

ISBN 0-7910-6330-5

Chelsea House Publishers
1974 Sproul Road, Suite 400
Broomall, PA 19008-0914

www.chelseahouse.com

Contents

Editor's Note

This volume gathers together what in its editor's judgment represents the best criticism yet published upon the principal American women poets, from Anne Bradstreet to Louise Bogan. The editor is grateful to Karin Cope for her erudition and insight, which helped him in locating and choosing the essays included here. Three essays have been devoted to Emily Dickinson and two each to Marianne Moore and Louise Bogan. The remaining poets each receive one essay in criticism.

Anne Bradstreet, the first considerable American poet, is shrewdly analyzed by Jane Donahue Eberwein as a master of rhetoric who, like Emily Dickinson, "contrived to sound meek and vulnerable, even in the act of choosing among crowns." Dickinson herself is introduced here in an essay by Shira Wolosky that advances our apprehension of the poet's spiritual agon "with and against God . . . , the clash between his language and her own." Another aspect of this agon is illuminated by Joanne Feit Diehl in her study of language as defense in Dickinson, as the poet "explores the possibilities for a poetics that yields nothing to forces beyond the self." A trinity of Dickinsonian critiques is completed here by Sharon Cameron's analysis of the tangled relationships in the poetry between problematical representation, death, and the trope of boundary.

Gertrude Stein's poetry (and fictive prose) is examined by Randa K. Dubnick, who distinguishes between two modes of obscurity in Stein, one not unwillful, and one which "was a necessary consequence of the nature of her innovative experiment with language." H. D. (Hilda Doolittle), Stein's younger contemporary, receives consideration of a kind she would have welcomed, in Adalaide Morris's essay that relates Freud's mechanism of defense, projection, to the poet's visionary powers. On Marianne Moore, one of the major poets of H. D.'s generation, two very different but complementary essays are offered here. Bonnie Costello's innovative investigation of what Eliot, Jarrell, and Blackmur had termed Moore's "feminine" language concludes rightly that: "No container will hold her gusto." Humility, affection, and reserve are thus judged not to be "feminine" or passive qualities "but dynamic and vital modes of response." David Bromwich concentrates on Moore's affinities with the early Stevens and the early Eliot, like her explorers of the border between the visual and the visionary.

Two essays on Louise Bogan present very different emphases. Diane Wood Middlebrook analyzes Bogan's private mythology that "expresses a felt contradiction between writing and living a woman's life." Sandra Cookson, investigating quest images in Bogart, uncovers a pattern of repression in Bogan in which, as Bogan puts it, "the repressed becomes the poem."

Introduction

I

A tradition of poets that includes Emily Dickinson, Marianne Moore, and Elizabeth Bishop has a palpable distinction, but it may be too soon to speak or write of a canon of "American Women Poets." The sixteen American and two Canadian poets studied in these volumes are not chosen arbitrarily, yet considerations of the books' lengths as well as of the poets' canonical probability have entered into my selection. I regret the omission of Léonie Adams, Muriel Rukeyser, Sandra McPherson, Grace Schulman, Josephine Miles, Maxine Kumin, Mona Van Duyn, and several others, while various critics and readers might have included Amy Lowell, Sara Teasdale, Elinor Wylie, Edna St. Vincent Millay, and a large group of our contemporaries. But the eighteen poets studied here do seem a central grouping, and the canonical process is always an ongoing one anyway. Future editions of these volumes may be relied upon to correct emphases and clarify choices.

Two distinguished critics of literature by women, Sandra M. Gilbert and Susan Gubar, have taught us to speak of "the tradition in English," yet with characteristic fairness they quote the great poet Elizabeth Bishop's denial of such a tradition:

> Undoubtedly gender does play an important part in the making of any art, but art is art and to separate writings, paintings, musical compositions, etc., into two sexes is to emphasize values in them that are *not* art.

Bishop, a subtle intellect, makes clear that gender is a source of *values* in the genesis of art, but asserts that such values are not in themselves

1

aesthetic. Though my inclination is to agree with her, I am wary of arguing against the tendency of origins to turn into ends or aims in the genealogy of imagination. Since I myself am frequently misunderstood on this point by feminist critics (though never, I am happy to say, by Gilbert and Gubar) I have a certain desire to illuminate the matter. Most Western poetry has been what Gertrude Stein called "patriarchal poetry," and most Western criticism necessarily has been patriarchal also. If Dr. Samuel Johnson, William Hazlitt, Ralph Waldo Emerson, and Dr. Sigmund Freud are to be considered patriarchal, then I as their ephebe presumably must be patriarchal also. So be it. But such a coloring or troping of critical stance is descriptive rather than prescriptive. Most strong Western poets, for whatever reasons, have been male: Homer and the Yahwist presumably, and certainly Virgil, Lucretius, Horace, on through Dante, Petrarch, and Chaucer to Shakespeare, Spenser, Milton, Pope, Wordsworth, Goethe, Shelley, Leopardi, Hugo, Whitman, Baudelaire, Browning, Yeats, Rilke, Stevens, and so many more. To this day, the only woman poet in English of that stature is Dickinson. Not every poet studied in these volumes seem to me of proven achievement; I have grave reservations about Plath and one or two others. Moore and Bishop, while hardly comparable to Dickinson, seem to me beyond dispute, and so do Jay Macpherson, May Swenson, and Vicki Hearne, but there are problematic aspects to many of the others.

However, there are values also, in nearly all the others, that seem to me rather different from the qualities of their strongest male contemporaries, and some of those differences do ensue from a vision, an experiential and rhetorical stance, that has its origin in sexual difference. To locate the differences in stance seems to me the admirable enterprise of the best feminist literary criticism. That polemic and ideology should be so overt in much feminist literary criticism is understandable, and unfortunately aesthetic considerations sometimes are submerged in political and programmatic designs, but nothing is got for nothing, and I foresee that the emphases of feminist criticism will be modified by the success of that criticism. Though I will attempt to isolate differences in vision from male precursors in the two poets I will discuss in this introduction, I am aware that I am a patriarchal critic, and I will not attempt to mask my own sense of the dilemmas confronted by women poets and poetry in what follows.

II

It is appropriate that the first considerable American poet should have been a woman, Anne Bradstreet, who addressed her own book with a charming sense of the difference involved in being a woman poet:

> If for thy father asked, say thou hadst none;
> And for thy mother, she alas is poor,
> Which caused her thus to send thee out of door.

A comparison of Bradstreet with Quarles, her indubitable if unexciting precursor, would reveal his greater skill at craft and her far more interesting poetic and human personality. Whether one wishes to believe, with the feminist critic Wendy Martin, that Bradstreet's poetry constitutes a mode of "subversive piety" may depend upon the ideological perspective of the individual reader. But she certainly had more wit, vitality, and humanity, in herself and in her poems, than Quarles possessed.

No American poet, except Walt Whitman, to this day is Emily Dickinson's peer, so that in moving from Bradstreet to Dickinson we enter upon the mystery of what will always remain, beyond all ironies, the American Sublime. Attempts to find women precursors for Dickinson are not likely ever to prove persuasive. Her agon, immense and capable, is with Emerson and with the High Romantic poets, and ultimately with the Bible itself. To undertake such a struggle is beyond the capacity of any American poet except for Dickinson and Whitman, even of Wallace Stevens. Whitman's subtle inventiveness, his uncanny mastery of figuration and nuances of diction, above all his astonishing powers of regenerating multiple selves out of his own abyss of being, more than compensate for his relative lack of cognitive strength. Dickinson is cognitively so endowed, and so original, that her only peers among poets writing in English might be Shakespeare, Milton, and Blake. Like them, she reconceptualizes very nearly every idea she considers, and more in the overt mode of Milton and of Blake than in Shakespeare's extraordinary and deftly misleading manner. Like Milton and the High Romantics, she excels at the difficult art of making herself prior to what genetically precedes her. Consider the remarkable poem 290:

> Of Bronze—and Blaze—
> The North—Tonight—

So adequate—it forms—
So preconcerted with itself—
So distant—to alarms—
An Unconcern so sovereign
To Universe, or me—
Infects my simple spirit
With Taints of Majesty—
Till I take vaster attitudes—
And strut upon my stem—
Disdaining Men, and Oxygen,
For Arrogance of them—

My splendors, are Menagerie—
But their Competeless Show
Will entertain the Centuries
When I, am long ago,
An Island in dishonored Grass—
Whom none but Beetles—know.

This overtly is "about" the northern lights, but actually is mediated by Emerson's essay, "The Poet" (1843):

For it is not metres, but a metre-making argument, that makes a poem,—a thought so passionate and alive, that, like the spirit of a plant or an animal, it has an architecture of its own, and adorns nature with a new thing. The thought and the form are equal in order of time, but in the order of genesis the thought is prior to the form. The poet has a new thought: he has a whole new experience to unfold; he will tell us how it was with him, and all men will be the richer in his fortune. For, the experience of each new age requires a new confession, and the world seems always waiting for its poet. I remember, when I was young, how much I was moved one morning by tidings that genius had appeared in a youth who sat near me at table. He had left his work, and gone rambling none knew whither, and had written hundreds of lines, but could not tell whether that which was in him was therein told: he could tell nothing but that all was changed,—man, beast, heaven, earth, and sea. How gladly we listened! how credulous! Society seemed to be compromised. We sat in the aurora of a sunrise which was to put out all the stars. Boston seemed to be at twice the distance it had the night before, or was much farther than that. Rome, —what was Rome? Plutarch and Shakespeare were in the yellow leaf, and Homer no more should be heard of. It is much to know that poetry has been written this very day, under this very roof, by your side. What! that wonderful spirit has not expired! these stony moments are still sparkling and animated! I had fancied that the oracles were all silent, and nature had spent her fires, and behold! all night, from every pore, these fine auroras have been streaming.

Emerson is frolicking here, and yet his thought is so passionate and alive, his meter-making argument so compelling, that his little fable of the youth has its darker side also. The image of the aurora begins here as dawn, indeed an apocalyptic sunrise that might dim all the stars for good, but by a marvelous crossing is transformed into the aurora borealis proper, streaming from every pore of the night. The northern lights therefore represent, for Emerson, a reversal of belatedness into earliness, executed here with superb irony, since the belatedness belongs to Shakespeare and Homer, and the earliness to "a youth who sat near me at table."

Dickinson, frequently deft at taking hints from Emerson and then swerving away from them (in a process ably studied by Joanne Feit Diehl), seems to have taken the hint with more than usual dialectical agility in "Of Bronze—and Blaze—." I no longer agree with Charles R. Anderson's strong commentary upon this poem, which interprets its teaching as being that "the mortal poet corrupts his true nature if he attempts to be divine" and that "the poet must remain earth-bound." That tends to negate Dickinson's subtler ironies, which dominate the poem. The North, meaning the night sky and the auroras streaming through it, is so adequate as to overwhelm what might seem adequate desire to Dickinson, and infects her "simple spirit" with sublime longings. Her own bronze and blaze becomes the rhetorical stance of her poetry, which rises to the heights ("vaster attitudes") in order to manifest a sovereign unconcern all her own. Certainly the crucial irony is in "And strut upon my stem," which is a negative or downward metamorphosis, but only of the natural woman, as it were, and not of the poet. To say that her Splendors are Menagerie is indeed to admit that she is a performer, but the ancient Pindaric assertion of canonical renown and poetic survival follows with enormous authority. To be a "Competelesss Show," able to entertain the centuries, indeed is to be preconcerted with oneself, to be distant to alarms, even to the prophecy of one's organic fate.

Why do we apprehend, beyond error, that "Of Bronze—and Blaze" was written by a woman? In a way more singular and persuasive than any other woman poet has managed (at least since Sappho), Dickinson in scores of her strongest poems compels us to confront the part that gender plays in her poetic identity:

> The Tint I cannot take—is best—
> The Color too remote
> That I could show it in Bazaar—
> A Guinea at a sight—
>
> The fine—impalpable Array—
> That swaggers on the eye
> Like Cleopatra's Company—
> Repeated—in the sky—
>
> The Moments of Dominion
> That happen on the Soul
> And leave it with a Discontent
> Too exquisite—to tell—
>
> The eager look—on Landscapes—
> As if they just repressed
> Some Secret—that was pushing
> Like Chariots—in the Vest—
>
> The Pleading of the Summer—
> That other Prank—of Snow—
> That Cushions Mystery with Tulle,
> For fear the Squirrels—know.
>
> Their Graspless manners—mock us—
> Until the Cheated Eye
> Shuts arrogantly—in the Grave
> Another way—to see—

"Of Bronze—and Blaze" does not quite name the auroras, which is a typical procedure for Dickinson. "The Tint I cannot take—is best" goes further and avoids naming anything. American male theorists and poets from Emerson and Whitman through Stevens and W. C. Williams are programmatic in urging an unnaming upon us, and Stevens in particular achieves some of his greatest effects in that mode:

> This is nothing until in a single man contained,
> Nothing until this named thing nameless is
> And is destroyed. He opens the door of his house
>
> On flames. The scholar of one candle sees
> An Arctic effulgence flaring on the frame
> Of everything he is. And he feels afraid.

This is the crisis of "The Auroras of Autumn," where "this named thing" is the aurora borealis, which flames forth to frighten the poet or scholar of one candle and so undoes his attempt to enact the program of unnaming. But Dickinson, shrewdly exploiting her identity as woman poet, chooses another way to see, a way that unnames without defiance or struggle. The best tint is what she cannot take, too remote for showing, impalpable, too exquisite to tell, secret, graspless. Such a tint seems unavailable to the eye of the male poet, even to a Keats or a Shelley, even to Wordsworth's extraordinary mediation between the visual and the visionary. No woman poet since Dickinson has had the power to teach us so urgently and intuifively that women need not see as men see, need not will as men will, need not appropriate for themselves as men perhaps need to do. Freud, when he sadly admitted that women were a mystery, echoed the bafflement of Milton, and might have been echoing Blake. Only three men who wrote in English—Chaucer, Shakespeare, Samuel Richardson—seem able to convey the sense of a difference between women and men in a way comparable to the greatest women writers in the language, Jane Austen, George Eliot, Dickinson. If Austen is comparable to Chaucer as a craftsman in irony and George Eliot comparable to Richardson as a moral psychologist of the Protestant temperament, then Dickinson is quite comparable to some of the subtlest aspects of Shakespearean representation. Without Shakespeare, our sense of reality would be much diminished. Without Dickinson, our sense of reality might not be diminished, but we would know far less than we do about the sufferings and the satisfactions of a really isolated consciousness at its highest powers, particularly if it were the consciousness of a woman.

JANE DONAHUE EBERWEIN

"No rhet'ric we expect":
Argumentation in Bradstreet's "The Prologue"

For an acknowledgment of a poet's simple capacities and modest literary goals, Anne Bradstreet's "The Prologue" elicits strangely varied responses—especially in regard to voice and tone. Is the poet humbly submissive or bitterly angry? Is she self-deprecating and self-denigrating, as some readers find, or a prefeminist champion of her sex? Both extremes find textual justification, depending on the weight one accords her admittedly blemished muse or her anticipated parsley wreath. Perhaps, as Elizabeth Wade White and Robert Arner have suggested, the poem divides structurally and tonally at stanza five, with the first half lamenting the poet's inferiority to male writers and the second half asserting, nonetheless, her right as a woman to express herself in verse. The tension between Bradstreet's modest disclaimers and her spirited self-defense runs through the poem, however; it may be found implicitly in the first stanza and explicitly in the last, and it permeates the language and logic of all "The Prologue." Only by reading the poem as consistently ironic can we hope to appreciate Bradstreet's conscious artfulness in deploying both sides of the argument: inviting both male and female champions (and the vast majority of more tolerant readers) to approach her writing with respect.

As the name indicates, this is a prologue designed to introduce the author to her readers while whetting their interest in the more substantive

From *Early American Literature 16*, no. 1 (Spring 1981). © 1981 by University of Massachusetts.

poems to follow. She proceeds by negation, telling what she cannot hope to do:

> To sing of wars, of captains, and of kings,
> Of cities founded, commonwealths begun,
> For my mean pen are too superior things.

But, if we expect her to anticipate Barlow in turning from lofty historical themes to choose "a virgin theme, unconscious of the Muse," we will be unprepared for the succeeding poems. "The Prologue" was never meant to introduce Bradstreet's love poems or meditations; it was written directly for "The Four Monarchies" and was then prefixed to the four quaternions as well as the historical surveys in the opening section of *The Tenth Muse*. Despite her disclaimer, then, Bradstreet proceeded directly to write on the subjects she so pointedly reserved for poets and historians. The opening lines introduce an ironic counterpointing of claimed incapacity and demonstrated command which would enliven the whole poem.

The key to Bradstreet's strategy in preceding her lengthy, laborious, learned scholarly poems with this engaging prologue comes in the opening of stanza three: "From schoolboy's tongue no rhet'ric we expect." Like so many parts of the poem, this line has dual implications. We do not, in fact, count on hearing eloquent orations from schoolchildren, but we must recall that Bradstreet's contemporaries expected, in the sense of looked forward to, such skill as a probable outcome of the boy's education. From grammar, the student would proceed in course through the rest of the trivium: logic and rhetoric. In likening herself to the schoolboy, the poet suggests her own capacity to advance in the verbal arts—especially the art of persuasion. When we do not expect rhetoric, we may not even notice it; but we can be influenced by it, despite ourselves. As Henry Peacham wrote in the 1593 *Garden of Eloquence*, "By the benefit of this excellent gift, (I meane of apt speech given by nature, and guided by Art) wisedome appeareth in her beautie, sheweth her maiestie, and exerciseth her power, working in the minde of the hearer, partly by a pleasant proportion . . . and partly by the secret and mightie power of perswasion after a most wonderfull manner." Bradstreet praised apt speech given by nature and guided by Art in "The Prologue" and demonstrated it as well, keeping a pleasant proportion between instruction and delight to achieve a secret but significant power of persuasion. By recognizing her dexterity in manipulating logic and rhetoric, by remembering Rosamund Rosenmeier's caution that we must read Bradstreet as "someone accustomed to thinking figurally," and by responding to her varied cultural allusions, we can appreciate the complexity and sophistication of her apparently simple argument.

Like most of Bradstreet's successful poems, "The Prologue" is an argument: an attempt to articulate and reconcile opposition by emphasizing discrepancies while hinting at unity. As Ann Stanford has noted, the histories which "The Prologue" introduces fail as literature partly because they lack the tension the poet knew how to achieve when she engaged an I-narrator in vigorous argumentation. Unlike the quaternions, in each of which the four speakers demonstrate a different argumentative method, "The Four Monarchies" proceeds by discursive, impersonal narration. Bradstreet may have needed the chance to spar off against assumed sexist opponents in order to release the energy and excitement her familiar readers would anticipate in a new grouping of her poems.

With whom is Bradstreet actually arguing here? Certainly not with Thomas Dudley and the circle of admiring friends among whom she circulated her manuscripts. Textual analysis shows no direct personal address until stanza seven, when she says, "Preeminence in all and each is yours" to an inclusive audience of the whole male sex; but the apostrophe in stanza eight addresses a different you, limited to the great poets: "ye high flown quills that soar the skies." Her debate, however, seems to be with other antagonists—each "carping tongue" who belittles "female wits." Who those carping tongues might be remains a question. Although Jeannine Hensley, Elizabeth Wade White, and Ann Stanford all assume the reality of such criticism, they offer no specific examples. Those who sympathize with the poet's presumed cultural isolation as a frontier woman artist speak of the pain she "must have" felt and the insults she "must have" endured—linking her with Anne Hutchinson and Anne Hopkins, two well-documented examples of Puritan women who suffered for their intellectual aspirations. Yet Hensley admits that "we have no contemporary reference to her or her poetry which is not somewhere between admiration and adulation." There is simply no evidence of the attacks to which she retorts in "The Prologue."

The carping tongues, probably imagined, offered a useful opportunity for forceful, witty expression in this ironic battle of the sexes. Straw men, they were set up only to be knocked down. None of the deference Bradstreet shows in passages of the poem was meant for them. Her expressions of humility, presumably sincere acknowledgments of inferiority, were directed to recognized literary greats: Du Bartas, her poetic model; Demosthenes; perhaps Virgil; and all "ye high flown quills that soar the skies, / And ever with your prey still catch your praise." Long before Franklin, Bradstreet discovered that one could achieve the appearance of humility (and its rhetorical effect in placating a suspicious audience) by emulating the loftiest models and confessing failure.

Unlike Bradstreet's formal debate poems in which the contenders successively advance their individual cases, "The Prologue" maintains argumentative tension by its deft ordering of assertions and its ambiguous juxtapositions of ideas. Bradstreet develops both cases together, often seeming to capitulate to her opposition. But any male supremacist who read happily along, imagining no threat to his smugness, would eventually find his case pressed to the point of absurdity, while a more alert or ironic reader would be delighted throughout by the poet's cleverness in charming while outwitting her antagonist. If "The Prologue" was intended to win readers for the histories while building affection and respect for the poet, it served its purpose.

Beginning boldly with her echo of Virgil, Bradstreet immediately disclaims her obvious purpose. She had, indeed, written of wars, captains, kings, cities, and commonwealths, though not in the epic strains a reader might expect from one who thought of poesy as "Calliope's own child." Reference to her "obscure lines" could hardly disguise her purpose, at least for any reader with enough foresight to glance ahead into the book. Like Chaucer's "I can namore," this statement deflects attention only slightly from the author's plan to develop the supposedly forsaken topic at great length.

Further developing the sense of authorial humility, Bradstreet moved into a sincere tribute to Du Bartas, still her poetic master. The admiration, however, was that which an aspiring writer of either sex might feel for an established poet. Such expressions of poetic inadequacy to a great theme and inferiority to a major writer were common among authors known to Bradstreet, and there is no reason to interpret her praise as specifically female submissiveness. In his dedicatory verse to *The Tenth Muse*, we should recall, John Woodbridge indited a parallel passage to acknowledge his inability to emulate Bradstreet herself.

> What I (poor silly I) prefix therefore,
> Can but do this, make yours admired the more;
> And if but only this I do attain,
> Content, that my disgrace may be your gain.

Praising Du Bartas's choice of subject matter, his "sugared lines," and even his "overfluent store" of verse, Bradstreet—"simple I"—called attention to qualities which she could reasonably hope to imitate according to her skill. And skill is a revealing word, placing emphasis on craftsmanship, which could be developed, rather than natural gifts, which might have been denied. "The Prologue" is itself a display of poetic skill, technically more artful than the histories or quaternions with their monotonous couplets. The stanzaic pattern, the sound effects, and the rhetorical devices of "The Prologue" consistently qualify its author's pretensions to simplicity.

The next stanza sounds more sincerely self-deprecating with its imagery of "broken strings" in a musical instrument and "a main defect" in an aesthetic structure. Bradstreet speaks of her "foolish, broken, blemished Muse" and acknowledges irreparable limitations. People have no right to expect music, she asserts, in cases where nature has denied some essential power.

Yet her next example, Demosthenes, reverses the conclusion drawn in stanza three. Surely a congenital speech impediment seems a natural defect precluding oratorical success. But art, in this case purposeful, concentrated, sustained self-discipline, led first to clarity and then to fluency and sweetness. With any natural endowment at all, then, Bradstreet shows that an ambitious artist can achieve excellence. Art corrects nature, except for the "weak or wounded brain" which "admits no cure." Readers who divide the poem structurally at this halfway point see the first four stanzas as submissive and self-abasing—especially the final line. Perhaps the statements are self-critical but only in the sense that she submits to the artistic claims of recognized literary masters and recognizes faults in herself which can be corrected through the stylistic apprenticeship on which she has already embarked, as anyone could discover by reading the poems introduced by "The Prologue." Only if she claims the weak and wounded brain as self-description need we interpret this part of the poem as an expression of defeat.

Note, however, that mention of weak and wounded brains leads Bradstreet directly to reflection on carping tongues, which may well articulate idiocy. At this point, she joins battle with her supposed critics and stops comparing herself with writers who deserve her respect. These scolds who would restrict a woman to domestic activities turn out to be contemptuous of thought and imagination in any form—not just when offered by a female wit. They refuse to look at evidence ("If what I do prove well . . ."), and they mistake skill for chance. Confronted with the analogy the Greeks drew between femininity and artistic inspiration as embodied in the Muses, they cut a Gordian knot with their brute disregard for cultural intricacies. Those who say that "The Greeks did nought, but play the fools and lie" demonstrate contempt for fiction and deadness to poetry. They can hardly be the readers she hoped to draw further into her manuscript, but in travestying their claims she might hope to entertain or even impress her proper audience.

In stanza seven Bradstreet spins out the clumsy assertions of her fancied enemies to the extreme limits of logical fallacy. "Let Greeks be Greeks, and women what they are," she begins as if to capitulate gracefully. But Greeks and women need not be regarded as mutually exclusive categories. Attentive readers, like John Woodbridge, could think of Sappho. The carpers, of course, could drift rapidly along, caught in a tidal wave of ironic concessions. Although it would be "but vain" for women "unjustly to wage war," it might at times be appropriate to rally female energies in justified aggression. The poet who seems to be calming tensions here and promising peace is the same author who later in *The Tenth Muse* let gracious young New England challenge her despondent mother with a decidedly militant call to arms:

> These are the days the Church's foes to crush,
> To root out Popelings head, tail, branch, and rush;
> Let's bring Baal's vestments forth to make a fire,
> Their miters, surplices, and all their tire,
> Copes, rochets, crosiers, and such empty trash,
> And let their names consume, but let the flash
> Light Christendom, and all the world to see
> We hate Rome's whore with all her trumpery.

Bradstreet completes the logical undoing of her opponents by wheeling in a veritable Trojan Horse to confirm the tentative peace. "Men can do best, and women know it well," she proclaims—right in the prologue to a series of history poems which will parade before her readers an astounding chronicle of disasters, defeats, and depravities involving both men and women rulers but featuring the generally more powerful males. Although Bradstreet gave greater attention to women rulers in her poems than she found in Raleigh's history, she never attempted to show one sex as morally or even politically superior in the use of power; certainly "The Four Monarchies" rebuts her generalization in "The Prologue," however, and indicates its irony. The crowning joke comes next, when she admits "Preeminence in all and each is yours." By extending claims of male supremacy to all areas of human experience, she seems to dismiss hopes for female excellence in government, oratory, and poetry while acknowledging male dominion in everything; presumably even needlework and childbearing.

This apparent capitulation to the irrational claims of her imagined critics violates common sense, of course, and conflicts as well with the argumentative pattern of the quaternions in which each element, humor, age, and season admits weaknesses as well as strengths. The resolution of these conflicts comes from a recognition of complementary functions, from awareness of multiple contributions to a final desired unity. The same reasoning characterizes Bradstreet's marriage poems, where husband and wife appear as mutually dependent and supportive partners. To restrict women from literature, then, or even from historical narration would be folly. The battle of the sexes, like the debates of the elements and humors, should never be won.

After this deft lobotomy of weak or wounded brains, Bradstreet concludes "The Prologue" with a modest but confident declaration of her literary hopes. In the final stanza she invokes the world's great writers in lines which themselves fly and flash with the eloquence of her praise. The masters soaring in the heavens may see her lines as "lowly," but she gives no indication that earthbound readers need concur. In comparison to a poet like Du Bartas or a rhetorician like Demosthenes, she is limited but hardly worthless. Her "mean and unrefined ore" highlights their "glist'ring gold" and may, with time, be enhanced by careful polishing.

The most striking image in this paean, however, is surely that of the "thyme or parsley wreath" Bradstreet requests in recognition of her poetry, discounting the traditional bay laurel. It seems a humble request: substitution of a kitchen herb for richer foliage. Bay leaves are also herbs, however, and there are cooks who plunge all three in the same aromatic pot. As far as honor goes, there may be less distinction here than the phrasing suggests. Elizabeth Wade White points out that thyme symbolized vitality and courage for the Greeks and that they sometimes honored athletes or dead heroes with the "fadeless foliage" of parsley wreaths. Even more familiar was the mythical background of the laurel as a symbol of poetry. In his verses "Upon Mrs. Anne Bradstreet Her Poems, Etc." prefaced to *The Tenth Muse*, John Rogers commended the Puritan poet for her avoidance of the wantonly lascivious topics provided by classical literature, specifically mentioning "How sage Apollo, Daphne hot pursues." C.B., in his introductory quatrain, wrote: "I cannot wonder at Apollo now, / That he with female laurel crowned his brow." The laurel crown commemorated Daphne, who was protectively transformed in her flight from lusty Apollo; so the bay leaves provided a female crown for male poets. The modesty that kept Anne Bradstreet from claiming such an honor, then, may have been more nearly allied to chastity than to humility. She may have felt sensitive to the mythic presentation of woman as simultaneously the object and victim of the god of poetry and the sign of glory for his disciples. It is clear, at any rate, that the concluding stanza expresses personal self-assurance as a poet, and the reader who has followed the stylistic, rhetorical, and logical devices by which she guides "The Prologue" from acknowledgment of her defects to assertion of her triumph is likely to accept the claim. Like Emily Dickinson, who contrasted "Carbon in the Coal" with "Carbon in the Gem" as queenly ornaments, Anne Bradstreet contrived to sound meek and vulnerable, even in the act of choosing among crowns.

SHIRA WOLOSKY

Emily Dickinson: A Voice of War

Emily Dickinson's poetry has rarely been approached in terms other than
the private and personal. Even when wider contexts to her work have been
admitted, they continue to be defined by her presumably self-enclosed and
eccentric sensibility. That sensibility is further portrayed—by biographers,
critics, and anthologists—as one of shy, frail timidity. Frightened by the
world and disappointed in her hopes, Dickinson, it is said, retreated into a
privacy that shielded her from exterior involvement. There, in accordance
with the particular interpretation adopted, she is established as a martyr: to
a lost love, to a neurotic state, to a religious ideal, or to her own literary
pursuits. But Dickinson's verse, contrary to traditional conceptions of it,
registers issues and events outside of her private sphere. Her poetry, when
approached without the assumption of her complete isolation, can be seen as
profoundly engaged in problems of the external world and aggressively so. It
presents a point of intersection of literary, cultural, and metaphysical
concerns, an arena in which conceptual structures and historical pressures
implicate and generate linguistic configuration.

Privacy and fear are certainly present in Dickinson's work, as are
anguish and morbid sensitivity. But their quality is different from that
generally presumed. The overwhelming effect of Dickinson's verse is not
delicacy. It is ferocity. Dickinson is an assertive and determined poet, as

From *Emily Dickinson: A Voice of War*. © 1984 by Yale University. Yale University Press,
1984.

17

much fury as maiden, whose retirement is a stance of attack, whose timidity is aggressive. Her poetry leaves an impression of defiance rather than detachment, and her poetic is neither helpless nor quaking. It is, rather, one of ironic twists, sudden stabs, and poison:

> Go slow, my soul, to feed thyself
> Upon his rare approach—
> Go rapid, lest Competing Death
> Prevail upon the Coach—
> Go timid, should his final eye
> Determine thee amiss—
> Go boldly—for thou paid'st his price
> Redemption—for a Kiss-

This poem, never anthologized, is characteristic. In it, Dickinson presents her patience and timidity—and unmasks them. In appearance a litany of instruction to her modest soul, the poem ends as an attack upon her subject. The final stroke denounces God as a traitor who demands a Judas kiss for his mercy. In light of this end, the poet's fear of judgment is revealed as a false deference before one unworthy to judge. Her consciousness that "Competing Death" may prevail spurs her, but not to penitence. Instead, she is inspired with a sense of injustice that her time is so limited. And the initial hope of Christ's appearance becomes by the end an accusation that the divine approach is far too rare. This is God the betrayer; but it is finally the poet who betrays him, who exposes his nature as unjustly hidden, prevailing upon man with unjust weapons and reigning as an unjust judge. But the poet, too, has weapons and judgments, and in this poem, it is she who prevails.

Dickinson's slow timidity, then, is present here. But it is present in all its strenuous power. She shows herself rapid and bold even in her shyness. What the poem suggests is that Dickinson, while she may be agonized, is, even more, agonistic. She actively wrestles with the problems her poetry addresses and accuses the universe of evils and contradictions she finds all too real. It further suggests her characteristic religious stance. This is one of struggle against God, whom she defies, but also toward him and with herself. For although she writes to denounce him, she invokes liturgical modes in order to do so. And God remains her subject. God is not dismissed. He continues to stand in relation to the poet's soul in contradictory assertion.

Dickinson's religious position remains an embattled one. But its importance to her work extends beyond overtly religious concerns into the fundamental technical and conceptual aspects of her poetic. Dickinson's verse forms have long attracted attention for their technical irregularities and suggest a distinct self-consciousness regarding language as a medium. Her poems typically present temporal and causal discontinuities, ateleological organizations, and irregular prosody. Examination of these formal characteristics suggests that departures from linguistic convention are a function of a growing doubt concerning traditional metaphysical sanctions for causality, teleology, and axiology. Such categories are implicit in conventional structures of articulation, as Nietzsche, for instance, points out. The possible collapse of such categories is a theme in many Dickinson poems, which present the world as it would appear without them. And it is a force governing the language of her poems, which works against sequence in time and space, against harmonies between disparate entities, and against continuous logic and full designations.

The linguistic self-consciousness implicit in Dickinson's treatment of poetic forms thus emerges as an expression of her concern with the metaphysical assumptions that promised to govern her world, but that came to seem inadequate. Metaphysical structures had purported to define the direction, order, and goal of existence—categories that remained essential to Dickinson and in terms of which she persisted in conceiving her world. Her doubts regarding these structures finally raised the whole question of linguistic meaning and of meaning in general. Her language, which reflects dissatisfaction with metaphysical systems in its configuration, finally came to address those systems, to explore directly their suppositions—and in so doing, to reflect on itself. Consciousness of language as a medium becomes consciousness of language as such, representing an increased focus on the process of signification and its possible governing principles.

Such an interest in language is not accidental. In Dickinson's tradition, the principles governing meaning had been conceived as linguistic, in terms proposed by the Logos structure. In this structure, the Logos stands between the world of eternity and that of time. Truth is identified with the former and is only accessible to the latter through a Logos that remains most strongly identified with the eternal world. Meaning, and the possibility of discourse, must rely on a positive relation between the two realms, with the transcendent world as the source and locus of significance.

In Dickinson's work, however, the two realms come to conflict; and the sanctions and structures of linguistic signification threaten to collapse. Such collapse is never quite realized in Dickinson's work. But her confrontation with it profoundly informs her conceptions of language and her poetic expression—and not only hers. The mutual implication of metaphysics and language has a particular force and clarity in her poetry. In this she is singular, but not solitary. Melville's waved fists at an enigmatic Deity; Hawthorne's sense of a resistant and incremental evil far more certain than any possible grace; Whitman's assertion of the divine self; and Emerson's proscription that the poet take up the vestments fallen from the priesthood all trace a growing instability in metaphysical structures once secure.

This instability becomes only more pronounced in later writers with linguistic consequences already suggested by Dickinson's verse. Literary movements such as symbolism, imagism, surrealism, dadaism, futurism, and concrete poetry render Dickinson's poetic less merely eccentric. What seemed personal symptom can instead be seen as symptomatic. And Dickinson's work particularly suggests such formal experiments to be a function of metaphysical crisis which is further expressed, both by her and by later poets, in meditations on language.

Recent criticism has come increasingly to consider this question of Dickinson in relation to other writers, both of her own and of subsequent periods. Her recognition by later poets, such as the American Imagistes, and the resemblance between her verse and verse written after her have begun to suggest affinities that qualify her hitherto unquestioned isolation. Thus Karl Keller, in *The Only Kangaroo among the Beauty*, examines Dickinson's work in the context of American traditions; David Porter, in *The Modern Idiom*, does so in the context of twentieth-century modernism. And feminist criticism particularly has progressed toward examining Dickinson in less constricting terms. Studies of the social realities of nineteenth-century America and of the actual pursuits of women within it, and the stratum of such concrete experience in Dickinson's poetry have broadened the perspectives of Dickinson criticism. Treatments of her as a woman writer have the added benefit of confronting her virginity and the sexuality of her poems as active powers within her identity and as more than signs of repression, aberration, and incompletion.

These studies, however, have continued to proceed, to a greater or lesser degree, from the premise of biographical reclusion. The contours of Dickinson's world are extended beyond her own psyche, but generally little further than her literary connections. Keller's book presents Dickinson exclusively in terms of American literary history, and Porter's, in terms of literary theory. Even the feminist approach in such a work as *The Madwoman in the Attic* tends to focus on Dickinson's literary affinities at the expense of any extraliterary contacts. But the context for Dickinson's work includes more than literary influences, just as it involves more than the sphere of her own home.

Because of her seclusion, it is assumed that whatever pain Dickinson felt, whatever questions disturbed her, must be defined by a privacy into which only literature could penetrate. The possibility that her uncertainties were not self-induced, and that her concerns were not entirely private, has never been explored. Yet poem after poem suggests that the self of the poet, however imperious, is not the sole boundary of her existence nor her sole concern:

> The Battle fought between the Soul
> And No Man—is the One
> Of all the Battles prevalent—
> By far the Greater One—
>
> No News of it is had abroad—
> Its Bodiless Campaign
> Establishes, and terminates—
> Invisible—Unknown—
>
> (P 594)

Dickinson's inner world is the subject of this poem. Here she depicts her personal turmoil and even particularly insists on its private nature. The soul's inner strife remains unpublicized. Yet, she declares, it is the most terrible combat. Invisible and bodiless, it is still the most bloody.

In presenting this image of inner strife, however, Dickinson does so in terms provided by the world outside her. The poem was written in 1862: the very period when Antietam and Bull Run had begun to reveal fully the horrors of the Civil War. There are in Dickinson's opus many poems that register, directly or indirectly, the civil conflagration raging around her. The notion that Dickinson's morbid fear of death and preoccupation with suffering may not have been entirely the product of her own idiosyncratic and more or less pathological imagination has never been considered. But in this poem, although Dickinson centers attention on her private world, she does so in terms drawn from the public one. The initiative even seems to lie, startling as this may be, in the public realm. The invisible and unknown struggle within the self is given a form determined by visible and known violence. Her personal conflict takes on military proportions, and in this it reflects actual events in the world of history. That the personal is foremost does not obviate the fact that, in 1862, the bodiless campaign within the poet's soul had an objective counterpart in physical and palpable warfare.

In Dickinson's work, then, metaphysical conflict is accompanied by historical trauma, and the two spheres further conjoin in a poetic remarkable for disjunctions and discontinuities. Emily Dickinson was not a librarian, remaining indoors in order to sort her reading and sift her emotions into little packets reminiscent of a card catalog. Her language, instead, records the converging crises in metaphysics and culture that can be felt in the work of other American writers and that become a profound preoccupation in writers subsequent to her. Dickinson's work presents with striking force the metaphysical revisions that so characterize modernity, as this is implicated by cultural instability and as this implicates linguistic structures. For the critique of metaphysics announced by Nietzsche has broad implications for language, which itself has a primary function and importance in traditional systems. The Logos concept, in its Johannine formulation, presented the whole possibility of intercourse between transcendence and immanence in linguistic terms. The process of signification was defined as originating in the divine Logos, and through the incarnate Logos as the avenue of its truth, as finally emerging within the immanent world. Human language was meaningful and possible only as it participated, through the Logos, in the transcendent realm. But Dickinson's work testifies to an increasing hiatus between transcendence and immanence, Logos and language. Such hiatus precipitates a conflict between human language and the traditional sources of its significance, which has only increased in strength since the time of her writing and which challenges the once accepted patterns for interpreting reality and rendering it coherent.

In Dickinson, these issues ultimately conjoin in a confrontation between the language identified with an immutable world and the immanent words of human language. The characteristic result is, in Dickinson, blasphemy:

> Ended, ere it begun—
> The Title was scarcely told
> When the Preface perished from Consciousness
> The Story, unrevealed—
>
> Had it been mine, to print!
> Had it been yours, to read!
> That it was not Our privilege
> The interdict of God—
>
> (P 1088)

Dickinson's concern with language is evident in this poem. But the poem also places this concern in the metaphysical terms that consistently frame it for her. Here, a text has been interrupted. It is barely announced before its potential unfolding is engulfed: "Ended, ere it begun." Indeed, such interruption is the poem's first utterance, formally placing its own end before its beginning. The text's termination is so immediate as to seem to precede its commencement, in a profound temporal inversion.

This text takes place in the sphere of human language, which is itself identified as the poet's own world—for "Story" here figures not only as text but as universe and experience within it. This text-as-world could have been—and should have been—realized by the poet's human power, fulfilled within her human world. She would have it printed and read. But this has been willfully prevented by God's interdiction, which here has a particularly verbal resonance. God's decree forbids the completion of the human text. Divine language counters human language. What should support her utterance instead disrupts it. Nor does the poet gracefully bow to a higher, if mysterious, power. The poem is an assault. It does not declare the independence of immanent language from divine decree, but rather asserts divine decree only to attack, defame, and denounce it.

The poem thus stands poised between apostasy and affirmation—a poise that is, however, unstable and combative. There is no trace here of a timid Dickinson. The attack is frontal. And it is a linguistic attack, both as an assault through poetry and as a poem in which defiant human language strives against, but remains facing, the divine Word.

In this, Dickinson stands at the threshold of a modernity in which such struggle becomes typical. Later poets, however, could reach toward some resolution of the conflict between human and divine utterance by attempting either to reaffirm the traditional bond between them or to construct new frameworks based upon premises altogether different from the traditional ones. Dickinson, too, attempts such resolutions, but she does so without final success. She remains caught between the claims of each linguistic/ metaphysical realm. The strife of this conflict, above all, informs her work. It does so not in a vacuum nor in a hermitage but in relation to the history that surrounds her. Nor does her strife render her helpless. She is furious with the God without whom she is unable to conceive her universe, but who, if responsible for a universe so incomprehensible, claims her enmity. Her poetry becomes the field of this combat with and against God. It registers, finally, the clash between his language and her own.

JOANNE FEIT DIEHL

"Ransom in a Voice":
Language as Defense in Dickinson's Poetry

I dwell in Possibility—
A fairer House than Prose—

"Let us sit at home with the cause," admonished Emerson in his seminal essay, "Self-Reliance." Of all the ambitious young Americans who took this essay to heart, none followed his advise so literally as Emily Dickinson or adhered to its demands more rigorously. She defined her version of the "cause" as a desire to reveal, through her poems, a responsive, wholly alive consciousness. No matter how frequently ignored or misunderstood, Dickinson continued speaking into the void. Whatever the particular origins of her sense of estrangement (and we need not look far to discover its most overt forms: absence from the ongoing cultural life of Boston and Concord, spiritual exclusion from the orthodoxy sweeping mid-century Amherst, misunderstanding by those she hoped would recognize and nurture her genius), the austere originality of Dickinson's poetry develops from the tenor of her reaction to such exclusions, from her conversion of a potentially crippling alienation into a conception of language that serves as a defense against what she perceived not simply as an antipathetic society, but also as an adversarial nature and an inscrutable, if not fundamentally hostile, deity. From this estrangement, Dickinson develops a deeply skeptical, indeed, an antithetical approach toward the world beyond the self. Her pervasive

From *Feminist Critics Read Emily Dickinson.* © 1983 by Indiana University Press.

skepticism toward both the world and language, moreover, foreshadows a distinctly modernist alienation. Although the reasons for Dickinson's and other nineteenth-century women poets' sense of exclusion from both nature and culture necessarily differ from the origins of rejection that fuel the modernist writers of our century, the character of their poetic responses presents a strong, albeit surprising resemblance. How Dickinson converts her estrangement into verbal power, just how her sense of alienation informs her vision of a defensive language that pushes the word ever closer to indecipherability, are questions that lead back into her work and forward to a consideration of the possible ties between a feminist poetics and modernism.

The greatest danger facing a poet is, of course, the danger of silence. That Dickinson resists this temptation is proof of her energies; that she makes her alienation the subject of many of her most brilliant poems, thus transforming estrangement into a source of power, testifies to the strength of her imagination. No poet can accomplish this transformation in a single gesture, nor is the transformation of estrangement into power, once accomplished, permanently assured. Thus, Dickinson's poems, not unexpectedly, document a cyclical process in which the "I" initially experiences a rejection that provokes rage followed by resentment. This anger on the poet's part climaxes in the poems' assertion of a fiercely won independence from the very force or substance that she had originally been denied. Despite her disavowal of such appetite, "Art thou the thing I wanted? / Begone—my Tooth has grown—" (1282), no final resolution or poetic satiety can be achieved because of the very nature of the conflicts generated by repeated banishment and denial. In her attempts to marshal internal power against such continued threats to her autonomy, Dickinson makes language her strongest weapon. The Word becomes her defense as she assigns it sufficient force to devastate her adversaries and exercise her will even against Divine power. In response to the exclusionary silence of a hostile, or at best, incomprehensible world and a threatening poetic adversary, Dickinson invokes the powers of language, asserting that her word may vie with the Divine for authority over herself and her experience. If the word becomes a weapon, it also possesses, as Dickinson is well aware, the capacity to find its victim within the self. To assert that what determines survival or destruction resides within the self is simultaneously to acknowledge internal authority while denigrating the threat of any and all external forces.

Dickinson appropriates power for her own linguistic purposes by, among other ways, drawing upon the authority orthodox Christianity ascribes to Christ. Adopting qualities associated with the Christian deity, and transforming these into a linguistic process that she describes as both more humane and equable than the Christian, Dickinson creates an alternative power potentially subversive of any external authority based upon the sovereignty of a male-identified divinity or predicated upon the supremacy of those within the religious fold. In her boldest poetic statement of these alternative powers—the choosing of her words over against the force of God—Dickinson explores the possibilities for a poetics that yields nothing to forces beyond the self.

> A Word made Flesh is seldom
> And tremblingly partook
> Nor then perhaps reported
> But have I not mistook
> Each one of us has tasted
> With ecstasies of stealth
> The very food debated
> To our specific strength—
>
> A Word that breathes distinctly
> Has not the power to die
> Cohesive as the Spirit
> It may expire if He—
> "Made Flesh and dwelt among us
> Could condescension be
> Like this consent of Language
> This loved Philology.
>
> (1651)

One experiences a power commensurate with the Divine depending upon one's own capacity: the Word lives, the human word, as the Spirit. That Dickinson here chooses the power of the human word over the power of the Divine becomes apparent in the closing lines. The "condescension" of Christ, with that word's concealed arrogance of *descent* does not approach the mutuality of relationships expressed by "consent," the power of a human word to meet the reader on equal terms. As I have argued elsewhere, this poem can be viewed as Dickinson's central statement about language, her role as poet, and her relationship to the Divine. The process of transubstantiation here serves as a trope investing the poet's word with godlike authority. In a stunning inversion of orthodoxy, Dickinson takes the Word of God and makes it her own, which then serves as the criterion for measuring all power outside the self. Transubstantiation thus becomes a trope for poetic inspiration. Combined with this discourse of religion is the language of appetite, which Dickinson frequently identifies with the poetic enterprise. This transference of authority—"The Word made Flesh"— describes an alternative drama of mutuality between desire and fulfillment absent in the relations that exist within a hieratic Christianity. So sweeping is the usurpation of orthodox powers into the self that by the poem's final stanza, traditional incarnation can only hope to match the reciprocal relationship that informs "beloved philology." The closing words echo their own meaning in a circle of love (*philo-logos*), the beloved love of the word.

Yet, if here the poetic word triumphs over LOGOS, elsewhere it assumes no such absolute or benign power, but is, instead, identified as functioning within an adversarial relationship, as a weapon used to defend the self against the self's own powers. Once such power resides solely within the single consciousness, once the poetic self attempts to replace external authority, the dangers for poetic identity grow more intimate and acute. As Dickinson remarks, "Jacob versus Esau, was a trifle in Litigation, compared to the Skirmish in my Mind—." Language, the usurping power of the imagination, becomes, then, both a weapon of salvation and the means for potential self-destruction. Dickinson underscores the lethal relationship between the potentially brilliant show of her Word (its destructive possibilities) in "She dealt her pretty words like blades," where language "glitters" and "shines" while it exposes, like a surgeon's knife, the nerves or "wantons with a Bone—". Such surgical "wanton"-ness may prove lethal to its victim. But this is a risk Dickinson must take if she is to direct her linguistic energies toward a confrontation with her personal and literary isolation, if she is to provide herself with a means for overcoming the strictures of circumstance.

The ground of poetry, alone, offers Dickinson the freedom to articulate her independence. Choosing to write from her perception of this alienated consciousness, she projects an inviolate territory where words, even if potentially self-destructive, are her weapons against limitation, orthodoxy, and a hostile world. Such an alternative territory emerges in the early poem, "There is a morn by men unseen—" (24). Here Dickinson describes a pastoral landscape but with a difference: process ceases, temporality fades, and, as in poem 1056, "Consciousness—is Noon." Characterizing this "mystic green" in terms of her own ambition, Dickinson seeks there a "morn by men unseen." Whether she is using "men" in the generic or the more specific, sex-related sense, she attests to an enchanted ground inhabited by "maids" who engage in their own "dance and game," those who participate in secret rituals of delight during their "holiday" (holy day).

> There is a morn by men unseen—
> Whose maids upon remoter green
> Keep their Seraphic May—
> And all day long, with dance and game,
> And gambol I may never name—
> Employ their holiday.

Whether the poet "may never name" these rituals because she does not know them or because she will not or cannot disclose them affects the interpretation of the remaining stanzas. However one decides to read the poem, and I will not attempt a full reading here, it is significant that Dickinson is invoking an alternative, sacred ground toward which she yearns to travel. Wishing to join that company of fairy maids who do not inhabit the earth, she finds in their magic "ring" a ground secure from the antipathetic forces that drove her from the daylight world of men and women. In a poem that itself describes a form of sacred play, one must take into account Dickinson's own play with words throughout the text. Puns and associative images create a complex web of meaning that reinforces the overall vision of the poem as a counter-revelation, another way for the poet to be, as opposed to the commonly received notion of poetic vocation and the daylight world of masculine orthodoxy. Not only is the holiday also a holy day, but the Chrysolite that shines in her alternative landscape is, perhaps, an alternative to Christ's light; the revels of the magic "maids" are a kind of play that replaces traditional "revelation."

> Like thee to dance—like thee to sing—
> People upon that mystic green—
> I ask, each new May Morn.
> I wait thy far, fantastic bells—
> Announcing me in other dells—
> Unto the different dawn!

Despite the jubilation of the closing stanza, this "different dawn" remains in the realm of ambition. The luminous powers of the "mystic green" are not yet experienced by the poet who *waits* for her call to election, to this counter-revelation of a natural, free-spirited, exuberant circle of other worldly "maids."

As this "different dawn" has yet to be attained, so Dickinson recognizes that she cannot stay in her self-made world of language forever. Her most impressive poems thus derive their energy from the conflict between the poetic self and a world she perceived as estranged, or "other." Yet, if nature is alien, society without comprehension of her poetic powers, the language Dickinson inherits is also, she recognizes, not fully her own. Language as she knows it is defined primarily by a long line of male poets—to rid her words of their literal meaning would be an act of liberation that would free her from a confining tradition, a gesture that would allow her access to a new mode of signification. Her quest for such a revision of language itself becomes a major subject for a number of her most remarkable poems and the beginning of a feminist poetics that treats the difficulties of a woman poet who struggles for the integrity of her own voice. By describing her experience of rejection in terms that only serve to deepen its ambiguities, Dickinson demonstrates the precariousness that governs her relationships to all outside the self, especially to nature and to God—the chief adversaries she must resist if she is to survive as woman and as poet. The terms of Dickinson's encounter with the world go beyond mere antagonism as God and nature turn against and actively pursue the inquisitive self.

> Nature and God—I neither knew
> Yet Both so well knew me
> They startled, like Executors
> Of My identity.
>
> Yet Neither told—that I could learn—
> My Secret as secure
> As Herschel's private interest
> Or Mercury's affair—
>
> (835)

Here the ambiguities in Dickinson's relationships with external forces reveal themselves in a series of curiously inverted linguistic structures. First, note that the poem speaks of the I's relationship with nature and God in the past tense; whether this means that the relationship has subsequently altered or whether she is speaking of herself in the past in a eulogistic vein remains an open question. Although apparently a simple statement of her ignorance concerning God and nature, and their intimate knowledge of the "I," the poem is really more complex. For instance, after the opening lines assert that nature and God possess this knowledge, while she remains ignorant of them, she defines the character of this knowledge in terms of her response: "They startled, like Executors / Of My identity." In her choice of "executors," Dickinson begins the dichotomy that will set the poem against itself, for "executor" suggests both one who puts to death (perhaps explaining the posthumous tense of the poem), carrying out the verdict of society, and/or one who carries out the wishes of the deceased as expressed in her or his Will. Although the second alternative incorporates within its definition the sense of one who obeys, who thus subordinates himself to the wishes of an other, this acquiescence is precipitated by the death of the person who wrote the "will" and who now exercises that will through the very act of dying. "Executor" can, then, be either the agent of the victim's death or the one who protects her rights, sustains her will, after she has succumbed to other forces—most compellingly, the word may retain both these meanings and so operate dualistically, in an apparently antithetical relationship to itself. Thus, "executor" simultaneously contains both protective and potentially lethal meanings. The ambiguity associated with nature and God intensifies as Dickinson further complicates these relationships through additional syntactic complexities, the most obviously being her use of dashes and the pronoun "that," which discourages any single reading of the poem's final lines.

> Yet neither told—that I could learn—
> My Secret as secure
> As Herschel's private interest
> Or Mercury's affair—

The clause "that I could learn" again operates in two ways: first, as a parenthetical clarification—to the best of her knowledge, and second, nature and God did not tell their secret in ways so that she could learn. The reader cannot, moreover, be certain just what nature and God are refusing to disclose. The options might be these: either they will in good faith not reveal the "secret" information about the poet which would, she suggests, in some unnamed way, damage her were it told (thus she is protected by them as the deceased's wishes would be respected by her executors) and/or nature and God will not reveal to *her* what they know, preserving instead an inviolate secrecy. Within this second reading, "secure" functions as an ironic term, for the "I" cannot learn directly about either God or Nature, let alone about what they know of her; the secret is thus secured just because it is hidden from the self. What Herschel's private interest might be she cannot know, as Mercury's affair remains a mystery. These closing lines are themselves enigmatic in their brevity, but equally suggestive as well. The reader does not know, for example, to which Herschel the poem refers—to the distinguished astronomer, William, or to his remarkable sister and collaborator, Caroline, who discovered eight comets in her lifetime, or to William's son, John. Each of these names does, however, recall not simply an astronomer, but a scientist who discovered a celestial body hitherto unknown. A conjectural reading of

"As Herschel's private interest" suggests that if Herschel's (any of the Herschels) public interests were so vast, how great might his/her secret interest have been; the speaker's secret is as secure as Herschel's because it also is cosmological in scope and as much a part of the hitherto unknown. The closing line with its reference to Mercury makes both the astronomical connection to Herschel and the link back to the Roman god, a pagan deity as opposed to the Judeo-Christian presence with whom the poem opens. But Mercury has other important connotations for this context as well: the planet is closest to the sun and extremely hard to view from the earth. (In what was most probably an apocryphal story, Copernicus on his deathbed reportedly stated that his one regret was never to have observed Mercury.) Moreover, because of its position in relation to the sun, one side of Mercury is constantly in light, the other in total darkness. Thus, Mercury could keep its secrets in two senses—as the planet so hard to see from the earth and as one that keeps half its form in constant night. The allusion to the pagan identity of Mercury functions ironically: as the messenger, the one who brings news, Mercury would disclose rather than withhold secret knowledge. In larger terms, two meanings operate antithetically here; the first more overt, perhaps, than the second, but both equally sustained through the poem's syntax and diction, creating an unresolvable tension rather than a resolution of interpretation. Such interpretative indeterminacy, moreover, places the reader in a position analogous to that of the "I" of the poem. Dickinson informs us of the terms in which she understands her predicament but gives no clear notion of exactly where her power or knowledge might reside.

Such interpretative ambiguities, brilliant as they may be, are a sign of a deeper ambivalence that manifests itself in the linguistic and syntactic complexities informing Dickinson's often richly multivalent texts. And yet, the extremely delicate process of articulating such indeterminacy is in itself the source of authority that surpasses nature's mystery by naming it. Whether such obscuring strategies have their origin in a deliberate desire to obscure or in an ironic evasiveness, or in both, no reader can ascertain; more alarming, such indeterminacy of language, despite the authoritative force of individual poems, may signal the potential breakdown of the word's capacity to bear the pressures of simultaneous, antithetical meanings that deconstruct each other.

Confronting her own awareness of the deconstructive possibilities in language, Dickinson finds that her weapons, her words, are double-edged. If language may serve as defense against an alien world and a rejecting father-God, it may, in the very act of its expression, further expose the sources of conflict that war within the self. Respect for the word and recognition of its power lead to a concomitant fear the language may turn precipitously, unannounced, against its author. If to "hurt" is "Not Steel's Affair" (479), when steel is the synecdochical knife of language, the word can be trusted neither to spare nor to protect; language may not only captivate— it may, alas, also condemn.

II

Such a vision of language leads Dickinson to an understanding of the world and her epistemological relation to it that is at once potentially dangerous and dangerously modern, for her poems speak repeatedly of a sense of a dislocation that neither depends upon nor assumes a ground of common or shared experience. The roots of such an alienated imagination draw their sustenance from isolation—both intellectual and physical. But the result of such depleting circumstances is, remarkably, a poetry that not only manifests a penchant for ambiguity (the double-edged ironic mode) but reveals as well experimentation with the possibilities of language to convey mutually conflicting meanings as the word pushes toward, and indeed at times *over*, the limits of communal understanding. Exclusion thus offers Dickinson the occasion to adopt a radical approach to experience that prompts her to invent a startlingly modernist poetics. In a world where nothing is certain, all relationships can be shifted, reversed, subverted, or kept indeterminate because they rely for their definition upon an isolate, rebellious consciousness, which itself is in a state of flux. Such radical solipsism often leads to a vertiginous freedom, what Dickinson herself names "that precarious Gait / Some call experience." Dickinson's skeptical investigation of experience combined with her abiding sense of exclusion translates into poems that assert their defiance against the existing order and articulate a willful rejection of the very things she has most desired, what she has been denied. In this way, Dickinson's poems potentially free her to become "executor" of her own identity.

Although engendered by different anxieties, the skepticism often bordering on despair that precipitates so many of the major modernists' experiments finds a kindred manifestation in Dickinson's work. If the modernists turn to radical experimentation with language to reclaim poetry for contemporary experience (one thinks of Pound, of Eliot, of H. D.), to fashion a language adequate to a deeply altered, forever changed world, so, too, Dickinson, albeit in isolation and without the support gained from the knowledge of others striving toward a common goal, pits her language against the world in a gesture as defiant as that of any of those twentieth-century poets who were to follow. As a woman poet she experiences cultural rejection and isolation *earlier* than the male poets who will later feel themselves exiled by cataclysmic historical events beyond their control—the most fatefully being the turbulent changes wrought by the First World War and the cultural disruption that was its aftermath. These changes forced writers to confront an historical discontinuity between themselves and an irretrievable past. So, too, women poets had, generations earlier, felt themselves cut off from the post-Miltonic poetic tradition, which had never been theirs. Thus, one may begin to account for some of the indeterminate quality of Dickinson's poetics by viewing her as a proto-modernist whose radical ways were formed, in part, by a feminist impulse.

Dickinson's sense of dislocation emerges with an austere clarity in the following poem, with its strong Stevensian tone:

> Four Trees—upon a solitary Acre—
> Without Design
> Or Order, or Apparent Action—
> Maintain—
>
> The Sun—upon a Morning meets them—
> The Wind—
> No nearer Neighbor—have they—
> But God—
>
> The Acre gives them—Place—
> They—Him—Attention of Passer by—
> Of Shadow, or of Squirrel, haply—
> Or Boy—
>
> What Deed is Their's unto the General Nature—
> What Plan
> They severally—retard—or further—
> Unknown—

(742)

In this poem's strangely vacant opening, one hears the Stevensian "mind of winter," the listener who "nothing himself, beholds/Nothing that is not there and the nothing that is." This voice prophesies as well that quality of provisional apprehension that haunts Stevens's most austere poems. Dickinson presents a stark scene of four trees standing isolate in an otherwise bare acre, invoking this vision to suggest the absence of assured meaning either in the trees' relation to other natural facts or to an ordering principle beyond themselves—some unnamed teleological force. There remains, however, a slight demurral from this absence in the "apparent" of the poem's third line. Asking the question Robert Frost will pose in "Design" when he observes the minute death-drama taking place on the white "heal-all," Dickinson sustains the possibility that there may be a design that governs over against her provisional denial. The stanzas that follow elaborate this issue of motive or purpose beyond sheer physical presence. The sun "meets" (a word that suggests intent) the trees; yet, oddly, the effect of such a meeting is only to intensify the aura of isolation that demarcates the trees' existence. Distant light alone is this landscape's nearest neighbor—except God. Although the "but" that precedes "God" (stanza two, line four) would prepare the reader for a seemingly minor omission, an afterthought, it is here that the poem coyly confronts its central question, for the issue of the exclusion of God is an oversight of truly teleological significance. Despite this ironic maneuver, the poem resists any orthodox assertion of Divine omnipresence, proceeding instead to define other earthly relationships that are determined by chance and dependent upon the presence of an observer:

> The Acre gives them—Place—
> They—Him—Attention of Passer by—
> Of Shadow, or of Squirrel, haply—
> Or Boy—

"Shadow," "Squirrel," "Boy": the list moves from optical effect to sentient, hence potentially questioning, consciousness. In a movement that parallels the structure of the preceding stanza—in each case the final line introducing the crucial term with the offhandedness given an afterthought—the poem again evades as it draws attention to its own implications—this time, the impact of a human viewer's consciousness. Rather than resolve the underlying question of meaning, the problem of intelligence as well as the issue of belief, the closing stanza will not fully acknowledge the presence of a Divine or human observer who would imbue with meaning this bare landscape-vision, which thus remains equivocal and obscure.

Commenting more generally on the relationship between Dickinson and Stevens, Harold Bloom notes, "The connection with Stevens is that he and Dickinson, more than any other Americans, more than any other moderns, labor successfully to make the visible a little hard to see." Here Dickinson creates this obliqueness of vision by questioning the reality of the observing eye as well as the presence of an hierarchical power that would invest meaning, the clarity of intent, into the otherwise desolate landscape. This poem eschews any such recuperative possibility that would ascribe a specific significance to the scene, choosing instead to bear witness to a complete ignorance of the scene's function or its meaning. By rejecting the relationships asserted in the poem, the final stanza poses the essentially ontological question: for what purpose do these trees exist? "What Plan/ They severally—retard—or further—Unknown." The repeated "n" sounds separated by the long "o" of "unknown" re-sound the finality of the word's meaning and, simultaneously, the impossibility of ever achieving that meaning.

III

To live in such a world is to live, no matter how brilliantly, alone. Yet, if God will not reveal his meaning or the meaning of his world, there may yet be another faith to which Dickinson can turn, one based upon an alternative to the exclusive, rejecting patriarchal order she must herself renounce. This heterodox faith, or "other" way, may be founded upon the belief in the development of a tradition of women poets, distinct from that delineated by the male poetic tradition. In perhaps the most forthright and impassioned statement of this possible alternative faith, an order that would be founded upon the majesty of woman, Dickinson invokes the maternal forms of mountains as standard bearers of her especial truth. In contrast to those poems that sever the external manifestations of the world from an unknowable God's intent, here Dickinson maintains a connection between an alternative theodicy and the physical presence of natural forms. As one who felt herself inhabiting a world where order remains frustratingly provisional and God continuously hidden, how Dickinson must have yearned for the security of such imaginable, alternative relationships. In an imperative voice that, through its very assertiveness, conveys its desire to coerce geological forms into truth-telling mothers, Dickinson woos as she creates her distinct reality:

> Sweet Mountains—Ye tell Me no lie—
> Never deny Me—Never fly—
> Those same unvarying Eyes
> Turn on Me—When I fail—or feign,
> Or take the Royal names in vain—
> Their far—slow—Violet Gaze—
>
> My strong Madonnas—Cherish still—
> The Wayward Nun—beneath the Hill—

Whose service—is to You—
Her latest Worship—When the Day
Fades from the Firmament away—
To lift Her Brows on You—

(722)

Constancy, fidelity, and unconditional acceptance—those qualities which Dickinson found missing in orthodox Christianity, she now seeks among the monumental "Strong Madonnas." For such heresy, the taking of the "Royal names in vain" and her assuming the role of the "Wayward Nun," the "I" anticipates a reciprocal allegiance. This very waywardness ironically legitimizes the self's demand for such unwavering constancy on the part of the "sweet mountains," as heterodoxy is converted into belief in the alternative power of the maternal. As Sandra M. Gilbert and Susan Gubar state, "Surely these 'Strong Madonnas' are sisters of the mother Awe to whom, Dickinson told Higginson, she ran home as a child, and surely it was such mothers who enabled (and empowered) this poet to escape her Nobodaddy's requirements, if only in secret." And yet, this alternative power receives only conditional allegiance; the imperative tone of the poem's opening: "Sweet Mountains—Ye tell Me no lie—/ Never deny me—Never fly—" assumes the voice of a command. The poem asks for the belief of the mountains in the "I" who usurps Christ's role but adopts a diametrically opposite position, beneath the hill as Christ was at its summit. This "wayward nun" is, moreover, at once savior and worshipper. In the first stanza, the "I" undergoes trials of faith as she plays the part of defiant actor. (Note the negative terms in which these trials are described: "fail," "Feign," "or take the Royal names in vain.") She performs in these ways, the second stanza recounts, for the sake of the strong "Madonnas" whom she addresses as "My," thus making her the daughter of the savior's mother—Christ's sister forming an alternative religion of the mother: "Whose service—is to You—," rather than of the son. To see the mountains as madonnas is not simply to see religion in natural forms, but so to transform religion as to transplant it in nature. If the mountains in this poem appear as strong madonnas, they are elsewhere subsumed into the more general vision of a hostile natural world that can offer no solace. Even more disruptively, the mountains may turn volcanic, representing no outward hope but a power at once destructive and potent that smolders within the self. It is to "Vesuvius at home" that Dickinson grants her primary allegiance. All gods or goddesses beyond this mouldering self may receive intermittent recognition, but none earns the devotion Dickinson bestows upon her own power.

Such allegiance to one's strength, however, is not free from danger; rather, the stakes for poetic survival increase as trust in all external forms fades before the self-inflicting powers of the imagination. The tenuousness of all reality beyond the self, the difficulty of ascertaining any ontological certainty whatsoever—radically modernist dilemma—finally makes her immune to the solace of religious solutions, no matter how subversive. Instead, when Dickinson writes to her experience, she characteristically sees it as an adventure, a journey through rugged, hostile terrain toward an end both untested and potentially fatal. For companionship, she takes along only her consciousness. Dickinson elsewhere describes the climax of this travail; the terror she faces when confronting "The Forest of the Dead" renders her paralyzed before her goal, which is her end as well:

> Retreat—was out of Hope—
> Behind—a Sealed Route—
> Eternity's White Flag—Before—
> And God—at every Gate—
>
> (615)

The white flag of surrender and/or salvation may welcome the traveler or obscure the vision of God. But even prior to this moment of apocalyptic hesitation, the "routes" leading to it have been treacherous and fraught with danger. As a way of combating the potential devastation of such risks, Dickinson vests her faith in the only internal power upon which she may rely, upon the power of the transformative Word. Renunciation becomes a viable strategy for poetic survival only to the extent that she can continue to articulate her rejection in the form of writing poems. If, in all other spheres, "Renunciation—is a piercing Virtue," language itself is not to be denied, but instead given renewed and redefined power through the force of her alienated imagination.

Once the poet grants that her word may supplant God's, however, she must be prepared to face the dangers of such redirected authority, hence those poems that witness the treacherous capacities of language, a language that may (with the very probity that lends the Word its force) cause it to shake the foundations of the self. How language can function in this way, as transcendent and transforming reality, is a difficult and problematic question. Dickinson both relies upon the process of articulation to serve for a weapon against her sense of isolation and exile and paradoxically dreads what this very act of verbalization may reveal concerning her hidden (what we would now call "unconscious") self. Such turning against the self, which produces a split identity, is a direct result of Dickinson's poetic ambitions.

She fashions a poetics that functions as a counter-language eschewing communal identity, a poetics that depends upon, even as it attempts to transfigure the terms of, her exclusion.

IV

This concept of language as defense, as the only effective weapon in Dickinson's arsenal, develops into a strongly adversarial kind of poetics. A war rages in these poems, a war within the self for control over the potency of the word. Note the quasi-aggressive intimacy with which Dickinson describes such procedures:

> The Soul unto itself
> Is an imperial friend—
> Or the most agonizing Spy—
> An Enemy—could send—
>
> Secure against its own—
> No treason it can fear—
> Itself—it's Sovreign—of itself
> The Soul should stand in Awe—
>
> (683)

The repetition of "it's" serves to encode the doubling, the turning of self upon soul, the wrestling of intimate yet potentially antithetical identities. Out of such aggressive intimacy, there emerges awe, the same power Dickinson elsewhere identifies as the spur to her making poems. Even awe, however, contains within it its own paradoxical aspects: "I work to drive the awe away, Yet awe impels the work." What Dickinson asserts that she requires is the stimulus of defense, the sensation of warding off an external power that might destroy her. In response to such a threat, she reacts with a combination of fear and reverence that must be cast aside yet remains crucial to this process of composing poems. That awe is associated with the self's specific language-making function can be inferred from those poems that privilege the poetic act as they denigrate all authority that lies outside the single imagination.

In a hitherto largely neglected poem that directly addresses this conflict of world and word, a poem written during that great year of Dickinson's creative activity, 1862, she alludes to the process that will bestow joy upon the world; joy rising from the powers within the self. This regenerative process, however, leads inexorably to a chilling and personally devastating reversal. Particularly important is the role language assumes, functioning as the determinative power that creates a necessary distance between the self and the world as it staves off the world's destructive capacities. Dealing her "word of gold," Dickinson "dowers—all the World—." She transforms the world with her own resources. When she is robbed of her happiness, however, and finds in its stead only a barren existence, life becomes a "wilderness, which rolls back along (her) Golden lines," and, the poem implies, wipes them out. Language, with its transforming powers, extends over the landscape only to be vanquished by the emptiness of a world that reflects the poet's precipitating loss.

> It would never be Common—more—I said—
> Difference—had begun—
> Many a bitterness—had been—
> But that old sort—was done—
>
> Or—if it sometime—showed—as 'twill
> Upon the Downiest—Morn
> Such bliss—had I—for all the years
> 'Twould give an Easier—pain
>
> I'd so much joy—I told it—Red—
> Upon my simple Cheek—
> I felt it publish—in my Eye—
> 'Twas needless—any speak—
>
> I walked—as wings—my body bore—
> The feet—I former used—
> Unnecessary—now to me—
> As boots—would be—to Birds—
>
> I put my pleasure all abroad—
> I dealt a word of Gold
> To every Creature—that I met—
> And Dowered—all the World—
>
> When—suddenly—my Riches shrank—
> A Goblin—drank my Dew—
> My Palaces—dropped tenantless—
> Myself—was beggared—too—

> I clutched at sounds—
> I groped at shapes—
> I touched the tops of Films—
> I felt the Wilderness roll back—
> Along my Golden lines—
>
> The Sackcloth—hangs upon the nail—
> The Frock I used to wear—
> But where my moment of Brocade—
> My—Drop—of India?
>
> (430)

The miraculous change Dickinson describes in the poem's opening four stanzas, the change she felt "publish—in [her] eye," extends to her infusing the world with her joy through language. In a series of deliberate gestures, she "puts" her pleasure all abroad, "deals" a word of Gold, and "dowers" all the World. In these successive phrases, the poem creates an active, purposive self, who draws on internal powers to fill the world with her "word of Gold," thus simultaneously conveying beauty and value to all around her. Once "beggared," in an alarming and abrupt reversal that recalls a fairy-tale narrative with its charmed inevitability, the "I" is suddenly bereft of riches, of dew. Wealth, formerly hers, has vanished, as has the "dew" that nurtured her; her palaces, now without occupants, "tenantless," drop, and she finds herself destitute. Clutching and groping in her desperation, she feels the return of the wilderness as it rolls back along *her* golden lines. These "lines" may signify both the inroads her former bounteous self has made on the world and the poetic lines formed by her words spun of gold—thus, the association between the powers of language and the sources of her capacity to transform her universe. Ironically, at the poem's close, the very lines that had earlier marked her extensive reach into the world now serve as tracks or "guide-lines" for the inescapable encroachment of the formerly banished wilderness. The specific linguistic activity she had performed in her bounteous days was an Adamic one: naming, apportioning, assigning a word to every creature she encountered:

> I dealt a word of Gold
> To every Creature—that I met—
> And Dowered—all the world.

This Edenic condition, which derives its authority from the poet's own transformation, her excess of joy, recedes as suddenly as it came, erased by the nameless wilderness, a region devoid either of human control or of organizing principle. With its clearly delineated connection between linguistic power and continuous war waged between the competing forces of self and world, this poem serves as a paradigmatic expression of the conflict that marks Dickinson's understanding of her relationship to everything outside herself. To see only two—the word equal in power to its adversary, the world—is to envision a dangerously austere, dialogic cosmos where internal energies either overcome the world or are themselves devastated by it.

Even when Dickinson's poems attest to losing in such confrontations, however, they nevertheless reveal the high ambition of the individual consciousness to transcend the inhibitory powers of rejection. By asserting that one no longer wishes for or requires what one has been denied—by, in other words, willfully embracing renunciation, Dickinson attempts to conquer the forces that oppose the self. In the province of language, however, to do without another's voice, to deny all external sources of "inspiration," demands an intellectual self-sufficiency that may prove its own undoing, for the threat remains that devoid of others' language, the poetic voice will be stifled by such defensive isolation. Dickinson writes of this poetic double-bind, expressing a condition which may prove attainable in the realm of the ideal rather than in any recognizable reality:

> To own the Art within the Soul
> The Soul to entertain
> With Silence as a Company
> And Festival maintain
>
> Is an unfurnished Circumstance
> Possession is to One
> As an Estate perpetual
> Or a reduceless Mine.
>
> (855)

The "Mine" that cannot be depleted would be the "mine" of the isolate self. Dickinson's possessive pronoun converts the terms of her deprivation into a potential resource whose hidden reserves will never fail because they lie buried deep within. To protect the imagination against the barrenness of circumstance, to guard herself against the deadening effects of a necessary isolation (the possibility that such an internal absence will produce linguistic autism), Dickinson draws upon the transformative capacities of the word. The word—her Word—thus may acquire the power to make things new as she seeks the possibility of redefining the terms of existence to coincide with the priorities of her individual consciousness. If language can achieve such authority, as it does only intermittently in Dickinson's poems, then it may indeed, as she asserts, challenge the preeminence of God's holy Word. To re-make the world according to her own image—this is the ambition of Dickinson's boldest poems. That she must renounce this attempt only to take it up once again, that she testifies to her own failures, does not diminish, but rather reaffirms the extent of her ambitions. For Dickinson imbues her poetic enterprise with a vision of language operating as defense against the pressures of rejection and exile that define her world. Here is a definition of poetry that possesses, like Blake's visionary language, the capacity to mold the terms of existence within the fires of her own imagination. Such a vision of language originates in the perceived absence of external allies and the poet's compensatory devotion not to the conditions of the world, but, instead, to what Dickinson called the "Art within the Soul." If there is "ransom in a voice," if the bounty that will restore the world to the Self resides within, then to speak in words that challenge the world is the only way a poet can endow and so change that world to make it yield to her authority. Recognizing that "all is the price of all," Dickinson creates in her self-imposed, domestic exile, a poetics of high ambition, a poetics that foreshadows the experimental, fiercely defiant voices of modernist literary experimentation. Dickinson explores the latent ambiguities of language to construct a deeply paradoxical, if, at times, bafflingly equivocal voice. By insisting upon the articulation of her own version of experience, she develops rhetorical strategies that break with tradition as they depend increasingly upon indeterminacies, upon the disruption of linguistic structures that would otherwise provide recognizable, coherent meanings.

Out of this alienation, Dickinson shapes a language that challenges the Western literary tradition's shared assumptions about the very character of figurative language itself, for she disrupts the relationship between the signifier and the signified in two ways: first by trying to replace the signified with the signifier, to transcend the world through her word, and second by using signs so that their meaning itself is not simply ironic, but self-deconstructing. Words that can be read this way, however, do not reduce in meaning, but approach an indecipherability that seeks not merely to disrupt communal meaning but to move past language's image-making power to reach the word as insoluble, irreducible construct that defies any referent, or any combination of referents. To let the Word replace the World in both meaning and the irreducible "I am that I am" of immanence, this is Dickinson's double project and its tie to a modernist poetics that rejects normative definitions to strive for an alternative order privileged by art. If the pressures that led Dickinson to such experimentation were extreme, so the defensive poetics she employs threatens to slip at any moment into self-disintegration. Yet it is here, at the brink of poetic indecipherability, where the risks of language are greatest, that Dickinson achieves her full power. Finally, her feminist poetics emerges as an experimental project that approaches modernist theories of art, for Dickinson shapes a revisionary language that pursues the possibilities of internally generated meanings as it resists the confines of figuration, the potential clarities of signification. Thus, Dickinson pursues as well a sublime if potentially fatal course as she discovers within the very indeterminacy of language a radically modern linguistic home.

SHARON CAMERON

Et in Arcadia Ego: Representation, Death, and the Problem of Boundary in Emily Dickinson

The events of the unconscious are timeless, that is, they are not ordered in time, are not changed by the passage of time, have no relation whatever to time.

—SIGMUND FREUD

The fact is that consciousness deteriorates as the result of any cerebral shock. Merely to faint is to annihilate it. How then is it possible to believe that the spirit survives the death of the body?

—MARCEL PROUST

The problem of boundaries is integral to some of our most profound concerns. What is the relationship between self and other, interior and exterior, literal and figural, past and present, time and timelessness? Were they not so crucial these questions would be pedestrian, and indeed how we answer them, whether we are able to answer them, is often an indication of the way in which we lead our lives. Jean Starobinski has recently pointed out that the connection we often make between history or past and interiority or depth is seductive precisely because it avoids the acknowledgment that some boundaries (in this case the one between past and present) render experience

From *Lyric Time: Dickinson and the Limits of Genre.* © 1979 by The Johns Hopkins University Press.

irrecoverable: "Making the most remote past coefficient to our most intimate depth is a way of refusing loss and separation, of preserving, in the crammed plenum we imagine history to be, every moment spent along the way. . . . To say that the individual constructed himself through his history is to say that the latter is cumulatively present in him and that even as it was elapsing, it was becoming internal structure." Such a conception may be regarded as a way of mediating between the absolute severance of past and present and their absolute fusion. For if the past is "inside us" rather than attending us, it is no longer necessarily subject to our conscious repossession. To be experienced again it must be re-presented. The past can be conceived, then, as having a diachronic progression that, once it comes into being, assumes synchronic structure. Such a conception both frees the self for future action by asserting that the past is safely contained behind or below the present, and simultaneously binds it by the selfsame fact of that containment. Like it or not, boundaries are not so easy to establish. While we frequently construe past and present by wedging a boundary between the parameters of each, as often in our conception of present and future, we hope to annihilate the severity of such boundaries, for could this be finessed, the present might be relieved of the indeterminacy that awaits it, and simultaneously gifted by the exhilarations of desired change.

I raise these issues in order to provide a context for, as well as to suggest the preliminary complexity of, characteristic problems of temporal boundary in Dickinson's poems. The most eschatological indication of boundary or division is, of course, death, and it is hence no accident that Dickinson's utterances hover around this subject with as much perseverance as the fly in one of her more noted poems. Indeed we might regard death as a special instance of the problem of boundary, representing the ultimate division, the extreme case, the infuriating challenge to a dream of synchrony. On the border of conception, the limits of experience, death both epitomizes the problem of boundary and offers itself as its severest manifestation. It is in this context that we shall examine Dickinson's death utterances, asking how the straying of a poem across impossible limits leads inevitably to the collapse of other boundaries, namely those that set themselves up as walls between figure and thing figured, between literal meanings and metaphoric ones. For if the problem Starobinski discusses may be construed as one of constructing boundaries, in Dickinson's death utterances, on which this chapter will focus, the problem is often one of destroying them. In the following pages, however, we shall see that the relationship between construction and destruction is a complex one—objects slip from one side of a line to another with the ease of a thought falling out of consciousness and rising back into it. And, as with consciousness, whose goal is to enlarge its own area of being, so with the life-space occupied by a poem that pushes with all its might against the line of death, in the hopes that it can, by however scant measure, enlarge its territory.

In part 2 of this [essay], I shall examine poems in which the question "Is death literal or figural?" does not admit of a simple or certain answer, in which death is neither a clearly phenomenological fact nor a clearly psychic phenomenon. In such instances we will see that it is difficult to distinguish between figure and thing figured because of their complex relationship to each other. In part 3 I shall turn briefly to poems that purport actually to mark the boundary between life and death and shall look, in conclusion, at those poems that trespass beyond it. I shall tentatively suppose that fusions between the literal and the figural (often represented in Dickinson's poems in terms of death and despair) are related to, and perhaps generative of, the temporal fusions that exist in larger scale in those poems where it is not clear on which side of the grave the speaker's utterance takes place. Finally, in examining these poems I shall want to ask how such fusions obscure the fact of death, blur its edges so that its future threat is undercut by the implicit assertion of its presence or prefigurement, and alternately to ask whether this prefigurement, ultimately subverted, throws death's outlines into sharper relief precisely by its distance from what, in the end, can only be intimated.

II

In many of Dickinson's poems, the relationship between death and despair is complex, not only because one may be the generative occasion for the other, but also and more significantly, because one is liable to be confused with the other. Thus in the following poem, while it is clear enough that the speaker has been reprieved from literal death, the psychic turmoil of its anticipation—or, in simple terms, the torture—so overwhelms the significance of what it anticipates that we are thrown off balance and can no longer specify the shape of the poem's predicament. Such a perplexity is acknowledged by the speaker herself, as the final question of the poem testifies:

> 'Twas like a Maelstrom, with a notch,
> That nearer, every Day,
> Kept narrowing its boiling Wheel
> Until the Agony
>
> Toyed coolly with the final inch
> Of your delirious Hem—

And you dropt, lost,
When something broke—
And let you from a Dream—

As if a Goblin with a Gauge—
Kept measuring the Hours—
Until you felt your Second
Weigh, helpless, in his Paws—

And not a Sinew—stirred—could help,
And sense was setting numb—
When God—remembered—and the Fiend
Let go, then, Overcome—

As if your Sentence stood—pronounced—
And you were frozen led
From Dungeon's luxury of Doubt
To Gibbets, and the Dead—

And when the Film had stitched your eyes
A Creature gasped "Reprieve"!
Which Anguish was the utterest—then—
To perish, or to live?

(P 414)

The anonymous creature who in the final analogy orders the halting of the death process seems, like the speaker, to be wrought to the breaking point; he is nothing akin to the demons who in calm "Toy coolly," practically, with the victim. Nor is he akin to the God whose calm borders on indifference. He seems rather to mediate between the two, as if only mediation could distinguish them. In fact it is not insignificant that the power which orders the reprieve should be of uncertain source, for the affliction is of uncertain source, and that uncertainty is reflected in the poem's diction, which rocks back and forth from one connotative sphere to another, as unsettled in its vocabulary for the experience as in the experience itself. This lack of clarity is illustrated in the initial image of the whirlpool. While it steers in the speaker's direction, we note that the "boiling Wheel" and the "notch" are both parts of the same cosmic machine whose complete shape is blanked out. As in a dream (and perhaps it is the dream feeling in the first stanza that prompts the explicit acknowledgment of dream in the next) the synecdochic distortion that isolates and magnifies is frightening precisely because it lacks a context. Disjoint, the only parts that can be seen are vengeful, annihilative. In stanza two the speaker is held upside down ("delirious") just perceptibly by the hem of her clothes, remaining only marginally in existence. What "breaks" in the stanza subsequently are the connections to that existence, and the speaker is delivered from the dream of this death, but delivered into what is unclear.

In the next four stanzas, the attempt to recapitulate a story whose meaning the speaker still does not know is laden with confusions of the earlier rendition. The impulse to tell and retell the same story has a quality of hysteria to it, for the implicit belief that to tell the story over will insure getting it straight is proved wrong. In the final lines the poem's focus shifts from the anticipation of death to a question about its status. If life is "like a Maelstrom, with a notch," and if what is being measured is human endurance, then "To perish" would at least end it. But the poem concludes, as it has been borne along, by the waves of its own exhaustion at the pervasiveness of psychic distress. The speaker may have been rescued from actual death but she seems as a consequence condemned to suffer the same torture to whose stages the poem's stanzas, we would have thought, promised her a terminal point.

While "'Twas like a Maelstrom with a notch" explores the border between life and death—its most articulate denomination of that border contained in the harrowing image of the eyes almost "stitched" permanently—it also raises the question of whether death is a metaphor for the torture or whether the torture is only a prelude to death. Insofar as the poem's final question relocates its subject or, at any rate, calls it into question, we not only ask with the speaker which anguish is most extreme, we also question our prior understanding of the generative experience for the representation. The entire poem, beginning with the second word, understood as a series of analogies by necessity, casts its subject into doubt. The fact of death and the psychic anguish that anticipates it are really no longer separate. In effectively annihilating the boundary between the two, Dickinson forces us to transcend a line that we know, in reality, it is impossible to transcend. With this verbal fusion she perhaps harbors the illusion that she has gained knowledge of what lies over the border. For an implicit, if secondary, assumption of the poem is that the unsurpassable psychic anguish will guarantee her safe or, at any rate, unsurprised passage to death.

If actual death can best be conjured by descriptions of acute pain, Dickinson frequently reverses the representational fusion by summoning psychic anguish in the explicit terms of death and burial:

I felt a Funeral, in my Brain,
And Mourners to and fro
Kept treading—treading—till it seemed
That Sense was breaking through—

And when they all were seated,
A Service, like a Drum—
Kept beating—beating—till I thought
My Mind was going numb—

And then I heard them lift a Box
And creak across my Soul
With those same Boots of Lead, again,
Then Space—began to toll,

As all the Heavens were a Bell,
And Being, but an Ear,
And I, and Silence, some strange Race
Wrecked, solitary, here—

And then a Plank in Reason, broke,
And I dropped down, and down—
And hit a World, at every plunge,
And Finished knowing—then—

(P 280)

We may speculate that the poem charts the stages in the speaker's loss of consciousness, and this loss of consciousness is a dramatization of the deadening forces that today would be known as repression. We may further suppose that the speaker is reconstructing—or currently knowing—an experience whose pain in the past rendered it impossible to know. We note that part of the strangeness of her speech lies in the fact that not only is the poem grammatically past tense, but it also seems emotionally past tense. It illustrates the way in which one can relate experience and, at the same time, suffer a disassociation from it. Of course in this case the experience itself is one of disassociation. Since the speaker adds no emotive comment to the recollection, it is as if even in the recounting the words did not penetrate the walls of her own understanding. That the poem is about knowledge and the consequence of its repression is clear enough from the poem's initial conceit, for people do not feel funerals and certainly not in the brain. In addition, as a consequence of the persistent downward motion of the poem, we see that the funeral is rendered in terms of a burial, and this fusion or confusion points to a parallel confusion between unconsciousness and death. The burial of something in the mind—of a thought or experience or wish—the rendering of it unconscious, lacks an etiology; its occasion and even content here remain unspecified. As a consequence our attention is fixed on the process itself.

Examining the conceit, we can speculate that the mourners represent that part of the self which fights to resurrect or keep alive the thought the speaker is trying to commit to burial. They stand for that part of the self which feels conflict about the repressive gesture. "Treading—treading—," the self in conflict goes over the same ground of its argument with itself, and sense threatens to dissolve, "break through—," because of the mind's inability to resolve its contradictory impulses. In the second stanza, on a literal level the participants of the funeral sit for the service and read words over the dead. On a figural level the confusion of the mind quiets to one unanimous voice issuing its consent to the burial of meaning. But the mind's unanimity, its single voice, is no less horrible. The speaker hears it as a drum: rhythmic, repetitious, numbing. In the fourth stanza, the repressive force lashes the speaker with retaliatory distortion: the "Heavens" and the cosmos they represent toll as one overwhelming "Bell"; "Being" is reduced to the "Ear" that must receive it. No longer fighting the repressive instinct (for the "Mourners" have disappeared, "Being" and "I" are united), the self is a victim passively awaiting its own annihilation. When the "Plank in Reason," the last stronghold to resist its own dissolution, gives, and the speaker plummets through successive levels of meaning (an acknowledgment that repression has degrees), the result is a death of consciousness. As J. V. Cunningham remarks, the poem is a representation of a "psychotic episode" at the end of which the speaker passes out.

But if we agree that the poem is not about actual death, why is the funeral rendered in such literal terms, terms that might well lead a careless reader to mistake its very subject? Paul de Man, distinguishing between irony and allegory, provides a suggestive answer. Allegory, he writes, involves "the tendency of the language toward narrative, the spreading out along the axis of an imaginary time in order to give duration to what is, in fact simultaneous within the subject." The structure of irony is the reverse of this form—the reduction of time to one single moment in which the self appears double or disjoint. Irony, de Man writes, is "*staccato* . . . a synchronic structure, while allegory appears as a successive mode capable of engendering duration as the illusion of a continuity that it knows to be illusory." Irony and allegory, he concludes, are two faces of the same experience, opposite ways of rendering sequence and doubleness. De Man's distinctions are illuminating for our

understanding of the fusions in "I felt a Funeral in my Brain," for the poem
exhibits a double sense of its own experience and of the form in which that
experience is to be rendered. With no terms of its own, it is through its very
disembodiment, its self-reflexive disassociation, that the experience wields
the power it does. If it could be made palpable and objectified, it might be
known and hence mastered. Thus the allegory of the funeral attempts to
exteriorize and give a temporal structure to what is in fact interior and
simultaneous. Because we see the stages of the funeral (stages that
correspond to steps that will complete the repressive instinct) we cannot help
but view repression in terms of death. Thus the funeral imagery, replete with
mourners, coffin, and service, seems both to distract from the poem's subject
of repression and to insist on the severity of its consequences. But it is in the
tension between the two modes of knowing and of representation, between
an allegorical structure and an ironic one, that the poem's interest lies. For
structure and sequence fall away in the ironic judgment of the poem's last
line, which suggests, if implicitly, that action (exteriority) and knowledge
(interiority) will always diverge. Even the attempt to reconstruct the
experience and do it over with a different consequence leads, as it did the first
time, to blankness. This divergence is further exemplified in the odd order
of the poem's events: the funeral precedes death, at least the death of
consciousness. Such inversion of normal sequence necessitates a figural
reading of the poem and makes perfect sense within it, for Dickinson seems
to be claiming we cannot "not know" in isolation and at will. What we
choose not to know, what we submerge, like the buried root of a plant that
sucks all water and life toward its source, pulls us down with a vengeance
toward it.

　　If "'Twas like a Maelstrom with a notch" suggests that agony may be a
metaphor for death, and "I felt a Funeral in my Brain" that death is a
metaphor for repressed agony, the problem of fusion becomes even more
complex in the following poem, where it is truly impossible to tell whether
death is a figure or the thing itself. In "'Tis so appalling it exhilarates," as in
other poems . . . in which naming is an indirect venture, this poem begins
with an elusive "it":

> 'Tis so appalling—it exhilarates—
> So over Horror, it half Captivates—
> The Soul stares after it, secure—
> A Sepulchre, fears frost, no more—
>
> To scan a Ghost, is faint—
> But grappling, conquers it—

How easy, Torment, now—
Suspense kept sawing so—

The Truth, is Bald, and Cold—
But that will hold—
If any are not sure—
We show them—prayer—
But we, who know,
Stop hoping, now—

Looking at Death, is Dying—
Just let go the Breath—
And not the pillow at your Cheek
So Slumbereth—

Others, Can wrestle—
Your's, is done—
And so of Wo, bleak dreaded—come,
It sets the Fright at liberty—
And Terror's free—
Gay, Ghastly, Holiday!

(P 281)

While the subject remains unspecified, its identity seems almost not to matter, for that obscurity is overpowered in significance by the initial formulation which suggests a relationship between extremity and exhilaration dread and release, excruciation and ease. The necessary arena for the free-play of terror is guaranteed by the absolute finality of the feared thing, and whether the finality is one of actual death or whether it is of a truth so "Bald" and "Cold—" as to precipitate the death of illusion is irrelevant. For to conceive of death seems to be to suffer its consequences, even if only in the imagination. "Looking at Death, is Dying—," or as Shakespeare wrote analogously in Sonnet 64 of the "ruin" implicit in the very "rumination" of loss: "This thought is as a death which cannot choose / But weep to have that which it fears to lose." In both instances the mind is liberated from hope and from the attendant anxiety about achieving its object. Since the task of Dickinson's poem is to distinguish between process and conclusion, intimation and knowledge, the dread of terror and its safe arrival, it rests its case on the implicit assertion that you cannot top or bottom a superlative. The content of the superlative thus matters very little; what must be appreciated is the consequence of mastering it.

In the poems discussed thus far in which Dickinson effects a fusion between death as figure and death as fact, the status of death—both called into question by the confusion between figure and fact and simultaneously dismissed by our inability to resolve it—is relegated to a secondary position, and what we are concerned with is a speaker's mastery of a condition that she understands no more than we do. In " 'Twas like a Maelstrom with a notch" the anticipatory state preceding death so partakes of death's characteristics that even on this side of death the speaker is not safe from them; in "I felt a Funeral in my Brain" the death of meaning blots consciousness out, brings a death to the mind so total that the body responds by losing cognizance of itself. In " 'Tis so appalling it exhilarates" any ultimate horror has the severity of death; that there is no distinction between the two seems to be precisely the lesson of the poem. In brief, all of these poems exemplify a duality that is both conscious of itself and dismissive of consciousness.

How such fusions of meaning occur is the explicit subject of the following poem in which Dickinson examines the very process whereby the synthesis we have been discussing comes into being:

> There's a certain Slant of light,
> Winter Afternoons—
> That oppresses, like the Heft
> Of Cathedral Tunes—
>
> Heavenly Hurt, it gives us—
> We can find no scar,
> But internal difference,
> Where the Meanings, are—
>
> None may teach it—Any—
> 'Tis the Seal Despair—
> An imperial affliction
> Sent us of the Air—
>
> When it comes, the Landscape listens—
> Shadows—hold their breath—
> When it goes, 'tis like the Distance
> On the look of Death—

> (P 258)

How does "light" come into relation with "Despair—" and "Despair—" into relation with "Death—"? What are the generative fusions of the poem and why is the grammar of its concluding lines itself so confusing? We note that light is a "Seal" or sign of despair and we remember that Dickinson was much too conscientious a reader of the Bible and particularly of the Book of Revelation not to have intended "the Seal Despair—" to point to an experience that was, if a secular experience can be so, both visionary and apocalyptic. In the Bible, however, while the self is "not worthy to open the scroll and break the seals" that will reveal divine agency, in the speaker's world meaning must be deduced within the privacy of a solitary consciousness. Thus "None may teach it [to] any [one else]"; "None may teach it any[thing]" (it is not subject to alteration); "None may teach it—[not] any[one]." But the "Meanings" of the event are not self-generated; if this is a poem about the solipsistic labor of experience, it is not about autism. To be credited as vision, despair must also seek its connection to the generative source outside itself. For light may seal despair in, make it internal and irrevocable, but the irrevocability, by a line of association that runs just under the poem's surface, prompts the larger thought of death.

In fact, the poem is about correlatives, about how interior transformations that are both invisible and immune to alteration from the outside world are at the same time generated by that world. The relationship between the "Slant of light" in the landscape and the "Seal Despair—" within may be clarified by an analogy to Erich Auerbach's distinction between figure and its fulfillment, for the "Slant of light" and the "Seal Despair—" are not in this poem merely premonitions of death, but are, in fact, kinds or *types* of death. Indeed it could be asserted that in the entire Dickinson canon, despair is often a *figura* for death, not as Auerbach uses the word to specify related historical events, but rather as he indicates the word to denote an event that prefigures an ultimate occurrence and at the same time is already imbued with its essence. Figural interpretation presupposes much greater equality between its terms than either allegory or symbol for, in the former, the sign is a mere form and, in the latter, the symbol is always fused with what it represents and can actually replace it. While it is true that figural interpretation ordinarily applies to historical events rather than to natural events, and while the "Slant of light" and the "Seal Despair—" are indeed natural and psychological events not separated by much time, they have a causal or prefigurative relationship to each other that is closer to the relationship implicit in the figural structure than to that in the symbolic one. Certainly it would be incorrect to say that they are symbols. "Light" and "Seal," however, are in relation to "Death—" as a premise is to a conclusion. Auerbach, speaking of the relationship between two historical events implicit in the figural structure, writes, "Both . . . have something provisional and incomplete about them; they point to one another and both point to something in the future, something still to come, which will be the actual, real, and definitive event." We may regard the "Slant of light" and the "Seal Despair—" as having just such a signatory relationship as that described above. For the light is indirect; it thus seeks a counterpart to help it deepen into meaning. The "definitive event" in the poem to which "light" and "Seal" point is, of course, "Death—." While we would expect the departure of the light to yield distance from the "look of Death—," instead the preposition "on" not only designates the space between the speaker and the light but also identifies that light as one cast by death, and in turn casting death on, or in the direction of, the speaker. The "Slant of light," recognized only at a distance—its meaning comprehended at the moment of its disappearance— is revelatory of "Death—", is "Death['s]—" prefiguration. Figure fuses with fact, interprets it, and what we initially called the confusion of the two now makes sense in the context of divination.

If the light is indeed one of death, then we have the answer to why and how it "oppresses" in the first stanza and to the earlier oblique comparison of it to "Cathedral Tunes—." What Dickinson achieves in the poem is truly remarkable, for she takes a traditional symbol and scours it so thoroughly of its traditional associations with life that before we get to the poem's conclusion the image leans in the direction of mystery, dread, and darkness. By the time we arrive at the final simile and at the direct association of light and death we are not so much surprised as relieved at the explicitness of the revelation. It is the indirect association of "light" and "Death—" (the "Slant" that pulls them together at first seemingly without purpose) that prompts "Despair—." We feel it indirectly, internally, obliquely. Were we to know it, it would be death. For Dickinson, death is the apocalyptic vision, the straightening of premonition into fact, figure into fulfillment.

The fusions I have been discussing either between literal reality and its metaphoric representation (where literal reality permanently assumes those metaphoric characteristics that seemed initially intended only to illuminate it) or between the more formal *figura* and its fulfillment (where events contain in a predictive relationship the essence as well as the form of each other) raise the question of whether we can ever know anything in its own terms, and suggest perhaps that knowledge is not, as we might have thought, absolute, but is rather always relational. If these fusions link the historical or natural world with the divine one, the analogue with the real thing, they are predicated on a structure of simultaneous correspondence rather than of linear progression. The truth that is "Bald, and Cold—" is death, it does not lead to it. The "certain Slant of light," although it prefigures death, also already contains its essence. The thing in other words is saturated in the terms of its own figuration. Given the synchrony of this relationship, we are not very far from those poems that strain to annihilate the boundaries of time itself and to treat death as if its very reality could be cast into the present tense, experienced, and somehow survived. The effort to know what cannot be known, to survive it, is thus carried one step further in those poems in which the speaker travels over the boundary from life to death to meet death on its own ground. Given the presumption of the quest, figural structure often gives way to allegory or at any rate to the acknowledgment of the inadequacy of simple analogue, for on the other side of death true knowledge can find no correspondences.

III

It was Heidegger who asserted that we perceive time only because we have to die. [Elsewhere, we have seen] how for Dickinson, too, despair or living death associates itself with timelessness, "When everything that ticked—has stopped—." In the following poem, actual death turns analogy into metaphor, the dead person imaged as a stopped clock:

> A Clock stopped—
> Not the Mantel's—
> Geneva's farthest skill
> Cant put the puppet bowing—
> That just now dangled still—
>
> An awe came on the Trinket!
> The Figures hunched, with pain—
> Then quivered out of Decimals—
> Into Degreeless Noon—
>
> It will not stir for Doctor's—
> This Pendulum of snow—
> This Shopman importunes it—
> While cool—concernless No—
>
> Nods from the Gilded pointers—
> Nods from the Seconds slim—
> Decades of Arrogance between
> The Dial life—
> And Him—
>
> (P 287)

The dead person's "Arrogance" inheres in his silence, his stoic resistance to the "importun[ing]" of those who would set him going again. Given the enormousness of his refusal, the task of vitalizing him is regarded as a mechanical feat that meets overwhelming failure. If life is a "Dial" measured by the degrees to which it can undergo transformation, death is inert, a "Pendulum of snow—." This, of course, is one way of figuring it—the riddle of the human being no longer alive and therefore unrecognizable as human. For the dead person is a "Trinket" and a "puppet," and comes closest to becoming a "Figure" only in its earlier proximity to the pain of temporality. If part of Dickinson's intention in the poem is to make us "guess what" or "guess who" the subject is, it is largely a consequence of her insistence on our participation in the mystery of death's temporal transcendence.

But despite Dickinson's depiction of the clock-person, life is not synonymous with time. For life endures, or fails to, in the face of time that is continually passing away. It is to rectify this discrepancy, to cure the difference between time and the life that is at odds with it, that Dickinson suggests a temporal transcendence more daring than that of death's. Thus in her proleptic utterances, the dead person becomes one with time either dramatically, as in the preceding poem of the stopped clock, or more subtly, by collapsing the boundaries between past, present, and future. Moreover, the speakers' failure to distinguish temporal categories, the predicated fusion *between* them, suggests an analogous fusion *with* them. In this second fusion internal or subjective time (that clock by which a self measures what is of importance to it) becomes one with external or objective time (which encompasses, disregards, and most usually opposes such private meanings). That external events rarely coincide with internal ones, that our inner thoughts have their own tempo and hence their own significance—can, for example, race at breakneck speed while the clock on the wall goes steadily as usual—are facts so obvious they barely require elaboration. Of the difference between internal and external time, Friedrich Kümmel has written: "If only internal time had reality, death would have no meaning and, conversely, where only external time ruled, life would come to an end." But the fusion between the two in Dickinson's poems lies precisely in the fact that although the speaker has died, life has not come to an end. As a consequence, the dead person, having transcended time, can speak from beyond the grave. For the dead person who is like the Roman god Janus (the god of gates and transitions, who looks with one face into the past and the other into the future), speech seems to be a function of the expansion of the present to include past and future, as well as of the synthesis of subjective and objective time. Put succinctly, the speaker has passed the boundary of life while, at the same time, retaining all of the characteristic features of life: memory, feeling, expectation, and the ability to speak and tell stories of these.

Erwin Panofsky provides us with an interesting counterpart to this phenomenon in the visual arts. In his essay "Poussin and the Elegiac Tradition, " Panofsky traces the transformation of the grammatically correct interpretation of the phrase *Et in Arcadia ego*, as it is represented in a painting by Guercino, to a misattribution of the phrase and a break in the medieval moralizing tradition, as it is represented in a painting by Poussin. Both paintings show human figures confronting death. But in Guercino's work the shepherds depicted are startled by their confrontation with death and the shock of their encounter seems naturally, as well as grammatically, to attribute the words "Even in Arcadia, there am I" to the death's-head, that is, to death itself. In Poussin's painting, we see four figures standing in front of a tomb, no longer in dramatic discovery of death, and attending tranquilly to speech that it therefore makes more sense to attribute not to the tomb but to the dead person who is buried within it. Thus it suddenly seems right to mistranslate the accompanying Latin phrase as "I, too, lived in Arcadia," that is to ascribe its words to a dead Arcadian shepherd or shepherdess. The misattribution of the Latin phrase prompted by Poussin's representation may do violence to Latin grammar but, Panofsky insists, it is in harmony with the new conception of the painting, which "projects the message of the Latin phrase from the present into the past—all the more forcibly as the behavior of the figures no longer expresses surprise and dismay but quiet, reminiscent meditation. . . . [With the] whole phrase projected into the past: what had been a menace has become a remembrance."

The transformation from terror to meditation, memento mori to elegy that Panofsky describes between Guercino's representation and Poussin's can be seen equally between those poems of Dickinson's that come upon and stop short of death's boundary and those poems that transcend it. In addition, the capacity to remember death rather than to anticipate it, to make past an experience of death that can really only be future, seems to have a similar consequence in Poussin's painting and in Dickinson's poems: in both cases it bequeaths speech to the dead person. We shall turn first to Dickinson's proleptic utterances (looking initially at three poems that stop short of the boundary line and, in so doing, mark it), then back to Panofsky's essay when, with more grounding in the questions it raises, we may explore its insights further. In scrutinizing Dickinson's proleptic poems, I shall be primarily interested in the two phenomena I have sketched above: the fusion of subjective and objective time, and the power of speech beyond the grave.

In the following poem in which the speaker documents the experience of near-death, the depiction is surrealistic, punctuated by the gaps in thought that attest to the terror of fragmentary comprehension:

That after Horror—that 'twas *us*—
That passed the mouldering Pier—
Just as the Granite Crumb let go—
Our Savior, by a Hair—

A second more, had dropped too deep
For Fisherman to plumb—
The very profile of the Thought
Puts Recollection numb—

The possibility—to pass
Without a Moment's Bell—
Into Conjecture's presence—
Is like a Face of Steel—
That suddenly looks into our's
With a metallic grin—
The Cordiality of Death—
Who drills his Welcome in—

                                                (P 286)

Indeed one might speculate that it is the speaker's lost grip on the land that makes *it* appear to suffer dissolution. The dream-like image of a "mouldering Pier—," eaten away partly by water, partly by the spectre of death, belongs to and marks the end of the earthly terrain. Before that spectre the earth itself is reduced to a "Granite Crumb." Since the first stanza represents a state of rapid transition and passage, it is fitting that what the speaker comprehend be partial and partially rendered. Thus although the first stanza's last line implies a subjunctive ("If we had dropped a hair further, we would have met our savior"), the assertion is truncated and elliptical in the extreme, utterance representing the split-second of a miss and its retrospective appreciation. But, in fact, the speaker is not able to penetrate the instant of near-annihilation. Scrutiny does not expand the experiential instant, cannot pry it apart for more substantial examination. The recollection, like the reality, will not open itself up. A "profile of the Thought" is the most that can be tolerated without the speaker's blacking out. In stanza two, as in the first stanza, we are conscious of how thin and inhospitable to knowledge the moment of transition appears even in memory. The speaker gains entry to the experience only by distorting it, by re-presenting it in terms blunt and crude enough to provide room for her exploration.

Only the concluding stanza accomplishes what the first two cannot. It acknowledges the reserve of the boundary line, that fact that it provides no warning or "Bell—" of the enormity of transformation it is facilitating. The stanza then freezes its own conception so that "Conjecture's presence—" (that which can only be present to us by conjecture, specifically death) hardens into static knowledge. In the last five lines of the poem all the earlier characteristics of the experience suddenly reverse themselves and what was evasive is now inevitable; what vague, now harrowingly delimited. The "Face of Steel—," the "metallic grin," the "drill" of the "Welcome" close upon the speaker in the half-lewd gesture that, as we have seen, frequently connects death and sexuality in Dickinson's work, and nail her down. In the first two stanzas she had been suggesting that she could not know this experience if she tried; in the last stanza it is clear that she cannot help but know it. The passage completed, even if only conceptually, guarantees all the inevitability that attends any certain state. Only the shadow line separating life from death, which may be glimpsed and touched but not seen or inhabited, is a featureless no man's land free of specific characteristics. At the end of the poem the speaker is still tottering on the edge of the line dividing life from death, but the strength of the completed conception no longer admits of any resolve to turn back.

The attempt to glimpse death's visage while escaping its grip, to know its features from a distance, to straddle the line between ignorance and knowledge, is an abortive one in the preceding poem, and Dickinson acknowledges that fact. One cannot have knowledge and be protected from its consequences at the same time. The "possibility—to pass" over the line is "like a Face of Steel—" precisely because of how absolutely it seals off the route back.

If "That after Horror that 'twas *us*" represents an involuntary and sudden arrival at the line that separates life from death, the following two utterances suggest more considered attempts to anticipate such a juncture and, through anticipation, to forestall its consequences. In "I read my sentence steadily," the wit of the intellectual construction hastens to announce its nonchalance at the "sentence" of death, but the poem's cavalier railery and its matter-of-fact evenness of tone are belied by the profusion of pronouns and the schism within the self that they imply:

> I read my sentence—steadily—
> Reviewed it with my eyes,
> To see that I made no mistake
> In it's extremest clause—
> The Date, and manner, of the shame—

And then the Pious Form
That "God have mercy" on the Soul
The Jury voted Him—
I made my soul familiar—with her extremity—
That at the last, it should not be a novel Agony—
But she, and Death, acquainted—
Meet tranquilly, as friends—
Salute, and pass, without a Hint—
And there, the Matter ends—

                                                    (P 412)

Charles Anderson's fine discussion of the poem as a dream-trial in which the mind discovers that the body has been condemned to death and, given no possibility of appeal, attempts to deal with the sentence by so fragmenting the self that it escapes realistic association with the condemned person renders further elaborate comment redundant. But in the context of our discussion, we should note that the purpose of the "Review" is to domesticate "extremity—," to make it "familiar—" so that the line separating life from death is apprehended prior to the speaker's encounter with it. In fact, the nature of her acquaintance with death remains deliberately unspecified, and the result is an intimation of an unsettling partnership, more strange for going unacknowledged ("without a Hint—"). We might simplify the problem by saying that acquaintance without recognition is what the speaker desires and hence depicts: to meet death without recognizing it, to be spared recognition, to have the body dissolve (as the pun in the last line smartly indicates) without the soul's witness to the dissolution, so neatly to dispose of the "Matter" (the subject and the body) that pain is an extravagance cleverly evaded. If the flippancy of the formulation and all the legal wrangling deny that the "Agony" of ending cannot, by definition, but be "novel," Dickinson faced it squarely in a more sober utterance:

Our journey had advanced—
Our feet were almost come
To that odd Fork in Being's Road—
Eternity—by Term—

Our pace took sudden awe—
Our feet—reluctant—led—
Before—were Cities—but Between—
The Forest of the Dead—

> Retreat—was out of Hope—
> Behind—a Sealed Route—
> Eternity's White Flag—Before—
> And God—at every Gate—
>
>   (P 615)

In an earlier poem whose narration of a journey away from life recalls "Our journey had advanced," Dickinson had written:

> 'Twas the old—road—through pain—
> That unfrequented—one—
> With many a turn—and thorn—
> That stops—at Heaven—
>
>   (P 344)

But we note significant differences between the two narrations. For one thing, the traveler in the first poem, as later stanzas indicate, is not the speaker; for another, the journey's end is, finally, "too out of sight—" to apprehend; but most important, since the terminal point in " 'Twas the old road" is heaven, the brink of the speaker's vision, the boundary point that prohibits further travel, remains just this side of death. Such a designation of boundary is, as we have seen, characteristic of the poems we have been examining. In "That after Horror that 'twas us," and even in poems whose subject is the relationship between figural and literal death ("I felt a Funeral in my Brain," and "'Twas like a Maelstrom with a notch"), the placement of boundary occurs at that moment prior to death—or, in the case of the former poem, prior to unconsciousness—which mediates between life and death. In "Our journey had advanced," however, as Geoffrey Hartman, Robert Weisbuch, and Harold Bloom have suggested, an interesting displacement is effected: death, no longer the terminus of experience, becomes instead a mediating point, a middle ground from whose territory a speaker can gaze further, into the reaches of eternity. The poem's premise, in other words, might be explained as follows: if death is not conclusion, is in fact only a step, albeit a significant one, along the way then it can be depicted as known or, at any rate, subject to knowledge. For the psychological requirement of such poems seems to be not that death be depicted as unknowable, but rather that some terminal point be depicted as unknowable. Once one adds a new element to the customary sequence, a "beyond" to death, one extends and amplifies the phenomenologically inhabitable territory, and relocates the crucial boundary point not at the moment of death, but rather after it.

In "Our journey had advanced," which almost asks to be read as a diagram subject to its own revision, our picture of the poem's geography alters with the speaker's own more sophisticated appreciation of it. The first stanza seems to imply a conventional terminal point to experience: one branch of the fork is "Being" itself, the other branch is "Eternity—" or death; "Eternity—" is an implied consequence of death, with an effective fusion between the two. However, this way of depicting it is apprehended as mistaken close-up. "Sudden awe—" is a consequence of the speaker's recognition that death and "Eternity—" are not the same; the fork cannot be directly traversed, and the mediating point that separates "Being" from "Eternity—!" has dimension and territory of its own. Indeed, as depicted, there is an implied vastness to "The Forest of the Dead—." What had seemed like a "Between—," a point that barely needed mention, has become a formidable space in its own right. Given such a recognition, the territory must now be mapped in new terms. The fork that, in stanza one, involved a simple and single split and that implicitly suggested options, in the concluding stanza straightens and narrows to preclude choice ("Retreat—was out of Hope—") and also to suggest that the road traversed is one-way ("Behind—a Sealed Route—"). What had been represented as a "Fork" is now more accurately depicted as a chronological progression: "Before—" (previous to this) "were Cities," but they are past. "Between—" (the boundary point swelled to new dimension by the housing of its inhabitants) is "The Forest of the Dead—." Death, in other words, is present. And "Eternity's White Flag—Before—" (ahead) is future.

The two opposite connotations of "Before—" (meaning "prior to" and "in front of") within so brief a space afford a mimetic parody of the poem's pattern of intersecting "identities" that, upon scrutiny, turn out to be different, as "Eternity—" is, for example, different from death, although in stanza one they are perceived implicitly as the same. What appears single or unitary in meaning and identity ("Eternity—" and death) is double; what double (the two-pronged fork of "Being" and "Eternity—") is at least triple, as the designations of "Cities—," "Forest," and "White Flag—" illustrate. For "Eternity—" is not "Term[inus]—," or at least not as the speaker initially thought, but rather lies before her. If, as we saw in the previous chapter, in "Behind Me—dips Eternity—/Before Me—Immortality—," the speaker is, rather simply, the "Term between—" the two, in this more complicated geography, "at the boundary" or "Before—" designates "on both sides of." For in "Our journey had advanced," the boundary line can be re-placed or dis-placed in direct proportion to the speaker's recognition that ending itself, neither stable nor certain, remains subject to perpetual re-definition. In a letter to the Norcross sisters, Dickinson had confessed: "I cannot tell how

Eternity seems." Then gesturing toward her own evasiveness: "It sweeps around me like a sea."

In "Our journey had advanced," the representations of boundary correct each other as vision sharpens into revelation and revelation, at the poem's conclusion, fades into blankness. The point at which the multiple conceptions of boundary intersect and the fact of the intersection is of significance, for the poem concludes by obliterating the very distinctions it has been at such pains to establish. White, that color enigmatic for interpretation in all of Dickinson's poems, is here a manifest emblem of inscrutability, a symbol purified of specific content. It signals the existence of eternity, marks it, and just as insistently seals it from view. If "Eternity's White Flag—" is the sign of meaning that cannot be divined at a distance, the poem's concluding line points to the agent of that meaning. But unlike the carefully charted areas of "Being," death and "Eternity—," "God—at every Gate," or ubiquitous presence, obscures distinction and insists on showing up the intersection of meanings about which I spoke earlier. The poem concludes with a suffusion of whiteness and vigilance, both of which overpower and imply the merging of the separate states previously articulated. The speaker's apprehension of "Eternity—" and of God's presiding presence over everything has not so much its own meaning as an effect of obliterating discrete meanings. Swallowed up in the enormousness of colorlessness and divine presence, the terminus of meaning and distinction intersects with the end of their necessity.

"That after Horror that 'twas *us*," "I read my sentence steadily," and "Our journey had advanced" allow us to linger in death's presence without actually going beyond it. Unlike the poems that fuse the literal and the figural and unlike those that effect temporal fusions between life and death, these utterances are halted from fusion by the very prohibition to knowledge that experience implies. The following two poems defy such prohibitions. While the temporal fusion between life and death is more apparently dramatic than any we have encountered so far, its result seems to throw death into a form that shrugs off comprehension or correspondence. Death, in these poems, though assumed and, in one instance, personified, is not fused or confused with anything; it is most distinctly itself, and in both of the poems I shall examine its purpose seems to be the implicit chastisement of the speaker for the boldness of the poems' very premise. Make the future present though she will, death's meaning still lingers beyond it. A speaker may put herself in a carriage with death and hand him the reins, but for all the intimacy this implies, the journey's end remains a mystery.

The crossing point between life and death is seen from a new perspective when a dead person reflects on the past-tense occurrence of the moment of her dying and, in so doing, reconstructs it as if it were present. Dying here is not projected or imagined. It is rather recollected:

> I heard a Fly buzz—when I died—
> The Stillness in the Room
> Was like the Stillness in the Air—
> Between the Heaves of Storm—
>
> The Eyes around—had wrung them dry—
> And Breaths were gathering firm
> For that last Onset—when the King
> Be witnessed—in the Room—
>
> I willed my Keepsakes—Signed away
> What portion of me be
> Assignable—and then it was
> There interposed a Fly—
>
> With Blue—uncertain stumbling Buzz—
> Between the light—and me—
> And then the Windows failed—and then
> I could not see to see—

> (P 465)

We must imagine the speaker looking back on an experience in which her expectations of death were foiled by its reality. The poem begins with the speaker's perception of the fly, not yet a central awareness both because of the way in which the fly manifests itself (as sound) and because of the degree to which it manifests itself (as a triviality). As a consequence of the speaker's belief in the magnitude of the event and the propriety with which it should be enacted, the fly seems merely indecorous, as yet a marginal disturbance, attracting her attention the way in which something we have not yet invested with meaning does. In a poem very much concerned with the question of vision, it is perhaps strange that the dominant concern in stanza one should be auditory. But upon reflection it makes sense, for the speaker is hearing a droning in the background before the source of the noise comes into view. The poem describes the way in which things come into view, slowly.

What is striking in the second stanza is the speaker's lack of involvement in the little drama that is being played out. She is acutely conscious that there will be a struggle with death, but she imagines it is the people around her who will undergo it. Her detachment and tranquility seem appropriate if we imagine them to come in the aftermath of pain, a subject that is absent in the poem and whose absence helps to place the experience at the moment before death. At such a moment, the speaker's concern is focused on others, for being the center of attention with all eyes upon her, she is at leisure to return the stare. Her concern with her audience continues in the third stanza and prompts the tone of officiousness there. Wanting to set things straight, the speaker wishes to add the finishing touches to her life, to conclude it the way one would a business deal. The desire to structure and control experience is not, however, carried out in total blindness, for she is clearly cognizant of those "Keepsakes—" not hers to give. Even at this point her conception of dying may be a preconception but it is not one founded on total ignorance.

The speaker has been imagining herself as a queen about to leave her people, conscious of the majesty of the occasion, presiding over it. She expects to witness death as majestic, too, or so one infers from the way in which she speaks of him in stanza two. The staginess of the conception, however, has little to do with what Charles Anderson calls "an ironic reversal of the conventional attitudes of [Dickinson's] time and place toward the significance of the moment of death." If it did, the poem would arbitrate between the social meanings and personal ones. But the conflict between preconception and perception takes place inside. Or rather preconception gives way only to darkness. For at the conclusion of the third stanza the fly "interpose[s], " coming between the speaker and the onlookers, between her predictive fantasy of the event and its reality, between life and death. The fact that the fly obscures the former allows the speaker to see the latter. Perspective suddenly shifts to the right thing: from the ritual of dying to the fact of death. It is, of course, the fly who obliterates the speaker's false notions of death, for it is with his coming that she realizes that she is the witness and he the king, that the ceremony is a "stumbling" one. It is from a perspective schooled by the fly that she writes.

As several previous discussions of the poem have acknowledged, the final stanza begins with a complicated synesthesia: "With Blue—uncertain stumbling Buzz—." The adjective "stumbling" (used customarily to describe only an action) here also describes a sound, and the adverb "uncertain" the quality of that sound. The fusion would not be so interesting if its effect were not to evoke that moment in perception when it is about to fail. As in a high fever, noises are amplified, the light in the room takes on strange hues, one effect seems indistinguishable from another. Although there is a more naturalistic explanation for the word "stumbling" (to describe the way in which flies go in and out of our hearing), the poem is so predicated on the phenomenon of displacement and projection (of the speaker's feelings onto the onlookers, of the final blindness onto the "Windows," of the fact of perception onto the experience of death) that the image here suggests another dramatic displacement—the fusion of the fly's death with her own. Thus flies when they are about to die move as if poisoned, sometimes hurl themselves against a ceiling, pause, then rise to circle again, then drop. At this moment the changes the speaker is undergoing are fused with their agent: her experience becomes one with the fly's. It is her observance of that fly, being mesmerized by it (in a quite literal sense now, since death is quite literal), that causes her mind to fumble at the world and lose grip of it. The final two lines "And then the Windows failed—and then / I could not see to see—" are brilliant in their underlining of the poem's central premise; namely that death is survived by perception, for in these lines we are told that there are two senses of vision, one of which remains to see and document the speaker's own blindness ("and then / I could not see to see—"). The poem thus penetrates to the invisible imagination which strengthens in response to the loss of visible sight.

I mentioned earlier that the poem presumes a shift of perspective, an enlightened change from the preconception of death to its perception. In order to assume that the speaker is educated by her experience, we must assume the fact of it: we must credit the death as a real one. But the fiction required by the poem renders it logically baffling. For although the poem seems to proceed in a linear fashion toward an end, its entire premise is based on the lack of finality of that end, the speaker who survives death to tell her story of it. We are hence left wondering: How does the poem imagine an ending? If it does not, what replaces a sense of an ending? How does it conceive of the relationship between past, present, and future? To address these questions adequately, we need to look at some theories of time against which the poem's own singular conception may more sharply be visible.

In *Cosmos and History*, Mircea Eliade writes of the primitive desire to make past and present coexist. What supersedes time is a life structured by the repetition of archetypal acts, structured, that is, by "categories and not . . . events. . . . although [the life] takes place in time, [it] does not bear the burden of time, does not record time's irreversibility; in other words, completely ignores what is especially characteristic and decisive in a consciousness of time. Like the mystic, like the religious man in general, the primitive lives in a continual present." In the primitive world that Eliade describes historical acts still occur, but their meaning is metahistorical. Events bear an associative or analogical relationship to each other. The replacement of analogues by unique events, events that guarantee a new present at every moment and, in so doing, render the past irretrievably past, is contingent upon the acknowledgment that experience has a terminal point.

One might, in fact, say it is the garden of Eden that teaches us it is impossible to conceive of a past purified by the attendant conception of its loss. For to understand the meaning of permanence is already to have surrendered the fact of it. If we imagine the Fall to be that moment when man first perceives past and future as forever exiled from the present, lying always outside of it, the new conception destroys the illusion of events as repeating themselves, moving reversibly or in a cyclical direction. Indeed the very premise of Christianity and its providential history depends upon such an eschatology, for while the Old Testament promises a divine judgment that will take place within history, the New Testament promises a judgment that will end it.

The impulse to see patterns in history is very close to the interpretation of events as patterned by ritual repetition or analogue, and in this respect history is a comparable fiction, that which provides significance to what would otherwise be mere chronicity. But the difference between ritual event and historical event lies in the latter's consciousness of the conclusion to all events. In *Christ and Time*, Oscar Cullmann distinguishes between *chronos*, or passing time, and *kairos*, "a point of time that has a special place in the execution of God's plan of salvation," that is, a crucial moment in the drama of eschatology, one that gains significance by its relation to the end. If a shift from the ritual organization of experience to its temporal organization necessitates the acknowledgment of time, many of whose moments are empty of significance, the fiction of history is a means of preserving and systematizing *kairos*, of attending to critical events of the past by regarding them as events of crisis. Imaginative fictions, less constrained because they are not under compulsion to be even selectively true, similarly rescue the world from a random succession of moments; in the world of the imagination the subject matter is always the interruption of daily events by the extraordinary. But *kairos* must come to terms with the facts of chronicity, with the ordinary generation of moments, and this inevitably involves the compunction to understand the very relationship between past, present, and future that ritual repudiates. Augustine spoke of the three temporal senses. as "the present of things past, the present of things present, and the present of things future." Attending to his mental synthesis of the three as he recited a psalm, he arrived at the following description:

> I am about to recite a psalm that I know. Before I begin, my
> expectation extends over the entire psalm. Once I have begun,
> my memory extends over as much of it as I shall separate off and

assign to the past. The life of this action of mine is distended into memory by reason of the part I have spoken and into forethought by reason of the part I am about to speak. But attention is actually present and that which was to be is borne along by it so as to become past. The more this is done and done again, so much the more is memory lengthened by a shortening of expectation, until the entire expectation is exhausted. When this is done the whole action is completed and passes into memory. What takes place in the whole psalm takes place also in each of its parts and in each of its syllables. The same thing holds for a longer action, of which perhaps the psalm is a small part. The same thing holds for a man's entire life, the parts of which are all the man's actions. The same thing holds throughout the whole age of the sons of men, the parts of which are the lives of all men.

Contrary to Augustine's attempt to distinguish between the three temporal senses, the intention of much modern poetry and fiction lies precisely in the effort to fuse past and present, meaningful event and trivia. Thus the distinction between mere chronicity and crucial event, which the historical fiction tried so hard to establish, has been effectively annihilated. As Robbe-Grillet writes in *For a New Novel,* "In the modern narrative, time seems to be cut off from its temporality. It no longer passes. It no longer completes anything. . . . Here space destroys time, and time sabotages space. Description makes no headway, contradicts itself, turns in circles. Moment denies continuity." We may say that the representation has gone full circle: from the primitive denial of time and the "pastness" of experience, to the creation of a historical fiction in which experience is obsessed with the fact that it must end—and, in which, therefore, the present is in constant need of understanding its relationship to the past that generated it and to the future in which it will conclude—and, finally, as some critics would have it, the return in modern literature to the representation of experience as timeless and mythic. But what if these ostensibly alternate ways of representing experience are, in fact, not alternate at all, but must be seen as mutually exclusive possibilities that therefore . . . always appear in contradictory relationship to each other? For to stop the succession of moments is, nonetheless, to have their inevitable passing firmly, even desperately, in mind.

If we date our perception of radical boundaries that forever seal us from worlds we forever long to inhabit with the Fall, then we cannot see the denial of temporal and spatial features of experience as a return to mythic or ritual primitivism since that route is unalterably sealed, but must ask what in its own right does such denial mean? With this question we find ourselves back at the specific questions raised in connection with Dickinson's "I heard a Fly buzz when I died," but now with a context in which to consider them, for there the poem denies the very eschatological fact that its meaning depends upon.

I mentioned earlier that one consequence of the absence of a fixed boundary line between life and death is the fusion of subjective and objective time. In "I heard a Fly buzz," in other words, we have no sense of subjective or interior time as substantially different from objective to exterior time. Perhaps this is always the case in the lyric, for the lyric—unlike the novel, whose task it is to legislate the conflict between social and personal realitypresents interior reality as if there were no other with which it must regretfully contend. Hence the sense of leisure about speech (even passionate speech) in the lyric. Marvell's lover (protests to the contrary) can woo his lady for as long as he likes; the borders of the poem withstand any external interruption and, as long as the reader's eyes are on the page, effectively banish it. Sir Walter Raleigh "give[s] the world the lie" with more fervored documentation than we can sustain in comparable moods of skepticism. Dylan Thomas's recollection of childhood in "Fern Hill" walls out for the duration of the poem the very adult world he claims he cannot be free of. Even Milton's dream of his dead wife, "my late espoused saint," disappears only when he violates recollection by seeking to prove its existence in reality: "But O as to embrace me she inclined / I waked, she fled, and day brought back my night." The poem, like Milton's vision, sustains its integrity for as long as one does not puncture it with the outside world. For the poem, like the vision, shrinks from mediation. Before the attempt at mediation with the social world, the poem ruptures, breaks off; it will not come into relation with, be on the same plane as, the social world. While this could, of course, be said of any imaginative fiction—talk to a character in a novel and he will not answer—no imaginative fiction is as resistant to the interruption of its interior speech as the lyric. For the lyric, unlike the drama or the novel, does not have to contend with authorial description, explanatory asides, or any other manipulative intrusion of its space. Nor need it weather the periodic interruptions guaranteed by act, scene, or chapter divisions. Most important, however, it must attend to no more than one (its own) speaking voice. This fact makes the self in the lyric unitary, and gives it the illusion of alone holding sway over the universe, there being, for all practical purposes, no one else, nothing else, to inhabit it.

As a consequence of the banishing of the social world, the network of lines that comprise the pressures of social or objective time are equally consigned to temporary obscurity. The consignment makes room for the poem by allowing it to hang, as it were, in front of social time much the way a painting hangs in front of a wall. While this covering procedure is, as I have been suggesting, a customary occurrence in all lyrics, it becomes noteworthy when a poem explicitly denies an aspect of social or objective fact that we know, on other terms, to be undeniable. The assertion that one can come back from the dead to tell one's story of it so clearly counters the possible that our attention is focused on the effective annihilation of reality; for in this case, the fiction not only "covers" reality, it also insists that reality does not exist. This may make "I heard a Fly buzz" appear to possess the characteristics Robbe-Grillet attributes to modern literature: the embrace of timeless, mythic reality, the externality and hence congruence of thought and event, all effective activity manifest on one plane. But appearance is, in this case, illusion. For the lyric which seems to evade social reality must at some point acknowledge its attachment to the social world which, however denied by the illusion of the lyric's freedom, must nonetheless be assured by its desire for intelligibility. At what point do illusion and reality intersect and how does illusion manage to camouflage the intersection with sufficient art to deny it? For since the relationship I have been describing is a covert one, it follows that in every fiction there will be a crucial tension between the fact of such a relationship and the lyric's efforts to deny, disguise, or transform it.

In order to maintain its status as fiction the lyric must assert its deviance from the strictures of reality and, at the same time, assert the unreliability of the adherence to the impossible. Thus not only tension but contradiction itself is at the heart of the lyric's power over us. . . .

The contradiction between social and private time is the lyric's generating impulse, for the self who would keep its own time, who would live in a world of perpetual *kairos* where events are significant because of the power one has to transform them, must acknowledge the less malleable dictates of the outside world, its scrupulous if simple-minded adherence to *chronos*. in "I heard a Fly buzz when I died," the collision between the two senses of time occurs at the poem's ending, and is just as resolutely uncommented upon by it. For the demands set by the fictional world of *kairos*, and by the equally clamoring world of *chronos*, make no concessions to each other. The most that can be hoped for is the discovery of the coincidence of the two, their temporary appearance at the same moment and along the same temporal plane. Hence in "I heard a Fly buzz," the moment of perception coincides with the moment of death at the poem's ending and, in so doing, effects a temporary rapprochement between the two. The conflict that it has been the poem's function to *manifest* here comes to an end. But we might more properly conclude not that the conflict has reached resolution, since by definition there is no resolution, but rather that it has momentarily played itself out. Indeed it is the genius of the poem to collapse the distinction between subjective and objective time, to assert that an eternity of consciousness and a finite consciousness painfully subject to instant termination at the mere caprice of an insensate world are time schemes compatible, even complementary. Thus two notions logically exclusive—that death is the end of life, specifically conceived of as loss of consciousness, and that perception is the end of life (consciousness continued, even heightened)—are in the poem stalwartly presented as if they were the same thing.

The relationship between perception (or consciousness) as terminus and death as terminus thus comes to be the implicit subject of the poem. The illusion that perception as finality replaces the finality of death so seems to prompt an exchange of the ordinary characteristics of each that perception assumes many of death's properties: secrecy, private apprehension, and closure. As a consequence of the intersection of perception and death, the boldness of the poem's flaunting of border is softened since its progression from the fact of death to the recollection of dying and back again to the moment of death leaves the reader at a conventional moment. It is as if the poem had moved along the same ground twice, but each time in an opposite direction: once from death back to life and, the second time, from life to death. Death, so often conceived by Dickinson as a journey, is here retraveled and hence presumed to be understood. In the previous chapter I suggested that the meaning of an experience could not be ascertained until its conclusion; hence the "Loaded Gun . . . / Without—the power to die—" (P 754) eludes interpretation. In these poems, too, completion is meaning now no longer from the point of view of the fragmentary life, but rather from the point of view of the life in touch with its own totality. If this is magical, Dickinson seems to assert that only from such magic can meaning be made. Like Eliade's description of the replacement of experience as event with experience as category, dying is here categorical rather than conclusive. That assumption is examined more explicitly in what is perhaps Dickinson's most complex utterance on the subject of death:

> Because I could not stop for Death—
> He kindly stopped for me—
> The Carriage held but just Ourselves—
> And Immortality.

> We slowly drove—He knew no haste
> And I had put away
> My labor and my leisure too,
> For His Civility—

We passed the School, where Children strove
At Recess—in the Ring—
We passed the Fields of Gazing Grain—
We passed the Setting Sun—

Or rather—He passed Us—
The Dews drew quivering and chill—
For only Gossamer, my Gown—
My Tippet—only Tulle—

We paused before a House that seemed
A Swelling of the Ground—
The Roof was scarcely visible—
The Cornice—in the Ground—

Since then—'tis Centuries—and yet
Feels shorter than the Day
I first surmised the Horses' Heads
Were toward Eternity—

(P 712)

Yvor Winters has spoken of the poem's subject as "the daily realization of the imminence of death—it is a poem of departure from life, an intensely conscious leave-taking." But in its final claim to actually experience death, Winters has found it fraudulent. There is, of course, a way out of or around the dilemma of posthumous speech and that is to suppose that the entire ride with death is, as the last stanza indicates, a "surmise," and " 'tis Centuries—," a colloquial hyperbole. But we ought not insist that the poem's interpretation pivot on the importance of this word. For we ignore its own struggle with extraordinary claims if we insist too quickly on its adherence to traditional limits.

In one respect, the speaker's assertions that she "could not stop for Death—" must be taken as the romantic protest of a self not yet disabused of the fantasy that her whims, however capricious, will withstand the larger temporal demands of the external world. Thus the first line, like any idiosyncratic representation of the world, must come to grips with the tyranny of more general meanings, not the least of which can be read in the inviolable stand of the universe, every bit as willful as the isolate self. But initially the world seems to cater to the self s needs; since the speaker does not have time (one implication of "could not stop") for death, she is deferred to by the world ("he kindly stopped for me—"). In another respect, we must see the first line not only as willful (had not time for) but also as the admission of a disabling fact (could not). The second line responds to the doubleness of conception. What, in other words, in one context is deference, in another is coercion, and since the poem balances tonally between these extremes it is important to note the dexterity with which they are compacted in the first two lines.

There is, of course, further sense in which death stops for the speaker, and that is in the fusion I alluded to earlier between interior and exterior senses of time, so that the consequence of the meeting in the carriage is the death of otherness. The poem presumes to rid death of its otherness, to familiarize it, literally to adopt its perspective and in so doing to effect a synthesis between self and other, internal time and the faster, more relentless beat of the world. Using more traditional terms to describe the union, Allen Tate speaks of the poem's "subtly interfused erotic motive, which the idea of death has presented to most romantic poets, love being a symbol interchangeable with death." It is true that the poem is charged with eroticism whose end or aim is union, perhaps as we conventionally know it, a synthesis of self and other for the explicit purpose of the transformation of other or, if that proves impossible, for the loss of self. Death's heralding phenomenon, the loss of self, would be almost welcomed if self at this point could be magically fused with other. . . .

Indeed the trinity of death, self, immortality, however ironic a parody of the holy paradigm, at least promises a conventional fulfillment of the idea that the body's end coincides with the soul's everlasting life. But, as in "Our journey had advanced," death so frequently conceptualized as identical with eternity here suffers a radical displacement from it. While both poems suggest a discrepancy between eternity and death, the former poem hedges on the question of where the speaker stands with respect to that discrepancy, at its conclusion seeming to locate her safely in front of or "before" death. "Because I could not stop for Death," on the other hand, pushes revision one step further, daring to leave the speaker stranded in the moment of death.

Along these revisionary lines, the ride to death that we might have supposed to take place through territory unknown, we discover in stanza three to reveal commonplace sights but now fused with spectacle. The path out of the world is also apparently the one through it and in the compression of the three images ("the School, where Children strove," "the Fields of Gazing Grain—," "the Setting Sun—") we are introduced to a new kind of visual shorthand. Perhaps what is extraordinary here is the elasticity of reference, how imposingly on the figural scale the images can weigh while, at the same time, never abandoning any of their quite literal specificity. Hence the sight of the children is a circumscribed one by virtue of the specificity of their placement "At Recess—in the Ring—" and, at the same time, the picture takes on the shadings of allegory. This referential flexibility or fusion of literal and figural meanings is potential in the suggestive connotations of the verb "strove," which is a metaphor in the context of the playground (that is, in its literal context) and a mere descriptive verb in the context of the implied larger world (that is, in its figural context). The "Fields of Gazing Grain—" also suggest a literal picture, but one that leans in the direction of emblem; thus the epithet "Gazing" has perhaps been anthropomorphized from the one-directional leaning of grain in the wind, the object of its gazing the speaker herself. The "Children" mark the presence of the world along one stage of the speaker's journey, the "Gazing Grain—" marks the passing of the world (its harkening after the speaker as she rides away from it), and the "Setting Sun—" marks its past. For at least as the third stanza conceives of it, the journey toward eternity is a series of successive and, in the case of the grain, displaced visions giving way finally to blankness.

But just as after the first two stanzas, we are again rescued in the fourth from any settled conception of this journey. As we were initially not to think of the journey taking place out of the world (and hence with the children we are brought back to it), the end of the third stanza having again moved us to the world's edge, we are redeemed from falling over it by the speaker's correction: "Or rather—He passed Us—." It is the defining movement of the poem to deliver us just over the boundary line between life and death and then to recall us. Thus while the poem gives the illusion of a one-directional movement, albeit a halting one, we discover upon closer scrutiny that the movements are multiple and, as in "I heard a Fly buzz when I died," constitutive of flux, back and forth over the boundary from life to death. Despite the correction, "Or rather—He passed Us—," the next lines register a response that would be entirely appropriate to the speaker's passing of the sun. "The Dews drew" round the speaker, her earthly clothes not only inadequate, but actually falling away in deference to the sensation of "chill—" that displaces them as she passes the boundary of the earth. Thus, on the one hand, "chill—" is a mere physiological response to the setting of the sun at night, on the other, it is a metaphor for the earlier assertion that the earth and earthly goods are being exchanged for something else. Implications in the poem, like the more explicit assertions, are contradictory and reflexive, circling back to underline the very premises they seem a moment ago to have denied. Given such ambiguity, we are constantly in a quandary about how to place the journey that, at any one point, undermines the very certainty of conception it has previously established. Something of the same ambiguity, and for similar reasons, is revealed in George Herbert's "Redemption":

Having been tenant long to a rich Lord,
Not thriving, I resolved to be bold,
And make a suit unto him, to afford
    A new small-rented lease, and cancell th' old.
In heaven at his manour I him sought:
They told me there, that he was lately gone
About some land, which he had dearly bought
    Long since on earth, to take possession.

I straight return'd, and knowing his great birth,
Sought him accordingly in great resorts;
In cities, theaters, gardens, parks and courts:
    At length I heard a ragged noise and mirth
Of theeves and murderers: there I him espied,
Who straight, *Your suit is granted*, said and died.

More boldly perhaps and with an acutely dramatic sense of its own contradictions, "Redemption" fuses past and present; earth and heaven; the feudal lord with his earthly mansion and the heavenly Lord with His divine estate; the lease of a new house and the lease afforded by the new dispensation; the speaker as individual man making a petition to God and as all mankind for whose collective sake Christ sacrificed His life. These fusions are complemented by a series of effective displacements each of which depends upon the disregard of conventional boundary. Thus, for example, the speaker travels to heaven (without dying) where he expects to find Christ (whose existence he could not possibly know about prior to the occurrence in the last line) and finding Him absent (on earth for the explicit purpose of granting the petition the speaker has not yet made to Him) the speaker returns to earth (mistakenly imagining that wealth houses divinity) only to be distracted by the "ragged noise and mirth" of the crucifixion itself and the simultaneity of Christ's death and man's redemption. The intent of such fusions and boundary crossings or, at any rate, their *primary* effect, is twofold: first, to cast the problem of man's salvation in inescapably personal terms that bring him into direct and literal relationship with Christ so that he finds himself both the explicit cause of the sacrifice and its only beneficiary; and second, to depict both the petition and its granting as unalterably present tense. No longer relegated to historical fact, in the timeless world of need and its fulfillment, the moment is charged with the history-making event of man's redemption, which converts past into an ineluctable present, and insists that meaning win its way free from generalization.

While Dickinson's representation of the ride with death is less histrionic, it is as insistent in our coming to terms with the personalization of the event and of its perpetual reenactment in the present. For the grave that is "paused before" in the fifth stanza, with the tombstone lying flat against the ground ("scarcely visible—"), is seen from the outside and then (by the transformation of spatial considerations into temporal ones) is passed by or through: "Since then—'tis Centuries—." The poem's concluding stanza both fulfills the traditional Christian notion that while the endurance of death is essential for the reaching of eternity, the two are not identical, and by splitting death and eternity with the space of "Centuries—," challenges that traditional notion. The poem that has thus far played havoc with our efforts to fix its journey in any conventional time or space, on this side of death or the other, concludes with an announcement about the origins of its speech, now explicitly equivocal: "'tis Centuries—and yet/Feels shorter than the Day." What in "There's a certain Slant of light" had been a clear relationship between figure and its fulfillment (a sense of perceptive enlightenment accruing from the movement of one to the other) is in this poem manifestly baffling. For one might observe that for all the apparent movement here, there are no real progressions in the poem at all. If the correction "We passed the Setting Sun—/Or rather—He passed Us—" may be construed as a confirmation of the slowness of the drive alluded to earlier in the poem, the last stanza seems to insist that the carriage is standing still, moving if at all, as we say, in place. For the predominant sense of this journey is not simply its endlessness; it is also the curious back and forth sweep of its images conveying, as they do, the perpetual return to what has been perpetually taken leave of.

Angus Fletcher, speaking in terms applicable to "Because I could not stop for Death," documents the characteristics of allegorical journeys as surrealistic in imagery (as for example, the "Gazing Grain—"), paratactic in rhythm or structure (as indeed we can hear in the acknowledged form of movement: "We passed . . . We passed . . . We passed . . . Or rather—He passed Us . . . We Paused . . ."), and almost always incomplete: "It is logically quite natural for the extension to be infinite, since by definition there is no such thing as the whole of any analogy; all analogies are incomplete, and incompletable, and allegory simply records this analogical relation in a dramatic or narrative form."

But while the poem has some of the characteristics of allegory, it nonetheless seems to defy such easy classification. Thus the utterance is not quite allegory because it is not strongly iconographic (its figures do not have a one-to-one correspondence with a representational base), and at the same time, these figures are sufficiently rigid to preclude the freeing up of associations that is characteristic of the symbol. We recall Coleridge's distinction between a symbolic and an allegorical structure. A symbol presupposes a unity with its object. It denies the separateness between subject and object by creating a synecdochic relationship between itself and the totality of what it represents; like the relationship between figure and thing figured discussed in the first part of this chapter, it is always part of that totality. Allegory, on the other hand, is a sign that refers to a specific meaning from which it continually remains detached. Through its abstract embodiment, the allegorical form makes the distance between itself and its original meaning clearly manifest. It accentuates the absolute cleavage between subject and object. Since the speaker in "Because I could not stop for Death" balances between the boast of knowledge and the confession of ignorance, between a oneness with death and an inescapable difference from it, we may regard the poem as a partial allegory. The inability to know eternity, the failure to be at one with it, is, we might say, what the allegory of "Because I could not stop for Death" makes manifest. The ride with death, though it espouses to reveal a future that is past, in fact casts both past and future in the indeterminate present of the last stanza. Unable to arrive at a fixed conception, it must rest on the bravado (and it implicitly knows this) of its initial claim. Thus death is not really civilized; the boundary between otherness and self, life and death, is crossed, but only in presumption, and we might regard this fact as the real confession of disappointment in the poem's last stanza.

Ahab, in *Moby-Dick*, whom Daniel Hoffman has characterized as having "The most allegorical mind of any character in American fiction" because of his willful insistence on reducing protean experience to his monomaniacal meaning for it, wished to strike through the "pasteboard mask" of appearances to reality. Ishmael, no less mesmerized by the mask, albeit attributing a different name to it, spoke of that image which man is drawn to in rivers and fountains as "the ungraspable phantom of life." Treat that "phantom" as symbol, however, and the self, rapt in the contemplation of its own reflection, falls toward it in fusion and, like Narcissus, drowns. *Moby-Dick* may in fact be viewed as a struggle between allegorical modes of perceiving the world and symbolic ones. The extremity of either choice is black magicthe egotistical projection of the self, or the resolute withholding of it. In *American Renaissance*, F. O. Matthiessen's suggestive discussion of the symbolic and allegorical biases of Melville and Hawthorne seems, at times, to intend a definition of the pervasive dialectic of nineteenth-century America, for in the one case man attempts to transform the world by reshaping it, in the other, he "deals with fixities." Paul de Man, too, imagines the dialectical pull between symbolizing structures and allegorizing ones to define Romanticism and also to characterize its moral overtones, for the belief in organic totality is a delusive myth. Elaborating on the distinction between allegory and symbol in the specific terms of the temporal difference that separates the self from that with which it desires to fuse, de Man calls to mind the dilemma of Dickinson's speaker in "Because I could not stop for Death": "Whereas the symbol postulates the possibility of an identity of identification, allegory designates primarily a distance in relation to its own origin, and, renouncing the nostalgia and the desire to coincide, it establishes its language in the void of this temporal distance. In so doing, it prevents the self from an illusory identification with the non-self, which is now fully, though painfully, recognized as a non-self." The self is not the thing it aspires to know. Nor can its representation of reality dissolve the distinction between the two.

I dwell on such issues because they provide a context for that curious shift from the assertion of knowledge in "Because I could not stop for Death—" to the confession of its failure, from the intimation that the ride to death defies the phenomenal characteristics of the world, to the admission that it does not. This pendulum that swings back and forth across the boundary separating life from death, time from timelessness, becomes the dialectic in which the self comes to terms with its impulse for fusion and identic relationship, and with the loss attendant upon the realization that such fusion is truly illusory. The self coming to terms with the fact of its mortality from which no fusion with death can rescue it cannot complete or make good on the certain knowledge that the poem's first stanza implicitly promised. The effort to make all events associative ones, or "repetitive," in the sense of identic (to recall Eliade's description of the primitive organization of experience) is to deny the most painful boundary between self and other that the world makes manifest, to cheat the world of its otherness and hence, of necessity, the self of its defining integrity.

Yet art does attempt such a cheat: it will make its voice heard, will *have* a voice where no voice can really be, and this willful fact brings us back, as I promised, to Panofsky's essay on how the phrase *Et in Arcadia ego*, once attributed to a death's-head, grew with Poussin's painting of the scene to be attributed to a dead person himself; how, concomitantly, what was once a matter of terror became merely an occasion for meditative speculation on the fact of death. In Guercino's painting of the death's-head the fact of terror and the unknown quality of death are wedded to each other. For it is clear that the skull which represents death is a mere emblem of it, a sign that conceals its meaning. Similarly, in those poems discussed in the first half of this chapter, death's appearance is incomplete and unknown, a "boiling Wheel" or a "Maelstrom, with a notch," and hence prompts terror. The soul is "secure" only in the presence of "A Sepulchre" for, in the terms of "There's a certain Slant of light," figural reality loses its indirection or "Slant" only when it straightens into the fulfillment of death. In lieu of that fulfillment, these poems collapse the distinction between subject and object, figure and thing figured, as if collapse into, or fusion with, the object in question might substitute for knowledge. In the proleptic utterances, however ("I heard a Fly buzz when I died" and "Because I could not stop for Death"), which speak as if from beyond the grave, the turmoil of the earlier poems has been smoothed into tranquillity, for in the beginning of "Because I could not stop for Death," as in Poussin's painting, death is no otherness and it does not create otherness by its occurrence; the dead person still assumes mortal shape and still possesses voice sufficient to speak. That terror should disappear as a consequence of knowledge gained about the thing feared is not especially surprising. But what if the nostalgia implicit in both Poussin's painting and Dickinson's poem is occasioned not simply by the loss of life, but also by the loss of self, its translation into a mere emblem of survival, no longer recognizable in human terms?

Dickinson's intuition that she must preserve an otherness in order to preserve a self abruptly distorts the seeming unity of personae in the carriage. The acknowledgment of time ("'tis Centuries—and yet/Feels shorter than the Day") is equally an acknowledgment that the desired and, for a time, achieved fusion between subjective and objective time will not hold. The speaker can finesse the illusion of such unity, but the last stanza points up all the problems with which it must come to terms. The experience of death still leaves eternity an unknown; the journey cannot be completed conceptually, is in need of an end that is not, and will never be, conceptually forthcoming. For allegory must come to terms with the conceptual inadequacy of its desire, with the real zero beyond which invention cannot go. Despite the fact that the allegoric impulse is contrary to the mimetic one—would rather perfect the world than represent it—it must nonetheless fall back on the same storehouse of images. Thus the transformation from the death's-head to the dead man who has words and, in Dickinson's poems, from the terror before death to the imaginative construction of speech after it, civilizes death in the only way we apparently know how. But such "civility" is an illusion. Death without the death of speech, death without the cessation of time—in a land of unlikeness, a true Arcadia, this is no place we know.

Where does the ride with Death and Immortality take place? And is it possible to say with any certainty how long—centuries or a day—it lasts? I suggested earlier that lyric time, although at some points coincidental with actual time, hangs in front of it observing only those properties of actuality that it chooses. Perhaps it would be more accurate to say not that the lyric defies the temporal-spatial axis but that it has its own referential axis, neither clearly future (though an utterance often implies its own continuous action) nor clearly past (though it often seems past because its own action is predicated on itself as on a history). " 'Tis so appalling—it exhilarates—/So over Horror, it half Captivates—/The Soul stares after it, secure—." "Stares," we might say, timelessly or for all time. Similarly, the "certain Slant of light,/ Winter Afternoons—/" "oppresses" with a present-tense verb of sufficient heft to secure both past and future under its aegis. "Slow tramp the Centuries,/And the Cycles wheel!" When and where are irrelevant questions. Even the past-tense "Because I could not stop for Death" brings us up short against the present of its disturbing conclusion. The speaker in the throes of the movement that pulls her forward seems to turn for a moment toward us and, in so doing, to stop the carriage's action allowing us to place it. And while "I heard a Fly buzz when I died" is narrated wholly in the past, it is no less adamant in its illusion that the incidents it relates are present. One might hazard the generalization that although Dickinson's poems on death assume the past tense with characteristic regularity precisely so that the death the speaker claims to have survived will be credited as a fait accompli, nonetheless, the very task of the entire poem is to re-present it.

George Wright, in "The Lyric Present: Simple Present Verbs in English Poems," offers conclusions to an important statistical study he has compiled on verb forms in the lyric. As the title of his essay implies, Wright documents the fact that the tense most characteristic of, and most frequently used in, the lyric is the simple present tense. But this present seems to contain a multiplicity of temporal features that we ordinarily think of as mutually exclusive. It is past-like as well as indicative of future. It locates action temporally, but not in time as we know it. Although timeless, this present tense implies duration. The distance cast by "the look of Death—" remains. Giving way to nothing else, it is what we return to every time we reread the poem. And, Wright suggests, the lyric not only implies temporal permanence and permanent temporal elusiveness, but a corresponding spatial dislocation as well, as its contradictions preserve the structure of the ambiguities that element it. A poem especially evasive about its spatial location is Yeats's "Among School Children," for if we ask where "Labour is blossoming or dancing," we are answered, but mysteriously:

> Labour is blossoming or dancing where
> The body is not bruised to pleasure soul,
> Nor beauty born out of its own despair,
> Nor blear-eyed wisdom out of midnight oil.

A present that houses the past as well as the future and that, moreover, evades spatial location and fixture is very close to the creation of a temporal myth built between past and future, real and imagined time, this world and some other. Keats's "Do I wake or sleep" poses a question about his state in the aftermath of the vision, but answer it either way and the vision still remains fixed, even in the permanence of its fleeting. The present tense is so characteristic of the lyric that Wright terms it "the lyric tense," and he adds that its assertion of presence may be the poem's dominant symbolic gesture—an idea we shall examine in the next chapter—as it transfixes reality so that reality remains caught precisely at the moment of its passing: "The lyric tense detail is almost always felt as symbolic, and as with Yeats's swans that drift or his birds that reel, the tense often appears at the most climactic moment, the moment at which some symbolic transformation, some metamorphosis takes place. . . . On such occasions the device of lyric tense seems not merely to frame but almost to *be* the metaphor."

Such metaphors inhere not simply in the slowing of action but also in the attribution of pivotal meaning to it, as if the poet assumed that, were action visible, the relational ties between subject and object might sharpen to clarity. These relations, the ones between subject and object, as well as between one temporal category and another, are, as I have been suggesting, compressed in the lyric or collapsed by it in what sometimes seems to be a mimetic gesture of the perceptual syntheses characteristic of thinking itself. Thus the poems are projective in nature, enacting the very displacements of experience. In them perception refuses to be riveted to one spot, shifts, as in "Our journey had advanced," to relocate itself in accordance with the progressive lessons of experience. The displacements we have seen (from the "Failed" windows in "I heard a Fly buzz when I died" to the "Gazing Grain—" in "Because I could not stop for Death") remind us how thoroughly the world remains saturated in our perceptual terms for it, how seductive syntheses and fusion are when we are overtaken by the starkness of the world's own terms. The color white, purged of meaning (which so haunts Dickinson's work, as we remember it haunts Melville's), is perhaps the way the world looks when we represent it accurately, but at such moments it is also bleached to nothing. The problem, of course, is how to give it coloration, to see it, as we say, in its own terms, for the very conception that something has its own terms is itself an anthropomorphic one. If the lyric shrinks from mediation with the outside world, it seeks no less to preserve the integrity of its own temporal fusions, for to mediate between them, to establish discrete barriers between past, present, and future is to distort the very synchrony of its knowledge. In Augustine's terms "the present of things past, the present of things present, and the present of things future" all have in common the shared moment of their acknowledgment.

Contradiction between social and personal time is, as I implied previously, the lyric's generating impulse, and Dickinson's proleptic utterances, by exaggerating these contradictions, draw our attention to them. The greatest contradiction lies in the lyric's fixity of its own present. This mythologizing of the lyric present, the insistence that present and, by implication, presence can achieve permanence is perhaps accounted for by the tenacious hold the past has on the present, by its dexterity in casting itself as if it still were. Hence the fusion between past and present is often so axiomatic as to escape attention, though in the next chapter we shall see that loss discovers its origin when space comes to intervene between the two. The present, here, then, seems permanent partly by virtue of how thoroughly it confuses itself with its own history, on the one hand, and its destiny, on the other. Unable to separate itself from what it has been and from what it desires to be, the present in Dickinson's poems (as if by association) projects even more daring fusions between the time before death and that after it. A passage from Beckett's *Malloy* which Wright calls our attention to indicates how natural such fusions are: "When I try and think riding I lose my balance and fall. I speak in the present tense, it is so easy to speak in the present tense, when speaking of the past. It is the mythological present, don't mind it." The present may be described as that moment in which all past moments (potentially) coincide with consciousness, just as the future only exists insofar as it can be conceived of or conjured by a consciousness that is present. The present is thus that fulcral moment that not only arbitrates between past and future but that also embodies them. For of themselves, both past and future may be conceived of as having subject without locution, spirit without body, the evasiveness of pure air. "Everything we say/of the past," wrote Wallace Stevens, "is description without place." Indeed, the same is true of our words for the future. Only the present has a sure space of its own.

In the poems discussed [elsewhere], death is eschewed, because it details the end of the self; here it is desired, but minus its consequences. Thus permanence (and hence an endless present) is attributed to death, and longed for in the form of fusion with it. Fusions are actively sought and achieved in the poems discussed in the first part of this chapter. In such poems, a state fuses with the terms of its own figuration, as death fuses with the image of light. In the proleptic utterances, however, where the fusion is sought perhaps even more strenuously because the stakes are higher, the gain of temporal fusion seems to necessitate the sacrifice of union between subject and object. The premise of these poems may be that temporal collapse will blur the distinction between subject and object, death and self, will make them one; the poems discover, however, that to preserve identity time and space must intervene. For the pain that binds the self to its own boundaries also defines it. What is restrictive in one context is definitional in another. Thus the poem may subject the world to reconstruction, but only one feature at a time. Temporal fusions *or* the fusion between subject and object—either may be ventured but not, apparently, at the same time. For knock down all the walls of the house at once and the structure crumbles to ruin.

Dickinson once wrote of "An Omen in the Bone/Of Death's tremendous nearness—" (P 532). Perhaps she took the omen for prophecy and with characteristic impatience pushed it toward a fulfillment she herself could appreciate. For her lyrics, as I have been suggesting, attempt to cross boundaries, to blur distinctions between life and death, time and timelessness, figure and its fulfillment, or, to put it more accurately, to wear a passage between them—which is the poem—and, in so doing, to seek refuge in a presence whose permanence will withstand temporal change. They thus go in search of the very mythical time that Wright tells us is characteristic of most lyric poems. For the idiosyncratic fusions Dickinson's lyrics make explicit, most lyrics imply. They record an event that, in Wright's words, "has happened—is happening—happens." In the mythological present the self goes forth bravely into places it does not and cannot know, dreaming the very landscapes to which it will forever be denied real access. It seeks symbolic correspondences and stumbles upon differences. It desires to break loose into timelessness and feels instead the weightless net of temporal ensnarement. It would give anything to become an otherness, but it must settle for itself. So it learns how to celebrate that self, even the confusions of its own contradictory impulses. In the process, and shaking itself free from all that would disembody it, the self finds a present, a being, and a voice. These the lyric memorializes.

RANDA K. DUBNICK

Two Types of Obscurity
in the Writings of Gertrude Stein

Many critics have tried to deal with the difficulties of Gertrude Stein's writing by labeling it "meaningless," "abstract," or "obscure." But such judgments often are inadequate and misleading in their failure to make some important distinctions. In the first place, not all of Stein's writing is obscure. And within that part of her work which is obscure, there are two distinct styles which might be characterized as "abstract," each of which represents a linguistically different kind of obscurity. The first of these two styles developed during the writing of *The Making of Americans* and reached maturity toward the end of that book (as well as in some of the literary "portraits" produced during that same time). The second style is best represented by Stein's *Tender Buttons*.

Stein called the first style *prose* and the second style *poetry*. As will be seen, her definition of each category, and her description of these two obscure styles seem to suggest some of the dualistic distinctions that structuralist thought (from Ferdinand de Saussure to Roman Jakobson and Roland Barthes) has made about language. What might be fruitful, then, and what the structuralist vocabulary seems to make possible, is an examination of the nature and stylistics of each of the two distinct ways in which Stein's writing moves towards the abstract and becomes obscure. All of Stein's writing can be viewed as made up of variations and combinations of the two

From *The Emporia State Research Studies* 24, no. 3 (Winter 1976). © 1976 by Emporia Kansas State College.

stylistic preoccupations represented by the participial style of *The Making of Americans* and the associational style of *Tender Buttons*. To understand the stylistics of Gertrude Stein's two basic types of obscurity, one must begin with an examination of these two works. Structuralist theories can aid in this examination by supplying a vocabulary as well as a framework that may identify the basis of her obscurity as her concern with the nature of language itself. This inquiry may lead to an understanding of the theoretical basis behind Stein's movement toward two kinds of abstraction. In this regard, a look at what was happening in painting, as Cubism also developed two obscure styles, may be helpful. The relationship between Stein's writing and Cubist painting, when seen from a structuralist perspective, seems to be based on common emphases on certain linguistic operations over others. What one discovers is that Stein's comparisons of her writing to the work of the Cubists do not belie a misguided attempt to apply to language artistic theories which are irrelevant and inappropriate to it, as some critics believe: rather, those comparisons represent concerns about the nature of language itself, concerns which are, therefore, appropriately explored within the realm of literature.

Gertrude Stein, in one of her famous lectures, explains the radical stylistic difference between *The Making of Americans* and *Tender Buttons* in terms of the distinction between prose (the main concern of which is the sentence) and poetry (the main concern of which is the noun):

> In *The Making of Americans* . . . a very long prose book made up of sentences and paragraphs . . . I had gotten rid of nouns and adjectives as much as possible by the method of living in adverbs, in pronouns, in adverbial clauses written or implied and in conjunctions. . . . really great written prose is bound to be made up more of verbs adverbs prepositional clauses and conjunctions than nouns. The vocabulary in prose of course is important if you like vocabulary is always important. . .

However:

> the vocabulary in respect to prose is less important than the parts of speech, and the internal balance and the movement within a given space.

On the other hand,

> Poetry has to do with vocabulary just as prose has not. . . . Poetry is I say essentially a vocabulary just as prose is essentially not. . . .

And what is the vocabulary of which poetry absolutely is. It is a vocabulary entirely based on the noun as prose is essentially and determinately and vigorously not based on the noun.

In asserting this different emphasis on, first, syntax and, then diction, Stein seems to be touching upon what structural linguists differentiate as the horizontal and vertical axes of language (as formulated by Saussure, Jakobson, and Barthes, with somewhat varying terminology). The horizontal axis links words contiguously. It is

a combination of signs which has space as a support. In the articulated language, this space is linear and irreversible (it is the "spoken chain"): two elements cannot be pronounced at the same time (*enter, against all, human life*): each term here derives it value from its opposition to what precedes and what follows; in the chain of speech, the terms are really united *in praesentia*.

When Stein says that the key element in prose is the sentence, and that verbs, prepositions, and conjunctions (which function to hold the syntax of the sentence together) are important in prose, she is implying an emphasis on the horizontal axis of language.

On the other hand, the vertical axis of language links words by associations based on similarity and/or opposition, and has to do with the selection of words.

"Beside the discourse (syntagmatic plane), the units which have something in common are associated in memory and thus form groups within which various relationships can be found": education can be associated, through its meaning, to *up-bringing* or *training*, and through its sound to *educate, education* or to *application, vindication.* . . . in each series unlike what happens at the syntagmatic level, the terms are united *in absentia*.

Stein characterizes poetry as concerned with vocabulary (and with the noun in particular). Hers is an oblique statement of the obvious observation that in poetry, word choice is of more concern than syntax, which is often suppressed, especially in modern poetry. The choice of a word from among a group of synonyms on the basis of qualities like rhythm and rhyme, or the choice of a poetic vocabulary from within an entire language, is an operation of selection. According to structural linguistic theories the operation of selection functions along the vertical axis of language.

As to Stein's remarks regarding the various parts of speech, Ronald Levinson points out in his article, "Gertrude Stein, William James, and Grammar," that Stein's theoretical formulation of the functions of the parts of speech was apparently greatly influenced by the theories of William James, who, in *Psychology*, compared the "stream of consciousness" to a series of "flights and perchings,"—the "perchings" being substantives ("occupied by sensorial imaginings"), and the "flights" being transitives ("thoughts of relating, static and dynamic"), which depend on verbs, prepositions, and conjunctions. As Levinson points out, Stein in her philosophy of grammar set forth in "Poetry and Grammar" echoes some of James' theories, especially in the distinction she makes between static words (nouns) and dynamic words (verbs, prepositions). What is original is her use of James' theories as the basis of a distinction between poetry and prose. Here, prose is based on verbs, prepositions, and conjunctions (the "flights"): the words that support syntax. These words function along the horizontal axis and have to do with contiguity: they combine to hold the words of the sentence in relation to one another. Poetry, on the other hand, is based on the noun or the substantive; the "perchings." Roman Jakobson's linguistic analysis of aphasia indicates that these parts of speech have to do with the operation of selection (the vertical axis). Thus, Stein's distinction between prose and poetry is based not merely upon stylistic or formal considerations, but rather on a distinction in emphasis upon what structuralists have since identified as two linguistic, and even mental, operations: similarity (or selection or system) and contiguity (or combination or syntagm).

Though one can see the germs of some of these ideas in James' theories as set forth in *Psychology*, Stein extends and applies them in her creative writing. James describes consciousness as a continuous flow, distinguishes between static and dynamic parts of speech, and discerns two types of association. The first is based on contiguity, meaning habitual association of things existing together in time and space. (This kind of association James identifies as performed even by animals.) The second type is based on similarity of entities not linked in space or time. However, James does not extend this distinction from the realm of association and use it to bifurcate the whole of linguistic operations along these lines as do the theories of structuralism.

Stein's contribution is the creation of an aesthetic based on James's theories and on pragmatism in general, as Robert Haas points out. Through this effort, she arrives at two types of obscurity which function, perhaps coincidentally, as practical illustrations of linguistic theories that were yet to be published at the time she was creating those two styles. (Even the first and most limited formulation of these structural theories in Ferdinand de

Saussure's *Course in General Linguistics* was not published until 1916, approximately four years after *Tender Buttons* was written, *circa* 1912.) Furthermore, her writing, which suppresses, first, the vertical axis at the expense of the horizontal axis, and, then, vice versa, foreshadows Jakobson's observations and, then, the other as it occurs in the speech of aphasic patients. Jakobson did not publish these observations until 1956 in "Two Aspects of Language and Two Types of Aphasic Disturbances." Of course, in aphasia, the suppression of either of the two linguistic operations of contiguity and similarity is entirely involuntary and pathological, while Stein's theoretical writings indicate that the creation of each of her two obscure styles was quite consciously undertaken for certain theoretical and aesthetic reasons—all arguments about "automatic writing" to the contrary!

The key stylistic interest in *The Making of Americans*, and in other works of Stein's participial style, is syntax. Grammatically correct but eccentric sentences spin themselves out and grow, clause linked to clause, until they are of paragraph length. She asserts that nothing "has ever been more exciting than diagramming sentences. . . . I like the feeling the everlasting feeling of sentences as they diagram themselves." Her long, repetitive sentences convey the feeling of process and duration, and of the time it gradually takes to get to know a person or to come to grips with an idea. She felt that sentences were not emotional (i.e., the syntax or "internal balance" of the sentence is a given) but that paragraphs were. She illustrates this principle by reference to her dog's drinking water from a dish. The paragraph is emotional in that it prolongs the duration of the idea or perception until the writer feels satisfied. This feeling of satisfaction is subjective and not arrived at by following rules of grammar By extending the sentence to the length approximately of a short paragraph, Stein was trying to achieve an emotional sentence. Many of the stylistic idiosyncrasies of her "participial" style function to extend the length of the sentence. What follows is a passage located near the end of *The Making of Americans:*

> Certainly he was one being living when he was being a being young one, he was often then quite certainly one being almost completely interested in being one being living, he was then quite often wanting to be one being completely interested in being one being living. He certainly then went on being living, he did this thing certainly all of his being living in being young living. He certainly when he was a young one was needing then sometimes to be sure that he was one being living, this is certainly what some being living are needing when they are ones being young ones in being living. David Hersland certainly was

one almost completely one being one being living when he was being a young one. Some he was knowing then were certainly being completely living then and being then being young ones in being living then, some were quite a good deal not being one being completely living then when they were being young ones in being living. David Hersland did a good deal of living in being living then when he was a young one. He was knowing very many men and very many knew him then. He remembered some of them in his later living and he did not remember some of them. He certainly was one almost completely then interested in being one being living then.

In this characteristic paragraph (consisting of only nine sentences), Stein uses many grammatical and stylistic strategies to extend the syntax and physical duration of the utterance. For example, one way to extend the syntax is to create very complex sentences, such as "Some he was knowing then were not quite completely being ones being living then, some were a quite a good deal not being ones being completely living then when they were being young ones in being living" *(Making of Americans)*. It is characteristic of her writing that, although she may link clause to clause, she often will suppress the use of relative pronouns such as "that" or "who." This method makes it more difficult to divide the sentences into individual clauses, forcing the reader to take a more active role in struggling to follow the sentence structure. Another simple, but less orthodox, means of extending the syntax is by fusing two or more sentences through the comma splice: "He certainly then went on being living, he did this thing certainly all of his being living in being young living" *(Making of Americans)*. (One should note, here, that the sparse use of commas also functions to make the reader work harder to follow the sentence.) Another device for stretching the sentence almost to paragraph length is the mechanistic linking together of many independent clauses by a series of conjunctions:

Some are certainly needing to be ones doing something and they are doing one thing and doing it again and again and again and again and they are doing another thing and they are doing it again and again and they are doing another thing and they are doing it again and again and again and such a one might have been one doing a very different thing then and doing that then each or any one of them and doing it again and again and again.
(Making of Americans)

Stein's first style is full of participles that function as nouns or adjectives and verb forms as well, a use which critics have termed a philosophical choice. Participles prolong the time span to achieve a sense of duration and process. Moreover, the participle, and particularly the gerund, also help portray the pragmatic conception of the world as a constantly on-going event. However, it should be noted that when Stein substitutes, "When he was being a young one" for "When he was young," the sentence is lengthened by two syllables. Her substitution of the participle for a simpler form of the verb has the cumulative effect of substantially lengthening the sentence, especially in view of the fact that, as Hoffman points out, "Probably more than half her verb forms use some form of the progressive ending." The Stein sentence is also lengthened by the fact that she so often insists on the "changing of an adjective into a substantive. Rather than saying 'Everybody is real,' she changes 'real' into 'a real one.' " Again, this method has the cumulative effect of lengthening the duration of the reading or the utterance.

In *The Making of Americans*, Stein stretches syntax almost to the breaking point and simultaneously limits her vocabulary. She moves farther and farther away from the concrete noun-centered vocabulary of the realistic novel. In part, the movement is due to her subject matter. *The Making of Americans* is a monumental attempt to create a chronicle of one family which could serve as an eternally valid history of all people, past, present, and future. Herein, she presents people as generalized types, and uses the characters in the novel to represent all human possibilities. This method led her from the essentially conventional narrative which dominates the beginning of the book to the generalized and theoretical kind of digression dispersed throughout the novel, but especially prominent towards the end of the book.

Although the long passage cited earlier concerns David Hersland, Stein has supplied very little concrete information about him because she was trying to turn particular and perhaps personal facts (the Hersland family is considered to be autobiographical by most critics) into universally valid generalizations. This effort is reflected in the dearth of conventional nouns and the wealth of pronouns. This is a move towards obscurity in that the referent of a pronoun is more vague than that of a noun. Verbals are used instead of conventional nouns and adjectives: "alive" becomes "being living." The same phrase is also used as a noun: David Hersland is interested in "being living" rather than in life. Probably this construction reflects Stein's desire to emphasize the transitive linguistic processes over the substantive ones in prose.

Conventional verbs are replaced by participles, which prolong and de-emphasize whatever action is being described. The participles contain very little concrete information. In the passage under discussion, there are only five participles, although each is repeated a number of times (*being, living, wanting, needing, knowing*). The least specific participles are those most often repeated. *Being* and *living* each occur nineteen times in the paragraph.

There are few conventional adjectives in the passage, aside from the participles. As for adverbs, *certainly* occurs a number of times, here, as it does throughout the book. Some critics think that Stein, in this case, is attempting to reassure herself and her reader of the universal validity of her typology. In addition, the fact that she must say *some, many*, and *a good deal* more and more often is seen as her growing recognition of the limitations of what she is doing. The adverb *then is* prevalent in the novel, perhaps related to her attempt to bring all knowledge gained over the passing of time into the present moment. It is also natural that a style which extends syntax will contain many relational words, like prepositions and conjunctions.

The stylistic concerns of Stein's early prose, in both *The Making of Americans* and the early (pre-1912) portraits, are the extension of syntax and the simultaneous circumscription of vocabulary, which is limited not merely in terms of the quantity of words, but also in the degree of specificity allowed to appear. The result is a very vague and generalized portrayal of the subject matter. Thus, *The Making of Americans* fits very neatly her requirements for prose. It is concerned with syntax, and contains many verbs, adverbs and conjunctions, while it reduces the vocabulary, and for the most part, eliminates conventional nouns in favor of pronouns and gerunds.

It is interesting to compare these observations about her prose style with Jakobson's observations about the two aspects of language as they relate to the speech of aphasics. Like Stein's writing, aphasia manifests two basic types of obscurity (although, of course, the obscurity in aphasia is pathological and involuntary, while that in Stein is a voluntary stylistic choice). Jakobson delineates two types of aphasia, each related to an inability to function in terms of one of the two linguistic axes which Roland Barthes has described as "system" (vertical axis) and "syntagm" (horizontal axis). Jakobson refers to these axes respectively as "selection" and "combination":

Any linguistic sign involves two modes of arrangement:

1) Combination. Any sign is made up of constituent signs and/or occurs only in combination with other signs. This means that any linguistic unit at one and the same time serves as a context for simpler units and/or finds its own context in a more complex linguistic unit. Hence any actual grouping of linguistic

units binds them into a superior unit: combination and contexture are two faces of the same operation.

2) Selection. A selection between alternatives implies the possibility of substituting one for the other, equivalent to the former in one respect and different from it in another. Actually selection and substitution are two faces of the same operation.

He points out further that "speech disturbances may affect in varying degrees the individual's capacity for combination and selection of linguistic units, and, indeed, the question of which of these two operations is chiefly impaired proves to be of far-reaching significance in describing, analyzing, and classifying the diverse forms of aphasia." Some of Jakobson's observations regarding the language produced by patients suffering from an inability to perform the operation of selection are somewhat similar to what can be observed in the prose style of *The Making of Americans* and the early portraits. This similarity is not really surprising, since Stein is herein voluntarily suppressing the operation of selection by severely limiting her vocabulary and attempting to eliminate nouns. Jakobson describes some of the speech patterns of aphasics suffering from a similarity disorder as follows:

> the more a word is dependent on the other words of the same sentence and the more it refers to the syntactical context, the less it is affected by the speech disturbance. Therefore words syntactically subordinated by grammatical agreement or government are more tenacious, whereas the main subordinating agent of the sentence, namely the subject, tends to be omitted. . . . Key words may be dropped or superseded by abstract anaphoric substitutes. A specific noun, as Freud noticed, is replaced by a very general one, for instances *machin, chose* in the speech of French aphasics. In a dialectal German sample of "amnesiac aphasia" observed by Goldstein, . . . *Ding* "thing" or *Stuckle* "piece" were substituted for all inanimate nouns, and *uberfahren* "perform" for verbs which were identifiable from the context or situation and therefore appeared superfluous to the patient.
>
> Words with an inherent reference to the context, like pronouns and pronominal adverbs, and words serving merely to construct the context, such as connectives and auxiliaries, are particularly prone to survive.

As it will be seen, some of Jakobson's observations about the language of aphasics with a contiguity disorder seem to indicate that this particular form of pathological obscurity shares certain characteristics with Stein's second stylistic interest, which she identified as poetry. For example, *Tender Buttons* represents a radical change from the early prose style of *The Making of Americans* and of other works to that which she called poetry. From prose, with its emphasis on syntax and its suppression of vocabulary, she moved to a concern for poetry with its emphasis on vocabulary and its suppression of syntax. This change manifests itself in a shift of linguistic emphasis from the operation of combination (horizontal axis) to the operation of selection (vertical axis).

Tender Buttons attained "a certain notoriety" in the press and attracted polemical criticism, perhaps because it seemed to "veer off into meaninglessness," at least in conventional terms. But the work is more than a literary curiosity. Its marked stylistic change appears to have been a breakthrough that influenced the direction of much of Stein's future work. "*Tender Buttons* represented her full scale break out of the prison of conventional form into the colorful realm of the sensitized imagination."

In *The Making of Americans*, her concerns were those of imposing order upon the world by classifying its inhabitants into universal and eternally valid types, of creating a history of all human possibilities. This goal called for a language that expressed generalities in a very precise way. Her attempts to portray the "bottom nature" of a person, the essence which lay behind his superficial particularity, continued in her early portraits.

> Gertrude Stein had tried numerous techniques in her previous efforts to match her conception of a person with a style. She had generalized and reduced her vocabulary in order to make true statements, however simpleminded. She had constructed long, cumulative sentences on the model of This-is-the-house-that-Jack built to convey the feeling of slowly becoming familiar with a person.

However, by the time Stein wrote *Tender Buttons*, her attention was no longer focused on the universals of experience, but now on the process of experiencing each moment in the present tense as it intersects with the consciousness. In *The Making of Americans*, she had subordinated particularity and individual differences to the type, an approach which she eventually abandoned. "But by rejecting her knowledge of types, she was faced with each experience as a unique thing, with even its importance unprejudiced, as simply different." She had simplified and generalized reality so as to impose an order upon it, but finally she "concluded that greater fidelity of representation might be achieved if she simply recorded the verbal responses her consciousness made to a particular subject, while minimizing her own manipulation of them."

In her lectures (written with the hindsight of many years, which perhaps lent her stylistic development more coherence than it had in actual fact), Stein discusses her new desire to see the world and return to the sensual particularity of experience as it was immediately available to her consciousness. After doing her portraits, she slowly became bothered by the fact that she was omitting a looking at the world. "So I began to do this thing, I tried to include color and movement, and what I do is . . . a volume called *Tender Buttons.*"

The Making of Americans, with its historical orientation and its goal of classifying people according to type, necessitated remembering the past. Classification is based on resemblances, on similarities, which must be held over time in the mind. In her early portraits, Stein freed herself of the narrative and dealt with the presentation of perceptions one moment at a time, but these perceptions were not dealt with "in the raw." They had to be edited, selected, and generalized so that the person could be analyzed and presented in his essential reality. However, in *Tender Buttons*, she came to terms with the chaotic nature of real experience and "the existential swarm of her impressions." The physical world is experienced as unique and immediate in each present moment as the consciousness receives data.

In any attempt to deal with Stein's writing, the word "abstract" is bound to come up. This term has been a problem in Stein criticism because it is not usually defined clearly. Even Michael Hoffman's book, *The Development of Abstractionism in the Writing of Gertrude Stein*, fails to come to terms with "abstract." Hoffman's definition of abstractionism is essentially the dictionary definition, "the act or process of leaving out of consideration one or more qualities of a complex object so as to attend to others." That Stein follows this approach, as any artist must, is obvious. However, this definition does not seem adequate to deal with important questions like Stein's refusal of verisimilitude. Because of the vague definition, Hoffman, thus, uses *abstract* to describe all of Stein's work without clarifying the distinctions between *non-representational, plastic, arbitrary,* and *abstract,* although he seems aware of the development of diverse styles in her writing. Stein's relationship to the Cubists, to whose work she compared her own, is an important question that cannot be examined without these kinds of distinctions. When Hoffman compares her work to that of the Cubists, he shares the common failure to be consistent and rigorous in his distinctions between the stages of Cubism as it developed over time. John Malcolm Brinnin, in *The Third Rose*, alone saw that developments in the Cubist styles (analytic and synthetic) parallel stages in Stein's stylistic development as well. This observation is potentially useful in clarifying the distinction between the two kinds of obscure writing that Stein produces.

Too often, the term *abstract*, when used in regard to Stein's writing, is taken to mean non-representational, which her writing almost never is. She never really abandons subject matter. In her early work, the subject matter was the representation of types of people, which appears to have led to an interest in the process of perception itself. In the style which *Tender Buttons* exemplifies, the subject matter is the intersection of the object with consciousness. As attention is focused on the process of perception, that process becomes as much a part of the subject matter as the object perceived. "As I say a motor goes inside and the car goes on, but my business my ultimate business as an artist was not with where the car goes as it goes but with the movement inside that is of the essence of its going." In fact, Stein insisted on subject matter and disapproved of abstract art. That the Cubists' work was never abstract, i.e., never non-representational, is not always clearly understood, and confuses the comparison of Stein's writing to some of the work of those painters.

Subject matter is certainly not abandoned in *Tender Buttons*, nor does that book "signal an abandonment of control. Her practice was to concentrate upon an object as it existed in her mind. . . . Gertrude Stein perceived that the object was immersed in a continuum of sound, color, and association, which it was her business to reconstitute in writing." In *Tender Buttons*, the subject matter was not limited to a description of the objective world, but included mimesis of the intersection of the real world with the consciousness of the artist.

Nevertheless, it is possible to assert that the vocabulary of her early writing moves towards abstraction, if one means that it moves away from the concrete, that it is very general and contains few concrete nouns and verbs of action:

> He was one being living, then when he was quite a young one, and some knew him then and he knew some then. He was one being living then and he was being one and some knew he was that one the one he was then and some did not know then that he was that one the one he was then.
>
> *(The Making of Americans)*

Tender Buttons has a less abstract vocabulary in that it contains many more concrete nouns, sensual adjectives, and action verbs than does her earlier style:

The stove is bigger. It was of a shape that made no audience bigger if the opening is assumed why should there not be kneeling. Any force which is bestowed on a floor shows rubbing. This is so nice and sweet and yet there comes the change, there comes the time to press more air. This does not mean the same as disappearance.

However, in a different sense, *Tender Buttons* taken as a whole is more abstract that *The Making of Americans* in that its words are used in a plastic, arbitrary way, and in that it is less concerned with traditional, discursive description.

In the previous centuries writers had managed pretty well by assembling a number of adjectives and adjectival clauses side by side; the reader "obeyed" by furnishing images and concepts in his mind and the resultant "thing" in the reader's mind corresponded fairly well with that in the writer's. Miss Stein felt that process did not work any more. Her painter friends were showing clearly that the corresponding method of "description" had broken down in painting and she was sure that it had broken down in writing. . . .

Miss Stein felt that writing must accomplish a revolution whereby it could report things as they were in themselves before our minds had appropriated them and robbed them of their objectivity "in pure existing." To this end she went about her house describing the objects she found there in the series of short "poems" which make up the volume called *Tender Buttons*.

As the concerns of Stein's writing gradually shift from an interest in orderly analysis of the world to an interest in the immediate perception of the world by the consciousness, her writing appears to deal more and more with the word itself: with the mental images called up by and associated with the word (signifieds), and with the qualities of words as things in themselves (signifiers). "Her imagination was stimulated then not by the object's particular qualities alone, but also by the associations it aroused . . . and by the words themselves as they took shape upon the page."

Perhaps coincidentally, a similar shift in emphasis was occurring in the painting of the Cubists around the time *Tender Buttons* was composed. Their earlier struggle, in Analytic Cubism, to see reality without the conventional and learned *trompe-l'oeil* of perspective focused their attention on the elements of composition and led them to the realization that the artist could use these elements arbitrarily rather than mimetically:

> in the winter of 1912–13 a fundamental change came about in the pictorial methods of the true Cubists. Whereas previously Braque and Picasso had analyzed and dissected the appearance of objects to discover a set of forms which would add up to their totality and provide the formal elements of a composition, now they found that they could begin by composing with purely pictorial elements (shaped forms, planes of color) and gradually endow them with an objective significance.

The Cubists had arrived at "the conclusion that they could create their own pictorial reality by building up towards it through a synthesis of different elements." That the elements of signification might have an importance in their own right and be used arbitrarily by the artist to create not a mirror of reality but an authentic new reality (the work of art as *tableau-objet*) was an important realization for this group and a conclusion that Stein seems to have arrived at, perhaps independently. Stein now realized that words need no longer be merely the means to the expression of another reality, but may become freed of their normal mimetic function (still retaining their meanings and associations) and be used plastically by the writer. In her lectures, she describes her growing concern with the quality of language as a thing in itself:

> I began to wonder at . . . just what one saw when one looked at anything . . . [Did] it make itself by description by a word that meant it or did it make itself by a word in itself. . . .
>
> I became more and more excited about how words which were the words which made whatever I looked at look like itself were not words that had in them any quality of description. . . .
>
> And the thing that excited me . . . is that the words that made what I looked at be itself were always words that to me very exactly related themselves to that thing . . . at which I was looking, but as often as not had as I say nothing whatever to do with what any words would do that described that thing.

Like the Cubists, Stein abandons conventional description of an object, although she is still concerned with the object as here "model," but she inverts the traditional descriptive relationship of word to object. Rather than the word evoking the mental image of the object, the object evokes words (associations, etc.) which the artist arbitrarily assembles into an independent linguistic object related to, but not descriptive of, the model or referent. In Analytic Cubism, the artist abstracts form from the given object and creates a representation of the object (however unconventional) on canvas. In Synthetic Cubism, forms have their genesis in the artist, although he uses them to create an object on the canvas. The function of the painting is no longer to describe or represent another reality, but to exist as a thing in itself. In Stein's early works *(The Making of Americans* and others, of her participial style), words are used to abstract generalities about the world to analyze or describe it on paper. However, in *Tender Buttons*, the words are not conventionally descriptive of the object, but have their genesis in the writer and in the associations which the object evokes in her. The function of the writing is not to describe the given object, but to become an entity in its own right.

In *Tender Buttons*, with the new attention to the immediately present moment and the abandoning of traditional description, Stein turned from her earlier "portraits" of people to the treatment of inanimate objects and seems to have felt some bond with the painters of still lives. Dealing with human beings "inevitably carried in its train realizing movements and expression and as such forced me into recognizing resemblances, and so forced remembering and in forcing remembering caused confusion of present with past and future time." Consequently, she turned from "portraits of men and women and children" to "portraits of food and rooms and everything because there I could avoid this difficulty of suggesting remembering more easily . . . than if I were to describe human beings." Stein also felt that this was a problem she shared with the painters:

> I began to make portraits of things and enclosures . . . because I
> needed to completely face the difficulty of how to include what
> is seen with hearing and listening and at first if I were to include
> a complicated listening and talking it would be too difficult to do.
> That is why painters paint still lives. You do see why they do.

Indeed, as the Cubists turned from an analysis of a given reality on canvas to a synthesis of a new reality from the pictorial elements, the Cubists, (Picasso especially), produced fewer portraits and more still lives. Perhaps the reason for this move is similar to the one that brought about the change in Stein's writing: dealing with inanimate objects allows the artist more freedom to treat the subject in an arbitrary manner. After all, the public expects a portrait to be a likeness of the model, who has the annoying habit of exhibiting his face in public, thus allowing it to be compared with the painting. But a still life is a small piece of reality that the artist arranges at will, and when he is finished, he can dismantle it, leaving the public nothing with which to compare the painting.

The new realization of Synthetic Cubism (that pictorial elements could be used arbitrarily) was marked by a return to color and texture in contrast to the predominantly grey paintings of Analytic Cubism. For Stein, the new interest in the sensory experiences of the present moment and the new-felt freedom in the use of words manifested itself in a richer, more sensual vocabulary, in contrast to the spare and spartan one of her earlier struggle to classify everyone into universal types. "The idea had entered her mind that lyricism contained a fuller measure of truth than could ever be encircled by making endless laboriously deliberate statements." The evocative power of the word called for more "decorative" approach. Freed from her concerns with remembering and classifying, she began to concentrate on the present moment and all of the phenomena therein, including the words called up by those phenomena and their effect upon her conscious mind. Thus, instead of the genderless pronouns, verbs of being, prepositions and conjunctions, and the virtual elimination of concrete words in her earlier style, there is a renaissance of the particular: concrete nouns, sensual adjectives, and specific verbs.

This new interest in the word itself, and especially in the noun and the associative powers of the word, was what Stein considered the essence of poetry. In *Tender Buttons* and other works that she held as poetry, the chief linguistic operation is association (given various labels by structuralists such as substitution, selection, system) and choice of words. The association of words and concepts by similarity or opposition, and the selection of a word from a group of synonyms, are operations that function along the vertical axis of language. Interestingly enough, the *Tender Buttons* style also suppresses syntax (the horizontal axis) while it is expanding vocabulary. Construction of syntax becomes increasingly fragmentary until syntax disappears altogether in some of the more extreme passages.

In *The Making of Americans*, the chief stylistic interest is syntax, but in *Tender Buttons*, the central concern seems to be diction, the selection of words based on association (in terms of both similarity and opposition). The long sentence-paragraph is abandoned as more attention is forced on the noun:

> after I had gone as far as I could in these long sentences and paragraphs . . . I then began very short thing . . . and I resolutely realized nouns and decided not to get around them but to meet them, to handle in short to refuse them by using them and in that way my real acquaintance with poetry was begun.

> I began to discover the names of things, that is . . . to discover the
> things . . . to see the things to look at and in so doing I had of
> course to name them not to give new names but to see that I
> could find out how to know that they were there by their names
> or by replacing their names. . . . They had their names and
> naturally I called them by the names they had and in doing so
> having begun looking at them I called them by their names with
> passion and that made poetry . . . it made the *Tender Buttons*.

However, as Stein begins to abandon her extension of the sentence and
enriches her use of diction, the result is not more conventional writing but
rather a new style, equally obscure, if not more so. It is even harder to read,
in the traditional sense, than her first obscure style, because, in part, there is
a disjunction between the two axes of language in this second style. One
word often does not appear to have any relationship to other words in the
sentence except in terms of their existence as pure words (in terms of
grammatical structure, or rhyme, or word play). Of course, words cannot be
divorced from their meanings; thus, each word (signifier) calls up a mental
image or idea (signified), but *Tender Buttons* cannot be read with a
conventional concern for subject matter because one cannot use the total
configurations of these mental constructs to reconstruct the "subject matter."
Sometimes a sentence in *Tender Buttons* may appear to have a normal syntax
and to be orthodox grammatically, yet the words selected do not relate to
each other in a traditional and discursive way. "The change of color is likely
and a difference a very little difference is prepared. Sugar is not a vegetable"
(Tender Buttons). These sentences are grammatically correct, though their
punctuation is not conventional. One may achieve the feeling that the
sentence would be perfectly comprehensible if the context were supplied.
Stein is using both syntax and diction, but because of the disjunction between
the two axes of language, the sentence does not "mean" in a conventional
way.

Sometimes in *Tender Buttons* Stein explores the patterns of speech,
repeating syntactical patterns, at the same time somewhat arbitrarily
plugging in terms from the pool of associated words in her vocabulary:

> Almost very likely there is no seduction, almost very likely there
> is no stream, certainly very likely the height is penetrated,
> certainly certainly the target is cleaned, come to set, come to
> refuse, come to surround, come slowly and age is not lessening.

She explores the rhythm and patterns of speech that are present, even when
discursive meaning is not. Like "Jabberwocky," this passage conveys a feeling

of speech, even though its words do not relate to each other in a conventional way.

In *Tender Buttons*, Stein's sentences become shorter as her emphasis shifts to diction and association rather than syntax. She explains in a lecture that lines of poetry are shorter than prose because

> such a way to express oneself is the natural way when one expresses oneself in loving the name of anything. Think what you do . . . when you love the name of anything really love its name. Inevitably you express yourself . . . in the way poetry expresses itself that is in short lines in repeating what you began in order to do it again. Think of how you talk to anything whose name is new to you a lover a baby a dog or a new land. . . . Do you not inevitably repeat what you call out and is that calling out not of necessity in short lines.

Often in *Tender Buttons*, lines that appear to be sentences are not sentences at all: "Cutting shade, cool spades and little last beds, make violet violet when." Obviously, this fragment promises to be a sentence until it is truncated by the period after "when," a word normally expected to introduce a subordinate clause. The disjunction between diction and syntax manifests itself in false predication. For example, how can shade, spades, and beds make violet? Here, each word is quite independent from those which precede and follow it in the speech chain, at least as far as the mental images or signifieds are concerned. (Obviously, however, there are relationships between some of the words in terms of sound.)

Stein uses punctuation in other ways to break up the continuity of the sentence: "This makes and eddy. Necessary" *(Tender Buttons)*. Also: "Cream cut. Anywhere crumb. Left hop chambers" *(Tender Buttons)*. She carries the disintegration of syntax even further, presenting a list within the horizontal structure of the sentence. (A list is usually a group of items associated with one another because they are similar in some way.) "Alas a doubt in case of more to go to say what is is cress. What it is. Mean. Potatoes. Loaves" *(Tender Buttons)*. In some of her writing following *Tender Buttons*, Stein even entirely abandoned syntax and made lists of words or phrases in vertical columns on the page.

Again, one observes that some of the stylistic phenomena of Stein's second "obscure" style, emphasizing vocabulary and the noun while suppressing syntax, are strikingly close to Jakobson's observations about the language of aphasics suffering from a contiguity disorder, in which ability to use syntax becomes weakened or disappears, leaving the patient with *only* a vocabulary in extreme cases:

The impairment of the ability to propositionalize, or, generally speaking, to combine simpler linguistic entities into more complex units, is actually confined to one type of aphasia. . . . There is no *wordlessness*, since the entity preserved in most of such cases is the *word*, which can be defined as the highest among the linguistic units compulsorily coded, i.e., we compose our own sentences and utterances out of the word stock supplied by the code.

This contexture-deficient aphasia, which could be termed contiguity disorder, diminishes the extent and variety of sentences. The syntactical rules organizing words into a higher unit are lost; this loss, called agrammatism, causes the degeneration of the sentence into a mere "word heap. . . ." Word order becomes chaotic; the ties of grammatical coordination and subordination . . . are dissolved. As might be expected, words endowed with purely grammatical functions, like conjunctions, prepositions, pronouns, and articles, disappear first, giving rise to the so-called "telegraphic style," whereas in the case of similarity disorder they are the most resistant. The less a word depends grammatically on the context, the stronger is its tenacity in the speech of aphasics with a contiguity disorder and the sooner it is dropped by patients with a similarity disorder. Thus the "kernel subject word" is the first to fall out of the sentence in cases of similarity disorder and conversely, it is the least destructible in the opposite type of aphasia.

In *Tender Buttons*, Stein's primary concern is words and their associations, and her selection of words often is imbued with a spirit of love and play:

Poetry is concerned with using with abusing, with losing with wanting, with denying with avoiding with adoring with replacing the noun. . . . Poetry is doing nothing but losing refusing and pleasing and betraying and caressing nouns.

Sometimes the selection of words is obviously related to the subject:

A Petticoat
A light white, a disgrace, an ink spot, a rosy charm.
(*Tender Buttons*)

Without too much effort, one detects the associations between word and object. Petticoats are lightweight and often white; a petticoat that shows is a disgrace which might provoke a modest blush. (Stein has been greatly overread, but it seems safe to identify the obvious and public association.)

Even when the associations of word to object are chiefly based on associated meanings, similarities of spelling and sound may play a role:

> A Method of a Cloak
> A single climb to a line, a straight exchange to a cane, a desperate adventure and courage and a clock . . . all this makes an attractive black silver.
>
> *(Tender Buttons)*

The "single climb to a line" might relate to the shape of the cloak, and the cane is related to the cloak as an object of apparel. (Both the cane and the cloak have a nostalgic, perhaps nineteenth-century flavor of elegance.) But the two phrases, "A single climb to a line" and "a straight exchange to a cane," have identical rhythmic patterns as well. The "desperate adventure" and "courage" might be related to the connotations of "cloak and dagger." Black may be the color of the clock which is "attractive;" perhaps silver was evoked by the sight of the lining of the cloak and the associated phrase, "silver lining." But clock seems to be associated with cloak because of the similarity in spelling and sound. In terms of association on the level of mental constructs (signifieds), Stein uses both association based on contiguity (defined by James as association of objects habitually found together in time and space, and identified by Jakobson as metonymy) and on similarity (which Jakobson identifies as metaphor.) Both kinds of association are operations of selection which function along the vertical axis of language. But the metaphorical type of association seems to predominate in *Tender Buttons*, as one might expect, given that "metaphor is alien to the similarity disorder and metonymy to the contiguity disorder." Moreover, the operation of association is stressed not only in terms of images and concepts (signifieds), but also in terms of the qualities of the words as words (signifiers).

Stein often plays with the qualities of words as *words* in *Tender Buttons* and chooses them on the basis of their associations with other words as signifiers. For instance, she oftens uses rhyme within the line: "all the joy in weak success, all the joyful tenderness, all the section and the tea, all the stouter symmetry. . . ." Similarly,

> Chicken
> Alas a dirty word, alas a dirty third, alas a dirty third alas a dirty bird.

and: "The sister was not a mister."

She also associates words on the basis of alliteration: "The sight of a reason, the same sight slighter, the sight of a simpler negative answer, the same sore sounder, the intention to wishing, the same splendor, the same furniture." She even uses onomatopoeia:

Chicken
Stick stick call then, stick stick sticking, sticking with a chicken.

Playing with the sounds and meanings of words also leads to puns, as in the following, seemingly evoking the associations of Washington, Wellington, and veal Wellington:

Veal
Very well very well. Washing is old, washing is washing.

Additional punning occurs in the following:

Milk
Climb up in sight climb in the whole utter needless and a guess
a whole guess is hanging. Hanging, hanging.

She even plays with the spelling of words: "and easy express e. c."

The devices used here are certainly traditional, or at least they seem so now: indirect associations of imagery, obliqueness, fragmented syntax, rhyme, rhythm, alliteration, etc. What is it, then, that so many have found upsetting? Perhaps it is the lack of discursive meaning or the fact that the "subject matter" cannot be reconstructed from the images like a jigsaw puzzle, but these may be inappropriate expectations with which to approach Stein's writing.

It is ironic that, in spite of Stein's intention in writing *Tender Buttons* to capture immediate experience while consciousness grapples with it, there have been so many problems in the reading of that book. One problem inherent in the work itself is the disjunction of the two axes of language making it almost impossible to read the work for conventional discursive content. Moreover, this problem leads to another: the effort of trying to "figure it out," to reconstruct the content, not only exhausts the reader, but overdistances him from the work itself. Such an effort is futile anyway, for *Tender Buttons* demands to be dealt with in its own terms. The reader is given none of the literary allusions that the reader of Pound, Eliot, or Joyce can hold on to. As for inventing glosses for the little pieces in *Tender Buttons*,

Sutherland points out that it is impossible and amusing to create them, but that "it is perfectly idle":

> Such a procedure puts the original in the position of being a riddle, a rhetorical complication of something rather unremarkable in itself. It would be rather like an exhibition of the original table tops, guitars, pipes, and people which were the subject matter of cubist paintings. The original subject matter is or was of importance to the painter as a source of sensations, relations, ideas, even, but it is not after all the beholder's business. The beholder's business is the picture in front of him, which is a new reality and something else, which does not add up to the nominal subject matter.

As Sutherland suggests, perhaps what the reader of Stein is required to do is to look *at* the work, rather than *through* it. One cannot look *through* it because it is an opaque, rather than transparent, style. If one does look *at* the work, what does one see in *Tender Buttons?* He sees the word presented as an entity in its own right. By forcing the reader to attend to the word, Stein makes the word seem new, again. In this effort, she does not ignore the meanings of words, as so may critics have claimed. However by presenting each word in an unusual context, she directs attention not only towards its sound but towards its sense as the reader is forced to grapple with each word, one at a time. One is forced to attend to the word, and to language, with a sense of bewilderment and perhaps with a sense of wonder and discovery:

> Nouns are the name of anything and anything is named, that is what Adam and Eve did and if you like it is what anybody does, but do they go on just using the name until perhaps they do not know what the name is or if they do know what the name is they do not care what the name is . . . . And what has that to do with poetry. A great deal I think . . . .

The role of poetry, then, is to give the word back its youth and vitality:

> you can love a name and if you love a name then saying that name any number of times only makes you love it more, more violently, more persistently, more tormentedly. Anybody knows how anybody calls out the name of anybody one loves. And so that is poetry really loving the name of anything. . . .

Stein's fascination with language, both its sound and its sense, and her interest in exploring the way it works are certainly evident in *Tender Buttons.* Her intuitive grasp of the principles of its operation is manifested not only in her theories, but also in the very nature of the two so very different kinds of obscure styles that she created.

Richard Bridgman and Edmund Wilson are among those critics who attribute the relative unintelligibility of Stein's work to her need to write about her private passions and her simultaneous need to be discreet about the nature of those passions. As Stein herself might have said, "Interesting, if true." But the only relevance of this sexually motivated evasiveness is that it may have served as an impetus for her innovations with language. In *The Making of Americans* (as well as in other works of the same style), she stretches the contiguity of the sentence as far as it will go without snapping, at the same time reducing, to a minimum the vocabulary available for selection. In *Tender Buttons* and similar works, the available vocabulary becomes practically limitless while the syntax is shortened, destroyed, and even disintegrated into lists. As Jakobson's observations about aphasia indicate, conventionally intelligible language can only occur when both aspects of language are fully operative. Although one can only speculate that Stein's innovations grew out of a desire and a need to be unintelligible, one can say less uncertainly that her obscurity was a necessary consequence of the nature of her innovative experiments with language.

ADALAIDE MORRIS

The Concept of Projection:
H. D.'s Visionary Powers

In April 1920, while staying with her friend Bryher in a hotel on the island of Corfu, H. D. had a vision which marked and measured the rest of her life. It set the aims, announced the means, and disclosed the dimensions of her great work, the visionary epics *Trilogy* and *Helen in Egypt*, and it seemed to guarantee her gift as seer and prophet. It would be twenty years from the Corfu vision to the poems that first grasp its promise, however, years of drift and anxiety in which H. D. would write and rewrite the story of her vision. By the time the event achieves final formulation in the first part of *Tribute to Freud*, it is clear that, however charged the vision's imagery, the plot we are to follow, the *mythos* of the matter, is its method: the miraculous projection of the images.

As H. D. explains in *Tribute to Freud*, the images she witnessed had the clarity, intensity, and authenticity of dream symbols and yet took shape not inside her mind but on the wall between the foot of her bed and the washstand. Because it was late afternoon and their side of the hotel was already dim and because the images were outlined in light, the shapes that appeared could not have been cast shadows. Neither accidental nor random, they formed with a stately, steady purpose, one after another, and seemed inscribed by the same hand. Their abstract, impersonal, rather conventional notation—a head in profile, a chalice, a ladder, an angel named Victory or

From *Contemporary Literature* 25, no. 4 (Winter 1984). © 1984 by the Board of Regents of the University of Wisconsin System. University of Wisconsin Press, 1984.

Niké—made them appear part of a picture-alphabet or heiroglyphic system, a supposition reinforced by their orderly succession, their syntax. For these reasons and because of the eerie, miraculous portentousness of the moment, H. D. calls this experience the "writing on the wall."

When Belshazzar witnessed the writing on his wall, he glimpsed along with the letters a part of the hand that wrote them. The origin of H. D.'s writing is, if equally mysterious, less simply formulated. The agent is not a hand but a projective process: the casting of an image onto a screen. The vision's earlier images, which appear entire, are like magic lantern slides; the later ones, which draw themselves in dots of light elongating into lines, resemble primitive movies.

The path from mind to wall is direct. It at first seems to follow what H. D. calls her "sustained crystal-gazing stare" an aching concentration that propels the image outward on her eyebeam. Because the vision rides on will, she must not flag: "if I let go," she thinks, "lessen the intensity of my stare and shut my eyes or even blink my eyes, to rest them, the pictures will fade out." When, however, she drops her head in her hands, exhausted, the process continues and Bryher, who has until now seen nothing, witnesses the final image. What she sees—H. D.'s Nikés elevated into the sun-disk—is so consistent with the preceding figures that H. D. compares it to "that 'determinative' that is used in the actual hieroglyph, the picture that contains the whole series of pictures in itself or helps clarify or explain them." With the power of the poet or prophet, H. D. has not only materialized the images of her psyche but cast them onto the consciousness of another and released her audience's own visionary capacities.

The images of the vision are described as flowing from, or at least through, H. D.'s psyche, yet their origin is obscured. What creates these slides or magic transparencies? Where do they come from? The answer given in *Tribute to Freud is* ambiguous. On the one hand, the images seem little different than the clips from memories or dream scenes that H. D. had earlier compared to "transparencies in a dark room, set before lighted candles." In this sense, however extraordinary, they would be "merely an extension of the artist's mind, a *picture* or an illustrated poem, taken out of the actual dream or daydream content and projected from within." On the other hand, in an interpretation H. D. clearly prefers, one sanctioned by the classical belief that gods speak through dreams and oracles, the images seem "projected from outside," messages from another world, another state of being.

Images as signs and warnings from her own subconscious, images as signs and wonders from another world; the artist as moving-picture machine, the artist as psychic, the artist as message-transmitter: what gives this odd combination of attributes unity and coherence, positions it within H. D.'s development, and makes it central to any interpretation of her work is the concept of projection. All the more apt for its abundant ambiguities, projection is the master metaphor of H. D.'s technique. Its operations connect the material, mental, and mystical realms and enact her belief that there is no physical reality that is not also psychic and spiritual. Without the energies of projection, H. D.'s work stalls and thins; with them, her writing has strength and brilliance. It is this excellence that the "projected pictures" at Corfu seem to promise.

The word *projection* appears throughout H. D.'s work. Though its meaning alters subtly and sometimes confusingly, it always marks an important moment in her creative process. From the verb meaning *to throw forward*, projection is the thrust that bridges two worlds. It is the movement across a borderline: between the mind and the wall, between the brain and the page, between inner and outer, between me and you, between states of being, across dimensions of time and space. The concept of projection informs H. D.'s transitions from Imagist to clairvoyant, to film theorist, analysand, and prophetic poet. What does it clarify at each stage? how does it change between stages? what light does it throw on the overall strategies and strengths of H. D.'s work? These will be the questions that guide our inquiry.

PROJECTION: THE ACT
OF THROWING OR SHOOTING FORWARD

"Cut the cackle!" "Go in fear of abstractions!" "Don't be 'viewy'!" Most memorable Imagist statements are prescriptions against a poetic tradition condemned as rigid, overblown, and unoriginal. Cackle is the chatter of conventional verse. It fills long lines with flourishes Pound called "rhetorical bustuous rumpus": platitudes, circumlocutions, and rolling, ornamental din. To theorists like Pound and T. E. Hulme, these flourishes were selfgenerated and self-sustained, cut off from the world they purported to present. In its eagerness to pronounce upon the world and in the vaporous grandeur of its pronouncements, cackle went in fear neither of abstractions nor of viewiness.

The cure for cackle is contact. Imagist theory privileges sight as fresh, accurate access to the exterior world. Sight is the acid bath that dissolves the sticky sludge of rhetoric. It connects us directly, so the Imagists argue, with the things of this world. Bad art, for Hulme, is "words divorced from any real vision," strings of conventional locutions, abstractions, "counters" which, like "x" and "y" in an algebraic formula, replace six pounds of cashews and four Florida oranges. Formulaic words, like algebraic symbols, can be manipulated according to laws independent of their meaning. Hulme's test of good poetry is whether the words turn back into things that we can see.

The major Imagist theorists echo each other on this point. "Each *word* must be an image *seen*, not a counter," Hulme legislates. "Language in a healthy state," T. S. Eliot insists, "presents the object, is so close to the object that the two are identical." For Pound, "the very essence" of a writer's work is "the application of word to thing." It was Pound who discovered, through the work of Ernest Fenollosa, the ur-pattern of the word-thing: the Chinese ideogram which was assumed to be direct, visibly concrete, natural rather than conventional, a picture language within which, as Fenollosa put it, "Thinking is *thinging.*"

The image of a thing, set into a poem, becomes for the Imagists the innocent word, the word that has somehow escaped the conventional, abstracting, mediating nature of language. The assumption of transparent expression is a correlate of the Bergsonian faith in the artist's direct intuition of the object. Where contemporary theorists hold that we see what we know, Imagists insist we know what we see. They find in vision the release from a shared system of signs into spontaneous, intuitive, unmediated apprehension of essences. Whatever her subsequent elaborations—and they are many' and strange—this belief in the possibility of essential intuitions, so central to Imagism, remains at the core of H. D.'s projective practice.

Projection is the act of throwing or shooting forward. Though the Imagists don't use the term, they depend on the concept. In the genesis of the Imagist poem, a thing in the world projects its essence onto the poet's consciousness; the poet imprints the image, or record of the thing, in a poem; and the poem, in turn, projects the image onto the reader's consciousness. The model for this, the simplest form of projection, is the magic lantern show. It is Hulme's concrete display of images that "always endeavours to arrest you, and to make you continuously see a physical thing"; it is Pound's *phanopoeia*, the technique by which "you use a word to throw a visual concept on to the reader's imagination."

H. D.'s *Sea Garden is* full of *phanopoeia*. The reader's visual imagination is bombarded by sand, tree-bark, salt tracks, silver dust, wood violets, and thin, stinging twigs—objects in a world of clear, hard-edged, gritty particularity. The images have an almost hallucinatory specificity. The view is tight, close-up, almost too bright: on the beach, "hard sand breaks, / and the grains of it / are clear as wine"; in the late afternoon sun, "each leaf / cuts another leaf on the grass"; night, when it comes, curls "the petals back from the stalk / . . . under till the rinds break, / back till each bent leaf/ is parted from its stalk." Break, cut, curl: these moments are doubly projective. H. D.'s images, forcibly cast onto the reader's imagination, themselves record moments in which one thing, thrown onto another, opens, releases, or transforms it. In *Sea Garden*, objects are perpetually twisted, lifted, flung, split, scattered, slashed, and stripped clear by rushing energies that enact the impact the poet wishes to exert on the reader's imagination.

The rushing energies are the sea, the sun, and the night, but in H. D.'s world these are more than fierce weather: they testify to a sacred power and promise in the universe. Unlike other of the Imagists, H. D. conceived of essence as god-stuff . To her, each intense natural fact is the trace of a spiritual force; each charged landscape enshrines a deity. Thus, in *Sea Garden*, dryads haunt the groves, nereids the waves; Priapus transfuses the orchard, Artemis courses the woods; Hermes marks the crossroads, and the mysterious Wind Sleepers roam searching for their altar. The world glows with sacred energy.

This radiance, however, like a Derridean sigh, marks a presence that is vanished or just vanishing. Gods do not manifest directly to mortals, but they do, like Apollo at Delphi, leave us signs, the afterglow of sacred presence. The speaker in *Sea Garden* *is* a supplicant in search of deities that are everywhere immanent in the landscape: they beckon, stand tense, await us a moment, then surge away, leaving behind heel prints, snapped stalks, and a charged silence. The poet, like a skilled tracker, moves from sign to sign in rapt, sagacious pursuit.

As embodiments of essence, the deities might seem mere metaphors, relics of the kind of claptrap the Imagists despised. H. D.'s work, however, is spare, stripped, as Pound said, of slither. In it, the gods function not as the poems' ornament but as their absent center. The deities are both cause and condition of this poetry; the poems do not work if we don't posit the reality of the presence they yearn toward.

The poems in *Sea Garden* are thrown out as bridges to the sacred. They project themselves toward the gods with a plea that the gods will in return appear to us. Poems like "Sea Gods," "Hermes of the Ways," "The Helmsman," and "The Shrine" address the gods directly, compelling them from immanence to manifestation: "For you will come," H. D. presses, "you will come, / you will answer our taut hearts, / . . . and cherish and shelter us." Projection as *phanopoeia*, a poetic technique, here, in H. D.'s first important modification, broadens into a technique of meditation or prayer: an imaging used to summon a being from another world.

PROJECTION: A REPRESENTATION ON A PLANE
SURFACE OF ANY PART OF THE CELESTIAL SPHERE

Except for three brief reviews in *The Egoist*, H. D. took little part in the barrage of Imagist treatises and evaluations. Contrasting strongly with the polemics she later wrote for the cinema, this silence had several sources. She was a new poet, unused to literary disputations, and, until the arrival of Amy Lowell, she was the only woman in a contentious group of men. In addition, she held a constricted position in the movement: if Hulme was its principal theorist and Pound its chief publicist, H. D. was from the first the Imagiste extraordinaire, the movement's most effective practitioner. Her poems stimulated and exemplified positions held by others.

A third, more significant source of H. D.'s silence, however, lies in her hesitations about Imagist doctrine. Her *Egoist* review of John Gould Fletcher's *Goblins and Pagodas*, for example, makes an obligatory bow to Imagist principles but is compelled by something else. "He uses the direct image, it is true," H. D. writes, "but he seems to use it as a means of evoking other and vaguer images—a pebble, as it were, dropped into a quiet pool, in order to start across the silent water, wave on wave of light, of colour, of sound." Fletcher attempts "a more difficult and, when successfully handled, richer form of art: not that of direct presentation, but that of suggestion." The goblins and pagodas that title his volume testify to visionary capacities. His art pursues not the solidity of physical things so much as the spiritual enigmas that radiate from them.

The next stage of H. D.'s development furthers her own shift from pebbles to their radiating rings: from the objects of this world to the phantasms of light, color, and sound surrounding them; from our three dimensions to the largest ring of all, the fourth dimension or celestial sphere surrounding us. In 1919, after her bonds with Pound, Aldington, and the other Imagists had cracked, after her alliance with Bryher had begun and her daughter Perdita had been born, H. D. had a series of intense psychic experiences. The visions of 1919 and 1920 undid any remaining traces of Imagist empiricism, affirmed a privileged role for the woman poet, and demonstrated H. D.'s clairvoyant powers. Applied to these experiences, the term *projection* registers not the poet's design on the reader or on the gods but rather the dynamics of clairvoyance. To this end H. D. extends the term by borrowing a metaphor from the art of cartography.

In the language of mapping, projection is the representation of a sphere on a flat surface. Like most figuration, projection simplifies, here reducing a curve to a plane. Two methods of charting the heavens clarify the distinction between general and cartographic projection. In the first sense, as Robert

Duncan in *The H. D. Book* observes, we make the night "a projected screen" by casting our mythologies into the heavens and rendering "the sky-dome above . . . the image of another configuration in the skull-dome below." Cartographers reverse this movement and project intersecting coordinate lines from the sky down to our earthly charts. This entry of another dimension into our familiar figuration is the equivalent in H. D.'s work of the process by which material from the celestial or astral planes manifests on the earthly plane. It is this that haunts and compels her.

H. D. experienced what she felt was an inrush of material from other dimensions at least four times in 1919–20, all after surviving her near-fatal childbirth and all in the steadying company of Bryher. The first, in late spring 1919, involved "the transcendental feeling of the two globes or the two transparent half-globes enclosing me"; the second was the apparition of an ideal figure on the voyage to Greece in 1920; the third and fourth in the hotel room at Corfu, were the projected pictures and a series of dance scenes conjured up for Bryher. Each of these seemed, as H. D. affirmed, "a godsend," an irradiation of the world of ordinary events and rules by an extraordinary grace.

The first of these experiences is described in *Notes on Thought and Vision*, a document composed for Havelock Ellis, whom H. D. and Bryher had been consulting and who subsequently accompanied them to Greece. Though rough and sometimes contradictory, these notes describe a matrix of creativity she calls the "jelly-fish" or "over-mind" state. The self is divided into body, mind, and over-mind. The artist-initiate begins, like the neophyte in the Eleusinian mysteries, with the body's desires and the brain's sensitivities, but the aim is to transcend these consciousnesses in the over-mind, the receptacle of mystical vision.

Like Ellis, H. D. begins her exposition with sexuality. All humans need physical relationships, she argues, but creative men and women crave them "to develop and draw forth their talents." The erotic personality, suffused with sympathetic, questing, and playful energies, is the artistic personality, par excellence, a hypothesis Ellis and H. D. both exemplify by evoking Leonardo da Vinci. Ellis, however, separates sexuality's primary reproductive function from a secondary spiritual function of "furthering the higher mental and emotional processes." H. D. counters this separation with a theory derived partly from the Eleusinian mysteries and partly from her own recent childbirth.

Complementing the "vision of the brain" is a force H. D. calls "vision of the womb." The term underscores the artist's receptive/procreative role. In the womb-brain, thoughts from another realm are received, nourished, brought to form, then projected out into the barrenness H. D. calls "the murky, dead, old, thousand-times explored old world." This model rewrites conventional phallic metaphors for creativity by depicting visionary consciousness as "a foetus in the body" which, after "grinding discomfort," is released in the miracle the mysteries celebrated as Kore's return. "Is it easier for a woman to attain this state of consciousness than for a man?" H. D. asks. Though both sexes possess this capacity, her formulation privileges her own particularly female experience of integration and regeneration.

Notes on Thought and Vision provide many explications of visionary consciousness, but the most pertinent to H. D.'s developing notion of projection are three ocular models. H. D.'s fascination with optics came from watching her father the astronomer and her grandfather the botanist gaze through lenses into a teeming world where before there had been only a blank. Each of her models postulates two kinds of vision, womb vision and brain vision, and each invents a way to adjust them so as to transform void to plenitude.

H. D.'s initial formulation describes the jellyfish state as enclosure in two caps of diving bells of consciousness, one over the forehead and one the the "love region." Each is a sort of amniotic sac, "like water, transparent, fluid yet with definite body, contained in a definite space . . . like a closed sea-plant, jelly-fish or anemone." This sack holds and nurtures the delicate, amorphous life of the over-mind, but it has a further function. Like a diver's mask or aquarium glass, the over-mind allows us to see the usually invisible inhabitants of the watery depths: here, H. D. explains, "thoughts pass and are visible like fish swimming under clear water."

The second formulation transforms these caps into dual lenses for a pair of psychic opera glasses. These, "properly adjusted, focused . . . bring the world of vision into consciousness. The two work separately, perceive separately, yet make one picture." What they see is the whole world of vision registered by the mystic, the philosopher, and the artist.

In the last and most evocative formulation, these lenses merge into a complexly constituted third eye. "The jelly-fish over my head," H. D. explains, "had become concentrated. . . . That is, all the spiritual energy seemed concentrated in the middle of my forehead, inside my skull, and it was small and giving out a very soft light, but not scattered light, light concentrated in itself as the light of a pearl would be." Like a crystal ball, this eye both receives and emits the force H. D. calls "over-world energy." It draws in, concentrates, then projects outward "pictures from the world of vision." This receptive/transmissive eye is the gift of vision, the pearl of great price.

The jellyfish eye opens the skull-dome. Into, out of, through this rupture pours all the prophetic soul-energy scientific materialism would deny and H. D.'s visions and visionary poetry affirm. Archetypal memories, dreams, the Corfu pictures all exemplify this projected vision, but a more excessive, startling instance is the sudden apparition of Peter Van Eck at the shiprail of the Borodino.

For more than twenty years, H. D. struggled to tell the story of Peter Van Eck, her code name for Peter Rodeck, architect, artist, spiritualist, and fellow passenger on the voyage to Greece. It formed the heart of a much rewritten novel entitled *Niké*, finally jettisoned in 1924. The most ample remaining accounts are in the pseudonymous short story "Mouse Island," published in 1932; in the analysis notebooks of 1933, published as part of *Tribute to Freud*; and in the unpublished autobiographical novel *The Majic Ring*, written in 1943–44.

It was sunset, neither day nor night, and the ocean was suffused with a soft violet-blue glow. The ship was approaching the Pillars of Hercules between the outer-waters of the Atlantic and the inner-sea of the Mediterranean. "We were crossing something," H. D. explains—a line, a boundary, perhaps a threshold. Alone at the rail of the Borodino, she stood "on the deck of a mythical ship as well, a ship that had no existence in the world of ordinary events and laws and rules." The sea was quiet, the boat moved smoothly, and the waves broke "in a thousand perfectly peaked wavelets like the waves in the background of a Botticelli." When she turned to search for Bryher, she saw a three-dimensional figure at the rail, a man who both was and was not Peter Van Eck. Taller, clearer, brighter than Van Eck, without his disfiguring scar and thick-rimmed glasses, this apparition summoned a band of leaping dolphins and disclosed, on the ship's seaward side, a chain of hilly islands. At the peak of the moment, H. D. reports, "his eyes, it seemed now, were my eyes. I was seeing his vision, what he (though I did not of course, realize it) was himself projecting. This was the promised land, the islands of the blest, the islands of Atlantis or of the Hesperides."

Was this a hallucination, a holographic illusion, an epiphany? If the latter, who was the being who directed or even impersonated Peter Van Eck? H. D. gives no consistent answer. *The Majic Ring* suggests it was "Anax Apollo, Helios, Lord of Magic and Prophecy and Music"; the letters to Silvia Dobson imply he was an astral double; the story "Mouse Island" compares him to Christ at Emmaus.

Whatever he was, all accounts agree he was a "projection" from another dimension into this one, a phenomenon for which "Mouse Island" gives the most extensive—and mechanical—explication. If each being is composed of two substances, "platinum sheet-metal over jellyfish" or body over soul, Van Eck's appearance was a "galvanized projection": soul-stuff shocked into form, transmitted through the third-eye opening in his skull, perceived through the opening in hers. "The inside could get out that way," the story tells us, "only when the top was broken. It was the transcendentalist inside that had met [Van Eck] in the storm on deck, when [Peter Van Eck] was downstairs in the smoking room."

The terminology is awkward, the physics creak, but the experience was real and haunted H. D. all her life. Van Eck's three-dimensionality was a kind of psychic *phanopoeia*—not all what Pound meant but very much H. D.'s technique in her later poetry. The visionary figures of *Trilogy*, the hordes of souls thronging *Helen in Egypt*, the angelic forces of *Hermetic Definition*, all are figures entering the imagination from another dimension and carrying with them the mysterious radiance by which H. D. gratefully remapped our "dead, old, thousand-times explored old world."

PROJECTION: THE DISPLAY OF MOTION
PICTURES BY CASTING AN IMAGE ON A SCREEN

When H. D. once again broached the Greek material in the 1940s, she reported that "the story, in its new form, began unwinding itself, like a roll of film that had been neatly stored in my brain, waiting for a propitious moment to be re-set in the projector and cast on a screen." This new twist to the term *projection* emerged from extensive experience. She had taken an exhilarating step into the technology of the cinema.

In spring 1929, when asked by *The Little Review* what she most liked to do, H. D. had no trouble answering. "I myself have learned to use the small projector," she replied, "and spend literally hundreds of hours alone in my apartment, making the mountains and village streets and my own acquaintances reel past me in the light and light and light." The projector belonged to POOL Productions, a company run by Bryher and Kenneth Macpherson, H. D.'s companions in film work in the late 1920s and early 1930s. H. D. wrote for their journal *Close Up*, acted in their films, did montage for one and publicity for two, and, finally, filled her contemporary poetry and fiction with images of light, focus, superimposition, and projection.

Most of H. D.'s film theory is in a series of essays composed for the first issues of *Close Up* and titled "The Cinema and the Classics." By "classics" H. D. meant, specifically, Greek culture and, more narrowly, the Greek amalgamation of the beautiful and the good. Despite Hollywood's fixation on "long drawn out embraces and the artificially enhanced thud-offs of galloping bronchoes" and despite "the gigantic Cyclops, the American Censor" who prettifies beauty and homogenizes goodness, cinema offers our best opportunity to recapture Greek wisdom. In the hands of the avant-garde, film repossesses the visionary consciousness of Athens, Delphi, and Eleusis. Here, at last, "miracles and godhead are *not* out of place, are not awkward"; it is "a perfect medium . . . at last granted us."

The word *medium* resonates through H. D.'s meditations. Film is an artistic medium, one occupying a medial position between the filmmaker's visual imagination and our own, but for H. D. it also functions as a psychic medium externalizing and making perceptible invisible inward intentions and coherencies. The announcement of the POOL film *Wing Beat*, starring H. D. and Kenneth Macpherson, promises "Telepathy and attraction, the reaching out, the very edge of dimensions in dimensions." Film reads and reveals the far reaches of our minds, and this connects it for H. D. with the Delphian dictate "Know Thyself." The mediumship, however, is more than telepathic. Cinema discloses the thoughts of the gods, their power, knowledge, and beauty. It may even, finally, disclose their very being, for here "Hermes, indicated in faint light, may step forward, outlined in semiobscurity, or simply dazzling the whole picture in a blaze of splendour. Helios may stand simply and restrained with uplifted arm."

Because film calls together in a dark room witnesses of charged hieratic images, images that make manifest what was mysterious, because it brings light to darkness and conveys the will of beauty and goodness, cinema is to us what the church was to H. D.'s ancestors and what the Delphic oracle was to the Greeks. The long two-part poem H. D. entitled "Projector" and published alongside her essays in *Close Up* names the Delphian Apollo as god of the cinema and envisions him reasserting his domain on a ray of image-bearing, world-creating light:

> This is his gift;
> light,
> light
> a wave
> that sweeps
> us
> from old fears
> and powers.

Just as Apollo claimed the power of prophecy at Delphi by slaying the monster Python, this projector-god destroys squalid commercialism and makes Hollywood into a "holy wood" where

souls upon the screen
live lives that might have been
live lives that ever are.

H. D.'s ecstatic poem greets Apollo as he begins his miracles. The poem's clipped, incantatory lines and detailed invocation of the Delphic paradigm, however, suggest something more than simple salutation. H. D.'s advocacy asserts a place and function for herself. Apollo at Delphi works through his oracle, the Pythoness, who is a medium between the god and the seeker. She has what *Notes on Thought and Vision* calls "womb vision," for it is she who receives, rings to form, and throws forth his knowledge. As the transmitter of the prophetic message, her position precedes and predicts H. D.'s. Who, then, is the poem's "Projector"? It is Apollo, light-bearer; it is his Delphic oracle; it is H. D. herself, the projector-poet; and perhaps it is also the machine in her apartment which, in a coincidence that doubtless delighted H. D., rested, like the Pythoness herself, upon a tripod—symbol of prophecy, prophetic utterance, occult or hidden knowledge.

PROJECTION: A DEFENSE MECHANISM IN WHICH THE INDIVIDUAL ATTRIBUTES AN IMPULSE OF HIS OWN TO SOME OTHER PERSON OR OBJECT IN THE OUTSIDE WORLD

Close Up did not push a particular doctrine. It contained accounts of German and Russian cinema, translations of Eisenstein, reviews of film exhibitions and avant-garde screenings, vituperations against Hollywood's censor, advice on the newest cameras and projectors, and assorted editorial pronouncements. As Anne Friedberg notes, however, one consistent strain in its pages is psychoanalytic theory. Many of the writers cite Freud; Dr. Hanns Sachs, Bryher's analyst and a member of Freud's inner circle, and lay analysts Barbara Low and Mary Chadwick contribute essays; and editor Kenneth Macpherson frequently elaborates his positions with psychoanalytic concepts. This interest illuminates Macpherson's own most ambitious project, the full-length film *Borderline*, in which H. D., disguised in the credits as Helga Doorn, plays a character caught between conscious and unconscious pressures. Her work on *Borderline* provides a glimpse into H. D.'s preoccupations some three years prior to her analysis with Freud.

Macpherson intended to take the film "into the labyrinth of the human mind, with its queer impulses and tricks, its unreliability, its stresses and obsessions, its half-formed deductions, its glibness, its occasional amnesia, its fantasy, suppression, and desires." The plot is a tangle of desire, murder, and bigotry. Astrid, the sensitive and worldly neurotic played by H. D., comes with her alcoholic husband Thorne to a small Swiss border town; in this limbo, she becomes obsessed with Pete, a giant, half-vagrant black man played by Paul Robeson, and is stabbed to death by Thorne in a crime for which the town persecutes Pete. The frayed atmosphere is exacerbated by the movie's silence, by the camera's raking of symbolic landscapes and faces gouged with light, and finally, by Astrid's staring into the camera—as if she were emptying her mind out onto the screen, or, even more uncomfortably, as if she were attempting a direct transfer of her psychic content into the mind of the viewer.

The unsigned, thirty-nine page publicity pamphlet, almost certainly written by H. D., reminds us that "Astrid, the woman, terribly incarnated, is 'astral' in effect." The earthly/astral border is only one more in a film deliberately situated on every possible margin: physical, social, racial, sexual, mental, even, since Macpherson and his company were displaced and uncredentialed, professional. The film's terrain is the limbo that H. D.'s projection-Imagist, clairvoyant, cinematic, or prophetic—always traversed.

If the stark, otherwordly sequences that punctuate *Borderline* have a hieroglyphic portentousness, it is because they in fact originated in picturewriting. As the pamphlet explains, Macpherson drew 910 pen-and-ink sketches giving detailed directions for each shot. Each was a light sculpture, a dream scene, a hieroglyph designed for projection, a "welding of the psychic or super-normal to the things of precise everyday existence." For H. D. this places *Borderline* in the same psychic category as the Corfu pictures and the charged dreams of her accounts of analysis: "For myself," she writes in *Tribute to Freud*, "I consider this sort of dream or projected picture or vision as a sort of halfway state between ordinary dream and the vision of those who, for lack of a more definite term, we must call psychics or clairvoyants."

"Borderline" is, of course, a psychoanalytic term designating the half-way state between neurosis and psychosis. H. D. would know the term from Bryher, who in the late 1920s was both studying and undergoing analysis, from lectures she and Bryher attended in Berlin during these years, from the general theoretic climate of *Close Up*, and finally, from the fact that Macpherson in titling his film doubtless had the technical term in mind. While playing on all its other nuances, however, the pamphlet shuns the psychoanalytic meaning and resituates the borderline so that it lies not between the neurotic and the psychotic but between the neurotic and the psychic. This gesture typifies H. D.'s complex attitude toward psychoanalysis.

"*Borderline* is a dream," the pamphlet pronounces, entering its summation, "and perhaps when we say that we have said everything. The film is the art of dream portrayal and perhaps when we say that we have achieved the definition, the synthesis toward which we have been striving." For H. D., dream was always interior projection, a cinematic exhibition of the mind's submerged content. Like *Borderline* and the Corfu pictures, dreams display "the *hieroglyph of the unconscious.*" It is for "open[ing] the field to the study of this vast, unexplored region" that H. D. would be forever grateful to Freud.

Accounts of dreams are, as it were, projections of projections, and H. D. was justly proud of her command of the intricate transmutation. It was not simple. "The dream-picture focussed and projected by the mind, may perhaps achieve something of the character of a magic-lantern slide and may `come true' in the projection," H. D. explains in *The Gift*, but to make it do so demands all the equipment developed by Freud: free association, command of the parallels between individual, biological, and racial development, and mastery of concepts like condensation, displacement, dramatization by visual imagery, superimposition, distortion, and screen memory. An admonitory passage from *The Gift* conveys H. D.'s delight in her descriptive skill:

> The dream, the memory, the unexpected related memories must be allowed to sway backward and forward, as if the sheet or screen upon which they are projected, blows and is rippled in the wind of whatever emotion or idea is entering a door, left open. The wind blows through the door, from outside, through long, long corridors of personal memory, of biological and of race-memory. Shut the door and you have a neat flat picture. Leave all the doors open and you are almost out-of-doors, almost within the un-walled province of the fourth-dimensional. This is creation in the truer sense, in *the wind bloweth where it listeth* way.

Her delight was matched—perhaps even sparked—by Freud's joy in the intense and haunting dreams of her two periods of analysis in 1933 and 1934. "[Freud] has embarrassed me," H. D. writes Bryher in April 1933, "by telling me I have a rare type of mind he seldom meets with, in which thought crystalizes out in dream in a very special way." In their sessions they pour over dream after enigmatic dream, Freud complimenting her on their "very 'beautiful' construction," their invention of symbols, their "almost perfect mythological state." The fact that so much of H. D.'s post-analysis writing places her before a luminous dream that she both creates and analyzes, participates in and watches, surely repeats the exhilarations of her contact with Freud.

In the analysis of her dreams, H. D. and Freud are colleagues who heed, adjust, and validate each other's interpretations, but much of the analysis material indicates another kind of relationship. Here H. D. is a small, confused seeker and Freud is the wise Hermit on the edge of the Forest of the Unknown, Asklepios the blameless healer, Herakles struggling with Death, Jeremiah discovering the well of living water, St. Michael who will slay the Dragon of her fears, even the infinitely old symbol weighing Psyche the soul in the Balance, even the Supreme Being. The formulations, as Freud taught us, call on another sort of projection: transference, or the process by which the patient directs toward the physician an intensity of feeling that is based on no real relation between them and can only be traced back to old fantasies rendered unconscious.

The first step in analysis, the establishment of transference, H. D. took easily, if somewhat ambiguously. To H. D., Freud became papa, the Professor, his study, like Professor Doolittle's, cluttered with erudite writings and "sacred objects"; to Freud, however, transference made him the gentle, intuitive mother. Both were right, for as Susan Friedman points out, "in an ultimate sense, he became both mother and father to her as he fused her mother's art and her father's science in the mysteries of psychoanalysis." Her transference love for Freud enabled H. D. to affirm herself as poet and visionary, release her blocked creativity, and write with passion and continuity throughout the rest of her life.

There was another, murkier transference in the analysis, however, one subject not to resolution but to repetition. This rendered every figure in her life a stand-in for someone else, every love a deflection, every trauma a replay of earlier disaster. The records of analysis swarm with formulae as Freud and H. D. decipher originary patterns beneath a palimpsest of repetition. Ellis as father, Freud as mother; Aldington as father, Bryher as mother; Rodeck as father, Bryher as mother; her "ideal" brothers Rodeck, Frances Gregg, and Bryher; her "real" brothers Pound, Aldington, and Macpherson—the list goes on and on. One fevered letter to Bryher in March 1933 indicates both the exuberance and the suspicion of futility beneath all this activity:

> My triangle is mother-brother-self. That is, early phallic-mother, baby brother or smaller brother and self. I have worked in and around that, I have HAD the baby with my mother, and been the phallic-baby, hence Moses in the bulrushes, I have HAD the baby with the brother, hence Cuthbert [Adlington], Cecil Grey, Kenneth etc. I have HAD the "illumination" or the back to the

womb WITH the brother, hence you and me in Corfu,
island=mother. . . . Well, well, well, I could go on and on and on,
demonstrating but once you get the first idea, all the other, later
diverse-looking manifestations fit in somehow. Savvy?????? It's
all too queer and at first, I felt life had been wasted in all this
repetition etc. but somehow F. seems to find it amusing,
sometimes.

Until the end of her life, H. D. deluged near strangers with intensities of
feeling belonging not to them but to their forerunners or even to the
forerunners of their forerunners. Here transference was a condition not of
cure but of compulsion.

Dreams and transference are projective in a general sense, but
psychoanalytic theory, of course, defines the term *projection* precisely: as a
defense mechanism that causes us to attribute an interior wish to a person or
object in the exterior world. This charged term formed an exemplary site for
the disagreement between Freud and H. D. about the nature of reality, and
here H. D. took Freud on, if not directly, nonetheless deftly.

The word *projection* occurs frequently in *Tribute to Freud*, but, like
"borderline" in the movie pamphlet, not once with its Freudian denotation.
The projected picture," images "projected" from the subconscious mind or
from outside, the strain of projection, the impact that "projected" a
dreamsequence: each use of the term points to the Corfu vision. Of all the
events that could have titled H. D.'s original account of analysis, her choice,
"Writing on the Wall," privileges and gives biblical sanction to the vision at
Corfu. The phrase draws our attention from the analytic to the mystical and
prepares our confrontation with the main question raised by the Corfu
pictures. Were they, as Freud maintained, a "dangerous 'symptom'," or were
they rather an upwelling of creativity, an inspiration, and a promise?

In Freud's use of the word, the "projected pictures" reduce to defensive
exteriorizations of unconscious material. In this sense they would be
desperate strategies of containment. By H. D.'s definition, however, the
projected pictures are precisely the opposite: they open the boundaries of the
self to another, higher reality, not in order to deny its operations but in order
to claim and be claimed by them. The pictures predict—or project into the
future—not a repetition of palimpsestic transferences but a transcendence, a
breakthrough into a new dimension. In her final image, the angel Niké
moving through a field of tents, H. D. recognizes the aftermath of the next
world war: "When that war had completed itself," she writes, "rung by rung
or year by year, I, personally (I felt), would be free, I myself would go on in
another, a winged dimension." This vision of 1920, recalled and reaffirmed

through analysis with Freud, predicts the transmutations wrought two decades later in the great poem H. D. would call her War Trilogy.

PROJECTION: THE CASTING OF SOME INGREDIENT INTO A CRUCIBLE; ESPECIALLY IN ALCHEMY, THE CASTING OF THE POWDER OF THE PHILOSOPHER'S STONE (POWDER OF PROJECTION) UPON A METAL IN FUSION TO EFFECT ITS TRANSMUTATION INTO GOLD OR SILVER

H. D.'s "Notes on Recent Writing," composed in 1949 for Norman Holmes Pearson, stresses the generation of *Trilogy* out of the ravages of World War Two. Throughout the Nazi air assault, H. D. had remained in London, close to the Hyde Park anti-aircraft batteries and in the thick of incendiary raids. Bombs—buzz bombs, fly bombs, oil bombs, doodle-bugs, and low, close V-1 rockets—in often nightly bombardments tore open apartments, leveled buildings, lodged unexploded shells in areaways and under pavements, and threw the survivors into unregistered dimensions of terror and powerlessness. "The fire has raged around the crystal," H. D. reported to Pearson. "The crystalline poetry to be projected, must of necessity, have that fire in it. You will find fire in *The Walls Do Not Fall*, *Tribute to the Angels* and *The Flowering of the Rod*. *Trilogy*, as we called the three volumes of poetry written during War II, seemed to project itself in time and out-of-time together. And with no effort."

After agonized blockage, H. D. was writing with assurance and speed, her typewriter clacking across the noise of the raids. In the last eight months of 1944 alone she composed three of her finest works: from May 17th to 31st, "Tribute to the Angels"; from September 19th to November 2nd, "Writing on the Wall"; from December 18th to 31st, "The Flowering of the Rod." The Freud memoir slid easily between the last two parts of *Trilogy*, for *Trilogy* performs, in its way, a kind of analysis. If, as Robert Duncan suggests, "in Freudian terms, the War is a manifestation of the latent content of the civilization and its discontents, a projection of the collective unconscious," *Trilogy* works to surface the terrors and redirect savage impulses to sublimer ends.

As in analysis, dream is the agent of transmutation. *Trilogy*, however, builds on a distinction made in "Writing on the Wall" between "trivial, confused dreams and . . . real dreams. The trivial dream bears the same relationship to the real as a column of gutter-press newsprint to a folio page of a play of Shakespeare." The enigmas of revelatory dreams emerge not from extravagantly repressed desire but from "the same source as the script

or Scripture, the Holy Writ or Word." Dream is the active force of the
sacred in human life. "Now it appears very clear," H. D. writes, "that the
Holy Ghost, / childhood's mysterious enigma, / is the Dream":

> it merges the distant future
> with most distant antiquity,
>
> states economically
> in a simple dream-equation
>
> the most profound philosophy,
> discloses the alchemist's secret
>
> and follows the Mage
> in the desert.

Each of the three parts of *Trilogy* generates a real dream, a vision of eternal
beings who reappear with the recovery of "the alchemist's secret," the
process through which destruction precedes and permits new, more perfect
life.

War executes a horrifying reverse alchemy. Rails are melted down and
made into guns, books are pulped for cartridge cases, the Word is absorbed
in the Sword, and people become "wolves, jackals, / mongrel curs." Casting
back to "most distant antiquity" in order to project "the distant future,"
H. D. turns to the early alchemists. Though our culture cartoons them as
greedy bunglers struggling to turn dung into gold, alchemists were scholars
of spiritual transformation. Alchemical formulas and philosophy structure
Trilogy and give the metaphor of *projection* its final precise and complex
elaboration.

Until modern chemistry's mechanical and quantitative postulates
replaced alchemy's organic, qualitative theory, four tenets seemed
self-evident. The universe, alchemists believed, was everywhere alive, all
matter possessing body, passion, and soul. Because substances appear, grow,
decay, diminish, and disappear, secondly, transmutation is considered the
essence of life. Third, all transmutation moves toward perfection: the seed
becomes a tree, the worm turns into a butterfly, grains of sand round into
pearls. In this process, the seed splits, the worm bursts, the sand vanishes,
thus demonstrating the fourth alchemical tenet: the belief that all creation
requires an initial act of destruction.

Projection is the final stage of an alchemical transmutation, the act that
precipitates new, more perfect form. All *Trilogy* moves toward the moment of

projection, but to understand this moment we must look briefly at the alchemists' explication of transformation. Like Aristotle, they believed that each substance consists of indeterminate prime matter and specific form impressed into it like a hot seal in wax. Changing a substance, therefore, was simply a matter of altering its "form." Ingredients were cast into a crucible, heated, and, in a process alchemists called "death" or "putrefaction," reduced to prime matter; then, after many intricate maneuvers—calcination, distillation, sublimation, fermentation, separation, and more—the specific form of a finer substance was projected into the crucible and new shape sprang forth. However audacious or even preposterous this procedure might now appear, to the alchemists it merely hastened a natural, universal process.

The magical act—or, as H. D. would remind us, the act of the Mage— was the making of the seed of perfection called the philosopher's stone or the elixir of life. Formulas were inherited, debated, obfuscated, adulterated, encoded, translated and mistranslated into and out of a dozen different languages, but the basic schema remained the same. To effect what was called "the alchemical marriage," sulphur, the male element, and mercury, the female element, were fused in the crucible and this union generated the philosopher's stone, "the Royal Child" which, like Christ, redeemed all life to its highest form. H. D.'s spiritual challenge in *Trilogy* is no less than the reawakening of this transmuting, projecting power: "the alchemist's key . . . / the elixir of life, the philosopher's stone" which "is yours if you surrender // sterile logic, trivial reason."

Nearly every image in Trilogy enacts a transmutation meant to convince us of the universality of the process and to draw our perception along a continuous line from the poem's smallest event to its largest. These images are holograms or discrete cells of the poem containing in code the plan of the whole. The archetypal alchemical transformation, for example, the changing of lead to gold, reappears in a casually inserted icon as "corn . . . enclosed in black-lead, / ploughed land." Washed by earth's waters, heated by sun's fire, and strewn with seed, black-lead land becomes gold corn. "This is no rune nor riddle," H. D. reiterates; "it is happening everywhere." In alchemical crucibles, under pressure, again and again, metamorphosis occurs: the mollusc shell holds a sand-grain, the egg-shell an egg; the heart-shell lodges a seed dropped by the phoenix; the cocoon houses a caterpillar, the shroud a worm preparing resurrection. Even the brain in its skull-case ferments and distills, dissolving sterile logic, generating new vision.

These images prepare our understanding of the poem's larger sweep. With properly cryptic encoding, the sections together retell the story of the making of the philosopher's stone. Each section contains a crucible, a purifying fire, and a double movement of destruction and creation; each moves us backward through time and inward across logic and custom, closer and closer to the culminating miracle of projection.

In "The Walls Do Not Fall," part one of the *Trilogy*, the crucible is the city of London, flattened by ceaseless pounding, filled with the shards of civilization, flaming with "Apocryphal fire." London's ruin makes it "the tomb, the temple," a matrix of death and rebirth in which Old Testament wrath and vengeance yield to a higher form of being. In a dream-vision, H. D. witnesses the reborn god whom she calles "Ra, Osiris, *Amen*":

> he is the world-father,
> father of past aeons,
>
> present and future equally;
> beardless, not at all like Jehovah.

This slender figure is the anointed son, the Christos, whose luminous amber eyes shine like transforming fire. With his entry into the poem, H. D. has half the alchemical formula, traditionally represented as the sun, fire, sulphur, the fathering principle.

In "Tribute to the Angels," part two of *Trilogy*, the crucible becomes the poem-bowl and the shards the word-fragments that survive as traces of the great traditions of female divinity. After proper invocations, with reverence for her materials and awe at the powers they hold, H. D. the poet-alchemist begins:

> Now polish the crucible
> and in the bowl distill
>
> a word most bitter, *marah*,
> a word bitterer still, *mar*,
>
> sea, brine, breaker, seducer,
> giver of life, giver of tears;
>
> Now polish the crucible
> and set the jet of flame
>
> under, till *marah-mar*
> are melted, fuse and join

and change and alter,
mer, mere, mère, mater, Maia, Mary,

Star of the Sea,
Mother.

This alchemical transaction creates a pulsing green-white, opalescent jewel which lives, breathes, and gives off "a vibration that we can not name." After distilling, purifying, and refining this force, after witnessing intermediate manifestations and meditating on "the moon-cycle . . . the moon-shell," H. D. has a dream-vision that closes this stage of her alchemy. It is an epiphany of the Lady, stripped of her myriad old forms—Isis, Astarte, Aset, Aphrodite, the old Eve, the Virgin Mary, "Our Lady of the Goldfinch, / Our Lady of the Candelabra"—and released into new, as yet unnamed power. She is without the bridegroom, without the child; she is not hieratic; she is "no symbolic figure." The book she carries "is not / the tome of the ancient wisdom" but "the unwritten volume of the new." This as yet uninscribed essence is the renewed stuff of the other half of the alchemical formula, traditionally represented as the moon, mercury, the mothering principle.

In "The Flowering of the Rod," part three of *Trilogy*, the crucible is not a place or a poem but the legend of resurrection: "a tale of a Fisherman, / a tale of a jar or jars," an ancient story which in its Christian form is "the same—different—the same attributes, / different yet the same as before." What the poet-alchemist must break down here is the familiar racist and misogynist reading of the scriptures that dismisses Kaspar as a dark heathen and Mary Magdalene as a devil-ridden harlot, making both peripheral to the real story. In H. D.'s rewriting, they are central. The first two parts of *Trilogy* had precipitated a new male and female principle; now, in part three, they meet in alchemical marriage to effect the miraculous transformation. Kaspar, who might be Abraham or an Angel or even God, is here a somewhat forgetful and fallible philosopher, dream-interpreter, astrologer, and alchemist from a long line of Arabs who knew "the secret of the sacred process of distillation." He carries with him a sealed jar of myrrh exuding a fragrance that is the eternal essence "of all flowering things together": the elixir of life, the seed of resurrection.

Kaspar was traveling to "a coronation and a funeral," like all alchemical transmutations "a double affair," when found by Mary Magdalene, avatar of H. D.'s "mer, mere, mère, mater, Maia, Mary, // Star of the Sea, / Mother." When he momentarily abandons his patriarchal stiffness and, assuming a posture of reverence, stoops to pick up Mary's scarf, he is granted a vision that reaches back to "the islands of the Blest" and "the lost centre-island,

Atlantis" and forward to "the whole scope and plan // of our and his civilization on this, / his and our earth." The spell he hears recovers the lost matriarchal genealogy, identifies Mary as heritor of *"Lilith born before Eve / and one born before Lilith, / and Eve"* (italics in original), and convinces Kaspar to yield her the precious myrrh. This act—in H. D.'s astonishing rewriting— seeds the resurrection. When Mary washes the feet of Christ, she anoints him with the elixir of life and insures that his crucifixion will be the first step in triumphant regeneration. Consecrated by Mary, Christ himself becomes the legendary philosopher's stone: the resurrection and the life.

Mary Magdalene's washing of the feet of Christ is the act of the alchemist: the projecting of the Mage's elixir onto substance prepared for transmutation. Behind the story of Kaspar and Mary is the old tale of sulphur and mercury; ahead of it is the work of the poet-alchemist who wanted to give us, through her combinations and recombinations of lost spells and legends, the power to transmute our own damaged civilization. The ultimate, audacious hope of *Trilogy* is that it might itself become an elixir of life, a resurrective power.

The mechanical philosophy that superseded alchemy posits a world of dead matter, matter without passion and without soul. This world of objects has often proved for its inhabitants a place of subjection, dejection, abjection, rejection—a place of energy twisted, repressed, or subverted. The nurturing universe H. D. glimpsed from the beginning of her career is profoundly different, a. world of immanence and immediacy that could be called a projective universe. As the glow of radium with its puzzle of energy resident in matter led Marie Curie through her discoveries, the image of projection served as a conceptual and aesthetic focus for H. D.'s developing inquiries. An instrument of verbal organization and a source of intellectual and spiritual energies, projection was an act, an intuition, and an integration. It opened into, achieved, and helped to maintain the coherence and direction of her lifelong redemptive quest.

BONNIE COSTELLO

The "'Feminine" Language of Marianne Moore

Several critics of Marianne Moore's poetry have remarked, directly or indirectly, on its "feminine" quality, although it is sometimes difficult to decide just what they mean by this. T. S. Eliot, for instance, concludes his 1923 essay on Moore with a statement he either seems to feel is self-explanatory or hasn't really examined: "And there is one final, and 'magnificent' compliment: Miss Moore's poetry is as 'feminine' as Christina Rossetti's, one never forgets that it is written by a woman; but with both one never thinks of this as anything but a positive virtue." What can he have in mind? Is it the "restraint" and "humility" that Randall Jarrell talks about in his essay on Moore, entitled "Her Shield"? Is it the ladylike quality, the "chastity" of taste (a term rarely applied to men) that R. P. Blackmur saw as both the virtue and defect of her work? Or perhaps Eliot was thinking of Moore's preoccupation with surfaces and objects of sense experience (especially trivial experience) which he and others have praised as her "genuineness" while they have distinguished genuineness from "greatness." Men write out of primitive or heroic occasions, women write out of everyday occasions. In his essay about Edna Saint Vincent Millay, "The Poet as Woman," John Crowe Ransom distinguishes Moore for having less "deficiency of masculinity," that is, (and he is explicit about this) "intellectual interest" than other women writers. Yet we feel a reserve of prejudice

From *Women and Language in Literature and Society.* © 1980 by Praeger Publishers.

influencing his view of her, even when his purpose is to applaud, as in "On Being Modern with Distinction." Woman's love, he says in the Millay essay, is a fixation to natural sense objects (woman can't transcend mundane experience). Woman's love is devoted (she has no self). Man has lapsed, since childhood, from natural feelings, and his mind thus grows apart from woman's (woman remains childish). Woman does not go to the office (she has the leisure to be idle and cultivate her tenderness). Woman is set in her "famous attitudes" (woman's mind is full of clichés and household truisms). These assumptions appear, under a gauze of affection, throughout criticism of Moore's poetry. Roy Harvey Pearce begins by praising Moore's modesty and ease, but his parenthetical criticisms make him sound a little insincere in wishing William Carlos Williams, Conrad Aiken, and E. E. Cummings had Moore's female virtue.

Surprisingly, in her staunchly feminist argument, Suzanne Juhasz agrees with the men, both in the way they read the poems and in how they evaluate them. Rather than reexamining the male standards she assumes them a priori. Rather than consider the possible complexity of Moore's predilections and the original strength of her verse, Juhasz accepts past interpretations and simply seeks to explain how Moore's social and historical situation might cause her to "retreat" into the "lesser" qualities of "spinsterly" writing for self-protection. Because she is looking for something else (confessional poetry), Juhasz completely misses the distinctiveness of, Moore's inventions. To Juhasz, insofar as Moore's stylistic devices are "feminine" they are defenses.

Moore's art does display much of the taste and manners, the "vanity" as well as the "nobler virtue" our society ascribes to women. She is a lover of ornamental surfaces; she is fascinated with fashion and wrote several articles on the subject; she is "gossipy" and chatty, passing on bits of hearsay and borrowed phrases; she is a collector of knickknacks, her poems are like overs tuffed cupboards, full of irrelevancies and distractions. Moore's life reflected the same tendencies and tastes. Her scrapbooks and library are full of literature on women's dress, interior design, jewelry, ornamental art. Her letters go on for paragraphs describing someone's living room, a new coat, a cat she is caring for. But somehow, when she is describing a friend's hat or a clay bird someone gave her, these particulars seem more important as *occasions* for imaginative response than for their conventional value.

Moore's critics have tended to identify her "feminine" qualities superficially, taking up her lexicon of virtues but applying their own definitions and prejudices to it. In context, I want to suggest, these qualities take on a special, powerful meaning, quite inverted in value. Moore purposely assumes the traditional "household" virtues and attributes in order to redefine them in the action of her poems. Moore's "feminine" virtues and manners do not glass-in or soften reality, do not trivialize experience or diminish the claims of the self, but on the contrary become in various ways the chief sources of energy in her work. Continually in her poetry and in her prose Moore shows a close relationship between moral and technical virtue. As Geoffrey Hartman has observed in a brief note on the poet, "her style does not embody a morality, it is one." The central morality of her style (and the chief source of its vitality) is a resistance to the complacencies of thought and language, to a tendency to accept given forms as descriptive of the world as it is. This is not a passive resistance, for it works in alliance with her mental voracity, continually readjusting the line and pushing against the limits of language. Moore's access to this central concern with the limits of language is through a conventional but redefined femininity. Or, conversely, the breaking up of our assumptions about certain types of virtue and manner is a natural instance of a larger concern for resisting complacencies of thought and language.

This is not, for Moore, an explicitly feminist issue. She nowhere indicates that she thinks of her poems or the values they advocate as particularly "feminine." In fact most of the animal figures that demonstrate these qualities are given male pronouns. But it seems only natural that Moore should select the attributes most readily applied to her as the focus of her efforts to rediscover language. Whether these qualities are a natural or inherited part of her femininity, however, one feels in reading her poems that a man could not have seen the potential in such qualities that Moore has seen and exploited.

One of Moore's favorite categories of virtue, observed throughout her poetry and criticism, is humility, with its analogues, restraint, and modesty. What a nineteenth-century reviewer said of the woman poet Felicia Hemans has been said in other ways (in the quotations above) of Moore: "she never forgets what is due feminine reserve." Indeed, Moore learned well the lesson of Bryn Mawr president Carey Thomas which she quotes in her essay on the "impassioned emancipator": she "behaved not with decorum but with marked decorum." This does not mean that Moore practiced humility without sincerity. Rather, she discovers in it a special value: "humility is a kind of armor." Critics usually take this to mean that by playing down the self, by making few overt claims to authority and power, we avoid subjecting ourselves to envy or attack. Moore's descriptiveness, her extensive use of quotation, her choice of peripheral subject matter, her circumlocution, are all pointed to as technical counterparts of her moral predilections. But what Moore, with Carey Thomas, understood is that strength and power are not necessarily stifled or even contained, but are on the contrary nurtured

through acts of self-protection. Aggressive, indecorous, intolerant behavior
wastes energy and creativity which can be better sustained and wielded with
a certain guardedness. She quotes Thomas's remark: "Bryn Mawr must not
be less guarded because it is good." Juhasz and others tend to see nothing but
the armor, neglecting what is achieved by its use. Moore compromises
nothing in her "self-protective" humility; she gains. Though the idea of
"feminine reserve" may conventionally imply an attitude appropriate to
inferiority, Moore does not even pretend to weakness. She shows humility to
be a reserve, in the sense of a reservoir of power. At the end of "In This Age
of Hard Trying," for instance, Moore shows how an apparent
"inconsequence of manner" is more effective and durable than aggressive
certitude. [All lines quoted from Marianne Moore's poetry are taken from
The Complete Poems of Marianne Moore (New York: Viking, 1967).]

IN THIS AGE OF HARD TRYING, NONCHALANCE IS GOOD AND

"really, it is not the
   business of the gods to bake clay pots." They did not
    do it in this instance. A few
      revolved upon the axes of their worth
as if excessive popularity might be a pot;

they did not venture the
   profession of humility. The polished wedge
    that might have split the firmament
      was dumb. At last it threw itself away
and falling down, conferred on some poor fool, a privilege.

"Taller by the length of
   a conversation of five hundred years than all
    the others," there was one whose tales
      of what could never have been actual—
were better than the haggish, uncompanionable drawl

of certitude; his by—
   play was more terrible in its effectiveness
    than the fiercest frontal attack.
      The staff, the bag, the feigned inconsequence
of manner, best bespeak that weapon, self-protectiveness.

Humility, a guarded manner, has the advantage of taking the listener
offguard. And Moore practices her point in a number of ways here. The

prosaic, conversational tone, the long, meandering, run-on lines and shifts of figurative level, give the impression of nonchalance. She is not, she seems to suggest, writing anything so grand as a poem. But the design is present, though unobtrusive, acting on our imaginations almost without alerting us. We hardly notice, though we subliminally hear, the careful rhymes, the subtly extended metaphor, the logic of the tale, so that the final lines have a special bold effect in their paradoxical clarity.

Moore's feminine humility, then, is designing: she wants to create and sustain an interest which overt self-assertion or pronounced form would snuff out. Moore's humility and restraint are not passive defenses but ways of gathering force, as a bow is pulled back in order to carry the arrow farther when it is finally released. Such motives and strategies are at work in many of her best poems, especially "The Plumet Basilisk," "The Frigate Pelican," "To a Snail," and "The Pangolin," poems about animals she admires for elusive strengths similar to those she displays in her writing. The end of humility is not self-protection for its own sake so much as "gusto," the spark released in the discovery of and enthusiasm for what is out of our control. In language, "humility is an indispensable teacher, enabling concentration to heighten gusto." Whereas humility associated with women usually implies something negative, a withdrawal, a deference, Moore shows its positive outcome. She is one woman for whom humility is not an end but a means of inspiration and expression.

Humility is not armor against the aggressions of the world on the self so much as against those of the self on the world, against the "disease, My Self," as she calls it. To impose the self and its accumulated structures on the world is to narrow the world and trap the self, a self-defeating gesture. "In Distrust of Merits" takes this theme up directly, but it is always present obliquely in Moore's verse. For her, humility "keeps the world large," preserves a place for something beyond the self that keeps us from complacency and satiation, consequently keeping us alive.

"His Shield" is the poem quoted most often in connection with Moore's idea of the armor of humility. She says it directly: "his shield was his humility." The poem warns against "greed and flattery," insisting that "freedom" is "the power of relinquishing what one would keep." Bravado does not please or improve anything, it simply attracts contenders, and wastes energy fighting them off. "Be dull, don't be envied or armed with a measuring rod." Don't attract envy by flaunting your achievement. This is a traditional code of femininity, but it usually implies that feminine achievement is incommensurate with envy or pride. Let us see how Moore understands her message.

The poem contrasts two kinds of armor, as several critics have pointed out. Moore finds that the spiny covering of the "edgehog miscalled hedgehog with all his edges out . . . won't do." Instead, "I'll wrap myself in salamander skin." The armor of "pig-fur" aggressing on the outside would scare things off. Its force is its inadequacy. But "asbestos" armor endures rather than extinguishes fire. It allows the outside world to enclose without annihilating the subject. Furthermore, it keeps the edges inside, keeps a fire alive internally rather than exhausting it in consuming ego. The ideal is "a lizard in the midst of flames, a firebrand that is life," who is, to use a phrase from Moore's critical essays, "galvanized against inertia." Where possession, and its verbal equivalent, singleminded assertion, imply stasis and complacency, survival and freedom require the constant readjustment of thought. At the level of the sentence, "humility" does not mean that one should be silent, but rather that language should continually be revised in the presence of what it cannot accommodate.

The utopia represented in the poem is an "unconquerable country of unpompous gusto." Power is not compromised, it is simply redistributed. Presbyter John, the hero of the poem, "styled himself but presbyter." Gusto is generated less out of self-aggrandizing conquest or consumption than out of awareness, out of a perpetually perceived difference between himself and the world, and the preservation of that difference and of desire. Resources are never used up in such a country.

Self-denial sounds like an odd basis for utopian experience, however. How can untapped wealth and power be considered as such? Moore manages to develop a sense of wealth without conquest through symbols of the potential effects of power. "Rubies large as tennis/balls conjoined in streams so/that the mountain seemed to bleed." The mountain only *seems* to bleed, but in doing so it marks a potential encounter. Emblematized strength is perpetual, exerted strength expires. Indeed, the emblem of external battle is only realized internally in the struggle for self-possession. The stream of blood, as the internalized warfare of humility, is only the blood stream, the "firebrand that is life."

If we think of the poet as presbyter, the vitality of Moore's lines comes from investing her thought in a presentation of the external world, hence so many poems in a descriptive mode which obliquely suggest a personal attitude. The oddity and apparent awkwardness of her lines comes from the sense of the inadequacy of the "measuring rod" to deal honestly with particulars. In language, "to relinquish what one would keep" is to continually resist available form. One way she does this is by having different forms displace each other to create a variegated surface. Images cut across each other to deny any rigid hierarchy. The "I" of the poem is swallowed up in description. Moral and discursive languages do not preside over the poem, but take their place in a range of languages: commercial, conversational, descriptive, metaphoric. While her lines expand and digress in pursuit of what is always posited as indefinable, they also create images of the self's internal activity, thereby steadying the flux of exploration. Thus, as Geoffrey Hartman has pointed out, "she achieves a dialogue of one, an ironic crossfire of statement that continually denies and reasserts the possibility of a selfless assertion of self . . . the armor she describes is the modesty whereby the self is made strong to resist itself, but also strong to assert its being against voracious dogmatism." The abnegation of self ultimately satisfies the self, for it widens the sphere of response, the self being continually discovered through response to the external world. It declares knowledge a matter of process rather than possession, and it ensures the continuance of that process. The aggressive self is identified in the conquest of one form over another, an impulse to narrow and exclude, which finally entraps the self in the form it has imposed. But the humble self flourishes in the multiplicity of form, identifying with none. It neither narrows its domain nor can be narrowed by the force of others, for it exists in resisting closure. Humility, restraint, paradoxically conduce to freedom.

The armor of humility appears as a recurrent theme and technique in the critical essays as well. "Humility, Concentration and Gusto" opens in the more than metaphorical context of war.

> In times like these we are tempted to disregard anything that has not a direct bearing on freedom; or should I say, an obvious bearing, for what is more persuasive than poetry, though as Robert Frost says, it works obliquely and delicately. Commander King-Hall, in his book *Total Victory*, is really saying that the pen is the sword when he says the object of war is to persuade the enemy to change his mind.

Such talk of persuasion would seem on the side of the porcupine's edgy, aggressive "battle dress." But what is persuasive, it turns out, what has bearing on freedom, is humility.

> We don't want war, but it does conduce to humility, as someone said in the foreword to an exhibition catalogue of his work, "With what shall the artist arm himself save with his humility?" Humility, indeed, is armor, for it realizes that it is impossible to be original in the sense of doing something that has never been thought of before. Originality is in any case a byproduct of

sincerity; that is to say, of feeling that is honest and accordingly rejects anything that might cloud the impression, such as unnecessary commas, modifying clauses, or delayed predicates.

One should not speak from ambition, then, but from honest feeling. The work, as one early critic of "female poetry" said, should "come from the heart, to be natural and true." Humility begins in this essay as a principle of simplicity and "quiet objectiveness," the reduction of self-assertion and the elevation of the external "impression." This is what Ransom "admired" in Millay, "a vein of poetry which is spontaneous, straightforward in diction, and excitingly womanlike; a distinguished objective record of a woman's mind." But humility becomes, as the essay goes on, a principle of difficulty standing for "the refusal to be false." When associated with "sincerity," the principle of humility and restraint becomes an agent of "gusto" by continually turning up a difference between the ways things are described and the way things are. "Gusto thrives on freedom," Moore explains, and freedom is preserved by failures of formal closure, by linguistic deviation. Daniel Berkeley Updike, Moore tells us, "has always seemed to me a phenomenon of eloquence because of the quiet objectiveness of his writing."

> And what he says of printing applies equally to poetry. It is true, is it not, that "style does not depend on decoration but on simplicity and proportion"? Nor can we dignify confusion by calling it baroque. Here, I may say, I am preaching to myself, since, when I am as complete as I like to be, I seem unable to get an effect plain enough.

But this is sophisticated humility on Moore's part. What is persuasive is her preaching to herself. Certainly we would not expect her to be less complete than she would like to be, so what might seem like ornament or excess in her verse is justified as honesty. Humility, which upholds an ideal of quiet objectiveness, of simplicity and proportion, also upholds sincerity, which will not force a perception into a dishonestly neat structure. What results from this ironic conflict is a lively play of impulses through a highly variegated, rebellious surface. Though she will not make public claims to "originality," her poems are certainly idiosyncratic and individual, and invite the interest of a public into the special world of a private enchantment.

Moore often speaks of her "natural reticence" in explaining the disobliging difficulty of some of her work. Conventionally, natural reticence belongs to woman's lesser capacity for logical assertion. As a supposedly intuitive rather than analytical creature, woman naturally has trouble being articulate: language is a system of codification and dissection. Moore herself says "feeling at its deepest tends to be inarticulate." But in her verse, once natural reticence gives way to speech it paradoxically causes an overflow of words.

The extreme digressiveness of surface in Moore's poetry has perplexed many critics. Juhasz sees it as deliberate evasiveness, her way "of not talking about what she is talking about and talking about what she is not talking about." Roy Harvey Pearce criticizes her "gossipy" quality and her "uncertainty as to direction." Though Pearce doesn't label these qualities "feminine" he implies as much, and Ransom is explicit. Woman's mind "has no direction or modulation except by its natural health." In other words, women live without purpose or focus beyond their immediate daily cares, to which they respond with inarticulate emotions. Their minds cannot sustain a logical argument or coherent structure because they have no powers of memory or projection, because they live in a continuous present.

Moore takes this digressive mode of thought and examines its special advantages. The mind that follows "its natural health" has a capacity for nuance which evades us where there is "too stern an intellectual emphasis." The "steam roller" mind crushes "all the particles down into close conformity." "As for butterflies, I can hardly conceive of one's attending upon you." The "aimless" mind, like "the magic flute" illogically weaves "what logic can't unweave." It is closer to the center of experience, alive to changes of an unconscious voice. It has a greater capacity for discovery, not blinded by its own hypotheses. It is more inclusive; it has more variety. Through her unwieldy, non-hierarchical structures, her elongated, loquacious sentences, Moore achieves a sense of "continuous present," a sense of the poem in process, the mind experiencing and discovering itself. Moore's prosody works to this same end, through inconspicuous syllabic measure, through dispersed rhyme and run-on lines. Ransom thinks women are always weak on form "because they are not strict enough and expert enough to manage forms, in their default of the discipline under which men are trained." Moore's form is indeed not uniform or abstractly applied; it depends upon movement and changes inflection, unleashing new impulses as they are called up.

Geoffrey Hartman has been unusually sensitive to the force of Moore's "gossipy" meanderings:

> one reads her poems less for their message (always suffused) than for the pleasure of seeing how style may become an act of the living—the infinitely inclusive and discriminating—mind.

This mind, or rather Miss Moore's, is "an enchanting thing," it takes us by its very irrelevancies. Here too everything is surface; she talks, so to say, from the top of her mind and represents herself as a gossip on the baroque scale. But secretly she is a magician, and distracts on purpose. While her message eludes us through under statement, the poem itself remains teasingly alive through the overstatement of its many tactics, till we accept the conventional rabbit, glorified by prestidigitation. Yet the magic of language becomes intensely moral on further acquaintance and her crazy-quilt of thoughts, quotations and sounds resolves into subtler units of meaning and rhythm. The free (but not formless) verse helps break up the automatic emphases of traditional syntax, and respects the more dynamic shifts of the inner, and not merely spoken voice.

Moore's elusive surfaces involve a moral prudence as well as an aesthetic one. She wants to dodge self-consciousness. What male critics have called a certain "fussiness" in Moore, she calls "unconscious fastidiousness" in which she finds "a great amount of poetry." What she seems to describe with the phrase is a kind of impulsive persistence in attempting to manage unmanageable material. Moore sees "unconscious fastidiousness" as an important part of the nurturing process, and imitates that process in her poems. Maternity is the subject of "The Paper Nautilus," and in comparing it to poetry she alters the conventional view of both. We conventionally think of maternal affection as a soft, graceful attitude, and similarly Moore's poetry has been prized, condescendingly, for its "relaxed ease." But the poem describes the process of nurture as a struggle beneath a surface of gentleness, a highly precarious restraint of power. Here unconscious fastidiousness means a high level of attentiveness without the imposition of rigid design which might impede natural development. The health of the eggs somehow depends upon maximum power and maximum restraint. The juxtaposition of "the ram's-horn cradled freight" and "a devilfish" and her eggs reinforces this tension. Later we are told of the shell's relative delicacy (like a wasp nest) and of its strength (like Ionic columns and the force of Parthenon sculpture). The tension described in holding back Hercules is clarified through a notion of a "fortress of love" but not relieved. We have metaphors of maximum impulse without the expiration of energy in action. The paper nautilus must "hide" her "freight" but not "crush" it. The same goes for poets. They too are "hindered to succeed."

> For authorities whose hopes
> are shaped by mercenaries?
> Writers entrapped by

> teatime fame and by
> commuters' comforts? Not for these
>   the paper nautilus
>   constructs her thin glass shell.

The poem starts by distinguishing two kinds of form, one which is complacent and commercial, generated by petty ambition, (and the association of mercenaries and commuters suggests a male domain) and another kind which will not "entrap" the writer or the audience. Appropriately, Moore will not "entrap" herself and her subject by restricting the tenor of this other kind. Rather, after an initial reference to writers, she shifts into a metaphor for metaphor itself: the shell in which our impression of the world can take shape without calcifying. But the shell is importantly the source and product of a maternal affection, a desire to nurture, in order finally to release the growing object. Her shell does not contain the eggs, or in terms of poetry, is not "the thing itself."

The feminine code of sacrifice says one must "relinquish what one would keep," and this is often applied to maternal relationships. But Moore changes this idea, in an artistic context, to a mode of freedom, not just a duty. Thus "the intensively watched eggs coming from/ the shell free it when they are freed." And the mother is free from her state of tension. Freedom, that is, requires differentiation.

We are curious when we sense something like ourselves yet different. Moore knows that observation is always in a way self-interested. Indeed, language is fundamentally of the self and not of the other, so self-expression is inevitable. Her mind follows likeness and finds difference, and again likeness, in the form of statements that are qualified, images which clash, rhymes that ate interrupted, deviating detail, almost any form of verbal differentiation. In the process she does not accomplish "objectification" (curiosity is not satisfied) but something more interesting: a composition which metes out likeness and difference, visual and aural as well as semantic. The composition has the rhetorical power both to make associations and to suggest its own limits, since these verbal differences are made to seem like the difference between the world and what we say about it. Moore's compositions are trails of associations which conduct the reader to their source. This identification occurs not only in our vicarious experience of her mental flux, but through her final, subtle self-portraiture. Moore begins by presenting an object apparently for its own sake, but in the process of describing it she borrows the object as a figure of her own activity. This self-portraiture is not the point of arrival of the poet's search for unity or for the thing itself, but a kind of parting embrace of words and things, a form of possession or appropriation that leaves the thing untouched while its ghost performs the function of analogy. Moore pursues the contours of objects for what she can discover of herself, but precisely because she learns about herself through observation of the external world, she can never declare her motive or speak of herself directly. "Imaginary possession" allows her to make associations without assumptions. She never gets to the point at which the idea subverts the observation.

The narcissists and sophisticates in the art world are the constant butt of Moore's satire, though they are "deaf to satire." In "Novices," for instance, she criticizes the "supertadpoles of expression" so attentive to their own egos

> so that they do not know "whether it is the buyer or the seller
> who gives the money"—
> an abstruse idea plain to none but the artist,
> the only seller who buys and holds on to the money.
> they write the sort of things that would in their judgment
> interest a lady;
> curious to know if we do not adore each letter of the alphabet
> that goes to make a word of it—.

These "Will Honeycombs" who "anatomize their work," whose art is highly rational and symmetrical, are "bored by the detailless perspective of the sea," too absorbed in flattering themselves with their intellectual conquests to recognize the irrational power of nature. Moore contrasts their style with "the spontaneous unforced passion of the Hebrew language," which derives its "tempestuous energy" from a complete surrender to the sublimity of nature. In their example Moore shows that the self grows larger by imaginatively embracing something beyond its rational control.

But Moore is not simply advocating unconscious spontaneity or self-annihilation. Moore's is a highly conscious art, its objects derived primarily from books, not wild nature. It is the activity of tracing an "other," of knowing it in relation to oneself, as similar and different, that interests her, and she has called the "imaginary possession." With imaginary possession the mind is free to make associations, but at the same time knows them as such and does not identify them as exclusive truths. The task of "When I Buy Pictures," for instance, is to give both the illusion of a figure in the world who does not affect it, and to make a gesture of possession, to bring what is seen under the control of language.

WHEN I BUY PICTURES

or what is closer to the truth

when I look at that of which I may regard myself as the
                                        imaginary possessor,
I fix upon what would give me pleasure in my average moments:
the satire upon curiosity in which no more is discernible
than the intensity of the mood;
or quite the opposite—the old thing, the medieval decorated hat-
        box,
in which there are hounds with waists diminishing like the waist
                                        of the hourglass,
and deer and birds and seated people;

The game of imaginary possession involves discretion and humility, not prohibition:

Too stern an intellectual emphasis upon this quality or that
                                detracts from one's enjoyment.
It must not wish to disarm anything; nor may the approved
                                triumph easily be honored—
that which is great because something else is small.

Of course these are not "average moments"; they are moments of luminosity, selected for their suggestiveness. The difference is that between selection which reveals a will and transformation which emblematizes a will. Moore does not simply direct her imagery toward a final or overarching intention. Her mind is attentive to the properties of each object and each word as it occurs. Age suggests images of age: hatboxes which bear images of old-fashioned hounds that are shaped like hourglasses whose waists remind her of time's waste and as these waists diminish the imagery narrows its reference to the matter of fact: deer, birds, and seated people. The coherence of a part takes her to the next, without rejecting the influence of the immediate details. But while avoiding "too stern an intellectual emphasis" a surprisingly complex range of associations, built upon the problems of time, distance and complexity, emerges in the movement from one image to the next, at no cost to the surface randomness of local association:

It may be no more than a square of parquetry; the literal
                                biography perhaps,
in letters standing well apart upon a parchment-like expanse;
an artichoke in six varieties of blue; the snipe-legged hieroglyphic
                                in three parts;
the silver fence protecting Adam's grave, or Michael taking
                                Adam by the wrist.

Parquetry, artichoke, biography, hieroglyphic are all patterns of one kind or another. The range is inclusive and humorous. These orders are mocked; but shown to be natural. "Literal biography" is a contradiction reduced to its formal elements, letters standing well apart. We are directed through meaningless "orders" to consider our desire for possession, and the poem moves to emblems of our fall. These unite the previously separate and random problems of time, distance, and complexity raised in the imagery. Poems suppose a hierarchy of elements, but the rhetoric of the list resists our locating ourselves anywhere in particular in the poem. Moore quite consciously tempts our desire for architectonic, mythic structures, our need to privilege the "heroic" moment. She wants these associations while she restrains them from blocking their natural contexts. One does not forfeit the self, then, one does not resign all "views"; one simply explores them discreetly.

Of course the poem itself is a picture for sale. The satire on curiosity is a picture of ourselves since it is, finally, the intensity of the mood which is at issue. Its "opposite," the picture of receding things, draws the curious figure on until it becomes a mirror ("when I look at that of which I may regard myself"). The self does get expressed, through its own enchantment with something else, and this, I think, is what Virginia Woolf means in *A Room of One's Own* when she speaks of a woman's ability to get close to the fountain of creative energy.

While Moore's poetry is in a way "impersonal," in that the self is not the focus or dominant presence, we feel the movement of a distinct personality throughout. Indeed, Moore's very resistance to formal closure becomes for her a means of self-revelation. The "minor defects" of form, as she called unassimilated elements, are marks of style. And it is in style that we know this poet, not in subject or assertion. Though she never advocates "originality," the ambition to supersede the forms others have created, she is a great defender of "idiosyncrasy," an inevitable expression of "honest vision," Idiosyncrasy is connected with sincerity, a kind of non-competitive, oblique presentation of self; it does not require a personal subject or a show of power; it challenges no one.

Emily Watts, in *The Poetry of American Women*, identifies Moore's verse with a tradition of "feminine realism." What she and other critics are pointing to in the use of this term is the combination of "mundane realities," "simple human and natural situations," and "natural sense objects," with ethical generalizations or "household morality." The feminine mind neatly integrates nature and morality. Randall Jarrell, for one, strongly objects to Moore's poetry on the basis of this integration. In clear sexual categories he challenges what he sees as Moore's domestic falsifications, upholding instead the male vision of amoral nature and its corresponding cosmic ambition.

But Moore has transformed the structure of feminine realism (which links observation lo ethical generalization) in a number of ways. While she does detail nature, she celebrates her subjects for their recalcitrance. And the morality that accompanies these pictures is one of resisting the mind's impulse to circumscribe experience. In "Sea Unicorns and Land Unicorns," (about the Unicorn Tapestries) Moore points out that the unicorn remains "a puzzle to the hunters." Only the virgin knows him:

> Thus this strange animal with its miraculous elusiveness,
> has come to be unique,
> "impossible to take alive,"
> tamed only by a lady inoffensive like itself—
> as curiously wild and gentle;

All the poems follow a dictum of resistance even while they move through an apparent structure of observation—moral, for they continually propose definitions only to unravel them. "Integration, too tough for infraction," integration of the mind and the external world, of ethos and nature, is the goal of Moore's poetry, not its claim. And it is based on "efforts of affection" and not on aggression. It is achieved through process, through an open-ended dialectic of observing and making observations, in a continuous present.

While Moore follows the tendency in "feminine realism" to keep an eye on the external object, she is distinctly modern in her awareness of the limits of language to present that object. Moore's "descriptions" break up the conventions of composition, not to protect the self but to bring language into a more adequate relationship to experience, to discover a new realism which resists the habits of mind and eye. But what such resistance to referential conventions does, finally, is bring us into a closer awareness of the surface of language. By blocking the easy transfer from word to picture of meaning, by continually shifting the flow of counters and intruding on conventions which we too readily naturalize, Moore reminds us that we are not actually seeing, but only reading. This technique is especially effective in her poem "An Octopus," a long description of a glacier that concludes with a moral of "relentless accuracy." The extreme difficulty of accurately perceiving the object creates a corresponding difficulty in the words. Often the lengthy and cumbersome sentences lose their syntactic hold on us. We forget the subject or antecedent in the tow of subordinate clauses. Colons and semicolons are suspended between groups without an easy sense of their relation. Appositions become subjects with their own appositions in turn.

Participial phrases go on for several lines until we cease even to anticipate their subjects. Where conventional "realism" trusts the parts of speech to represent reality, Moore's language continually demonstrates their failure. In its attempt to circumscribe the viscous presence, the language of "An Octopus," for instance, doubles back on itself with lines that refer outwardly to the objective experience, and inwardly to the experience of reading. "Completing the circle, you have been deceived into thinking that you have progressed." "Neatness of finish! Neatness of finish! Relentless accuracy is the nature of this octopus / with its capacity for fact." Such self-reflective imagery admits that ultimately the "morals" we derive are not natural but represent our efforts to come to terms with nature. In that sense all of Moore's ethical generalizations have to do with her poetic activity.

"Neatness of finish" and "relentless accuracy" sound, in isolation, like mundane lessons. But in the context of this poem they present an enormous challenge to the eye and mind. And Moore proves the point she is making, for instead of rounding off the description with this abstract conclusion, she returns to the particular. She adopts, in the end, a policy of accuracy more relentless than before:

> Is "tree" the word for these things
> "flat on the ground like vines"?
> some "bent in half circle with branches on one side
> suggesting dust-brushes, not trees;
> some finding strength in union, forming little stunted groves
> their flattened mats of branches shrunk in trying to escape"
> from the hard mountain "planed by ice and polished by the
>   wind"—
> the white volcano with no weather side;
> the lightning flashing at its base,
> rain falling in the valleys, and snow falling on the peak—
> the glassy octopus symmetrically pointed,
> its claw cut by the avalanche
> "with a sound like the crack of a rifle
> in a curtain of powdered snow launched like a waterfall."

The breathlessness of the passage pulls us away from the organizing frame of grammar and syntax and hurls us into the midst of detail. Ethical generalization is returned to the level of perception. And yet even in the midst of detail, the mind makes associations. In this case the associations simply remind us of the controlling presence of language. At the end of the mountain is a curtain of snow; at the end of the poem—is a curtain of snow, the page. Her humility denies both the claims of an achieved realist and those of an achieved moralist; but her struggle for integration is vital and rewarding.

Moore transforms and toughens our understanding of familiar virtues when she uses them as stylistic devices. Humility, affection, reverse, are not passive but dynamic and vital modes of response. They do not protect but rather sustain the self in experience. In her redefinition and revaluation of what have been seen as "feminine" modes of identity, Moore displays a larger, encompassing concern to avoid all complacencies of mind. No container will hold her gusto.

> You have been compelled by hags to spin
>   gold thread from straw and have heard men say:
> "There is a feminine temperament in direct contrast to ours
>
> which makes her do these things. Circumscribed by a
>   heritage of blindness and native
>   incompetence, she will become wise and will be forced to
>   give in.
> Compelled by experience, she will turn back;
>
> water seeks its own level":
>   and you have smiled. "Water in motion is far
>   from level." You have seen it, when obstacles happen to bar
> the path, rise automatically.

In describing Ireland, Moore has obliquely celebrated the resilient power of the "feminine temperament." Ireland survives and deepens its identity by a combination of persistence and responsiveness. By rising to meet the shapes experience presents rather than either retreating or imposing artificial forms, Moore sustains a vital, creative contact between her self and her surroundings.

DAVID BROMWICH

Emphatic Reticence
in Marianne Moore's Poems

A fault of every good criticism of Moore I have ever read is the assumption of a generalized familiarity with the poetry, an atmosphere-of-Mooreishness, which allows the quotations to be copious and admiring and yet seldom anchored in a parent poem. And perhaps we know the poetry well enough; but do we know the poems? Many readers will want to reply: "Oh certainly, I know what they're *like*; whimsical, helter-skelter; odds and ends, all in sharp focus; alive with incidental humor—every word an incident." Because I was tired of giving this answer myself, I made a list of poems. The following groups are neither exhaustive nor mutually exclusive; but they do make room for a different sort of answer.

>   *Riddles, anecdotes, squibs*: "To Statecraft Embalmed," "To Military Progress," "To a Steam Roller," "Silence"; with innumerable unrhymed epigrams, and divagations of a too-charitable satirist.
>   *Prayers; calls to fortitude*: "What Are Years?" "In Distrust of Merits," "By Disposition of Angels," and the bulk of the later poems (epitomised by "Blessed Is the Man," with its echoes of Eisenhower and Omar Khayyam).
>   *Trials of Ingenuity*: "The Plumet Basilisk," "The Fish,"

From *Poetry* 139, no. 6 (March 1982). © 1982 by the Modern Poetry Association.

"Peter," "England," "When I Buy Pictures," "The Labors of Hercules," "Snakes, Mongooses, Snake-Charmers, and the Like," "An Octopus," "Sojourn in the Whale," "The Student," "Spenser's Ireland," "Four Quartz Crystal Clocks," "Elephants," "His Shield."

Far-fetchers: "The Steeple-Jack," "The Hero," "The Jerboa," "The Frigate Pelican," "In the Days of Prismatic Color," "A Grave," "New York," "Marriage," "Virginia Britannia," "The Pangolin"; and, blameless outcast from the 1951 Collected Poems, "Melanchthon."

The most searching of her inventions belong to the last two groups. Wit, as *ingenium*, or the reasoning intelligence—as finder of hidden analogies, or master of the sociable challenge and repartee—here delights in testing its object for all uncharted incongruities, and a map showing every turn would be no help. Who, coming to the end of "Four Quartz Crystal Clocks," will say where we forget the smart touch of the colloquist, and find that we have learned something about science and the morality of play?

> The lemur-student can see
>   that an aye-aye is not
>
> an angwan-tibo, potto, or loris, The sea-
>   side burden should not embarrass
> the bell-boy with the buoy-ball
>   endeavoring to pass
> hotel patronesses; nor could a
>   practiced ear confuse the glass
>   eyes for taxidermists
>
> with eye-glasses from the optometrist. And as
>   MEridian-7 one-two
> one-two gives, each fifteenth second
>   in the same voice, the new
> data—"The time will be" so and so—
>   you realise that "when you
>   hear the signal," you'll be
>
> hearing Jupiter or jour pater, the day god—
>   the salvaged son of Father Time—
> telling the cannibal Chronos

(eater of his proxime
newborn progeny) that punctuality
is not a crime.

After such beautiful display one may still prefer the extravagant persuasion of the far-fetchers; and to justify the preference there is a decisive aphorism in "Armor's Undermining Modesty": "What is more precise than precision? Illusion." That poem more than any other was Moore's apology for her work, and to her its credo had an obvious application.

She was most satisfied, and hoped we would be, with poems that argued the necessity of some single illusion—poems in which, after enough scruples to disarm the skeptic, she could welcome the believing mind for its strengths, especially strength of sight. Any illusion that assisted life to its ends was perhaps another name for single-mindedness. In "The Steeple-Jack" this quality is what favors the not-native observer of a native place: the citizen for whom the author cares most is the one who may set "part of a novel" in the town she describes. Since Moore dropped the full title, "Part of a Novel, Part of a Poem, Part of a Play"—which covered two further poems in sequence, "The Student" and "The Hero"—"The Steeple-Jack" may now seem a more complacent piece of naturalism than it really is. But her decision was correct for other reasons. The three did not answer each other deeply enough, and "The Hero" had more in common with "The Jerboa" than with its companions. Like "The Jerboa," it bears witness to a personal ideal of ascetic heroism, some of whose elements Moore named in an essay on "Humility, Concentration, and Gusto." As the "Too Much" section of "The Jerboa" concludes with the desert and its real animals, unenvyingly remote from civilization and its toy ones—"one would not be he/ who has nothing but plenty"—so "The Hero" moves from the tourist laden with his collected wits to the different figure, rich without plenty, who can follow a personal liking:

He's not out
seeing a sight but the rock
crystal thing to see—the startling El Greco
brimming with inner light—
that covets nothing that it has let go.

These poems make as right a pair as "The Frigate Pelican" and "The Pangolin," in which an animal at once upsets and submits to be measured by the human scale of custom and value; or "New York" and "Virginia Britannia," one poem each for the North and South, in which the dream of paradise is close-woven with the dream of plunder. But the foregoing are all well-known or at least much-recognized poems, and this late in the history of Moore's reputation I would rather concentrate on three that seem to me too little read: "A Grave," "Marriage," and "In the Days of Prismatic Color."

"A Grave" is propositional in structure, categorical in mood, shorn of even such heterodox exuberances as Moore sometimes allows to flourish within the parallel rows of a catalogue. It is a poem about death, as dry as life can make it.

> Man looking into the sea,
> taking the view from those who have as much right to it as
> > you have to it yourself,
> it is human nature to stand in the middle of a thing,
> but you cannot stand in the middle of this;
> the sea has nothing to give but a well excavated grave.
> The firs stand in a procession, each with an emerald turkey-
> > foot at the top,
> reserved as their contours, saying nothing;
> repression, however, is not the most obvious characteristic of
> > the sea;
> the sea is a collector, quick to return a rapacious look.
> There are others besides you who have worn that look—
> whose expression is no longer a protest; the fish no longer
> > investigate them
> for their bones have not lasted:
> men lower nets, unconscious of the fact that they are
> > desecrating a grave,
> and row quickly away—the blades of the oars
> moving together like the feet of water-spiders as if there were
> > no such thing as death.
> The wrinkles progress among themselves in a phalanx—
> > beautiful under networks of foam,
> and fade breathlessly while the sea rustles in and out of the
> > seaweed:
> the birds swim through the air at top speed, emitting cat-calls
> > as heretofore—
> the tortoise-shell scourges about the feet of the cliffs, in motion
> > beneath them;
> and the ocean, under the pulsation of lighthouses and noise of
> > bell-buoys,
> advances as usual, looking as if it were not that ocean in which
> > dropped things are bound to sink—
> in which if they turn or twist, it is neither with volition nor
> > consciousness.

One sees the poem just as one hears it—a respectful monochrome, unflattering to man, of something larger than man: but how does it get this consistency of effect? One notes first the use of words at several removes from any lively particular, words like "unconscious," "volition," "characteristic," "contours," "repression," along with the careless drab music of the vernacular, "at top speed," "no such thing," "as much right to it," "the fact that," "as usual." T. S. Eliot would have had in mind words and phrases like these, when he praised Moore for having heard, in "the curious jargon produced in America by universal university education," one of the possible languages of men in a state of vivid sensation. And yet there seems, at a glance, hardly one vivid feature in this poem; it seems almost wrong to call it a poem. Only on the return visit that it somehow compels, and a step or so back from its subject, do certain details emerge from the flat continuous statement; and then it takes on quite suddenly the answering bluntness and unanswerable severity of an Aeschylean chorus: nothing could be more direct, more like words mean to surprise and unenchant, than "it is human nature to stand in the middle of a thing, / but you cannot stand in the middle of this"; and, "the sea is a collector, quick to return a rapacious look. / There are others besides you who have worn that look"; down to the theorem-like and almost affectless "dropped things are bound to sink." It would be hard to imagine any poem that sustained a more uncanny gravity. Under its law we naturally reserve for ourselves the few stage-properties of the sea, to make an interval of elation and release before the end: the sound of the bell-buoys and sight of the lighthouse, the "phalanx" of wrinkles beneath the foam, and birds swimming in the air, "emitting cat-calls as heretofore," with the ghostly tortoise-shell (no tortoise) moving among the cliffs below. Yet, much as these things may please us, the poem absorbs them without pleasure; and the detail we remember most irresistibly, a metaphor powerful enough to survive paraphrase, is also the most disquieting of all: the men, ignorant of death and of the figure they cut beside it, rowing quickly away from the thing they do not know is a grave, their oars "moving together like the feet of water-spiders as if there were no such thing as death." It is a long line without pause in which surely no reader has ever skipped one word. The entire poem must have been a favorite of Elizabeth Bishop's: some of it is still going in the background of "At the Fishhouses"; a smaller borrowing, but as gifted with appreciation and command as Bishop's use of a familiar Moore-genre in "The Man-Moth."

By an impartial observer, "Marriage" might be described as a duel of quotations. But we are none of us impartial; so let it be a male critic who says, In this poem man holds the chains and one woman, the words; yet she is cunning as a whisper and makes it seem, almost to the end, a remarkably equal match. The contestants are Adam and Eve, or the virtues of Adam and Eve. And Moore's Adam is the same as Milton's, though she does not tell us so; he whose first recorded words, to the first of women, are "Sole partner and sole part of all these joys," dull, sententious, and good, the temple of a selfless mastery. Who else could be let down so gently but so finally by Moore's reference to "the ease of the philosopher/ unfathered by a woman"? Many unkindnesses as well as (one feels) many liberties and general vexings, were required to move her to this. But steel against satire, Adam—the old and ever-renewed, in marriage—will be heard out; while Eve calmly wonders at

> the spiked hand
> that has an affection for one
> and proves it to the bone,
> impatient to assure you
> that impatience is a mark of independence
> not of bondage.

For, marrying, she has joined that locus

> 'of circular traditions and impostures,
> committing many spoils,'
> requiring all one's criminal ingenuity
> to avoid

—and, crushed by his single stroke of wit, his "Why not be alone together," she now dwells in those circles, a listener. The poet comes confusingly near a gesture of sentimental homage, when she speaks of

> This institution,
> perhaps one should say enterprise
> out of respect for which
> one says one need not change one's mind
> about a thing one has believed in,

but she recoils by the end, and transposes even this tentative melody into a more dubious key, with a minefield of sharps and flats:

> What can one do for them—
> these savages
> condemned to disaffect

all those who are not visionaries
alert to the silly task
of making people noble?

But this is not quite the end; we see the wife a last time, still listening to her husband, whose eloquence now has something of "the statesmanship / of an archaic Daniel Webster," proclaiming "Liberty and Union / now and forever"; yet another man, husband, orator, in a poem that has featured everyone from Adam to Edmund Burke. There is more bitterness than affection in this wind-up; it is an unexpected tone, for which we are glad: suitable, after all, to a poet whose refusal to be assured about her impatience was the making of her. Besides, in the masterly orchestration of the thing, a great many other voices have been heard—Bacon, Shakespeare, Pound, Richard Baxter, Charles Reade, and at last a voice close to Moore's own, which turns out to be La Fontaine:

Everything to do with love is mystery;
it is more than a day's work
to investigate this science.

There is in this more wonder than bitterness; and the quotations generally help Moore to keep her balance.

Psychology which explains everything
explains nothing
and we are still in doubt.

For every Adam there must be an Eve, who listens and smiles, and does not show her smile. The hurtful acuteness of some passages comes, notwithstanding the disclaimer, from the habitual care of a good and disturbing psychologist; and any writer who can describe Satan's investment in the serpent as "that invaluable accident / exonerating Adam," is none the worse for having a *parti pris*.

To square the account, she included in her *Selected Poems*, and reprinted ever after, a poem about Adam before Eve.

when there was no smoke and color was
fine, not with the refinement of early civilization art, but because
of its originality.

The poem, "In the Days of Prismatic Color," is alert to the snares of its myth; it knows that this sort of aboriginal earliness can never exist as its own contemporary; it is not born but comes to be original, when later eyes have seen it so. History alone, with memory, can make those days, and Moore writes out the history that her poem seems to deny, by adopting an idiom she has employed at other times—refined, self-conscious, derivative, *and fine*— and pressing it beyond any known reach of the abstract. We arrive at originality by this curious route; so that she can say, of Adam's solitude and perfect vision,

> obliqueness was a variation
> of the perpendicular, plain to see and
> to account for: it is no
> longer that; nor did the blue-red-yellow band
> of incandescence that was color keep its stripe.

That is science not poetry, we may say, too stupid to read our myths deviously; but the image stops us short: it is the first poetic rainbow in half a century that one can admire without embarrassment. This poem is no friend of complexity, which it admits may not be "a crime, but carry / it to the point of murkiness / and nothing is plain"; nor of sophistication, which it suspects of being "Principally throat," and "at the antipodes from the init / ial great truths." Yet it is wonderfully aware throughout that our originals though great can never be simple, except in their power to survive. We reduce them only from our need for something uncompounded to serve as the givens of thought and reliables of metaphor. But when they first appeared, before they could be remembered, there was always the stumbling, the obliqueness of the rude assault:

> "Part of it was crawling, part of it
> was about to crawl, the rest
>   was torpid in its lair." In the short-legged, fit-
> ful advance, the gurgling and all the minutiae—we have the
>   classic
> multitude of feet. To what purpose! Truth is no Apollo
>   Belvedere, no formal thing. The wave may go over it if
> it likes.
> Know that it will be there when it says,
>   "I shall be there when the wave has gone by."

In those lines originality becomes one with the self-confidence of genius anywhere. Seeing the naturalness of the transition, from "the gurgling and all the minutiae" to "the classic / multitude of feet," we are educated in how originals make their way, and incidentally shown a distinction Moore keeps in view all the time, between the precisionist's dreaming with one eye open and the formalist's interrogation with both eyes closed.

So far I have said nothing about Moore's verse forms—and after all, too much has been said by others. To most readers they probably still convey, for a little while, the sense of an absorbing peculiarity, like a friend's matinal fondness for mango juice. But one soon accepts them like any other convention, and once accepted they join the form of life with which the author has linked them permanently in our minds. Beyond that, what does anyone care about their appropriateness? They are uniquely suited, or unsuited, to the person who chose them, just as all poetry is; one can learn nothing more essential about Moore from her syllabic lay-outs than one can about Collins from the English-cucumber-shapee of an irregular ode: the important thing about both is that they are products of a given age and climate, streaked by the weather that followed, but undesirable or obsolete only in the dimmest of short runs. Moore herself, in "The Past Is The Present," says this best: "Ecstasy affords / the occasion and expediency determines the form." Yet an audience for whom modernism was never new may pass by her innovations unnoticing and therefore unalarmed; what they will want to have explained is her didactic freedom with aphorisms; for it is this that makes her remote not only from modernist practice but from all that has succeeded it. The causes of her uniqueness are rooted in what can sometimes feel like the land poetry forgot. I mean the Eighteenth Century— one of Moore's cherished haunts, and *not* her idea of the second fall of man, as it was to Pound and Eliot—when critics rashly spoke of "casting one's eye over mankind." Poems could then be praised for their sentiment. By this was generally meant the perfect utterance of a common feeling which no one could know was common until the poet made it so. Apart from poetry governed by the most relentless logical structure, sentiments might easily serve the purpose of classical *sententiae*: they were simply the best means by which the performer-with-words could recommend himself to the trust of his listeners. Moore's poems abound in wise feelings, which she often appears to set in place with an air of having left room for something of that sort, in case it should ask for admission. The reader who wonders at her daring must remember that among the writers she most admired were Pope, Johnson, Blake—and Shaw, a latecomer not at all strange to this company. She would have agreed with everyone who pointed out that a poem cannot be all poetry: only, she would have added, we ought in that case to change our definition of poetry. She did it more by example than precept, with "the physiognomy of conduct must not reveal the skeleton," and "Denunciations do not affect

/ the culprit; nor blows, but it / is torture to him not to be spoken to"; with "why dissect destiny with instruments / more highly specialized than components of destiny itself?" and "He can talk but insolently says nothing. What of it? / When one is frank, one's very presence is a compliment" and "The passion for setting people right is in itself an afflictive disease. / Distaste which takes no credit to itself is best."

Statements like these may look planted. But how different are they from those others, obviously at home in one place, which have a hardy existence on almost any soil? One does not need to know the title of the poem, "People's Surroundings," or the topic for discussion, the flats of Utah and Texas, to appreciate Moore's qualified love of "those cool sirs with the explicit sensory apparatus of common sense, / who know the exact distance between two points as the crow flies." In "Elephants," the relevant context can seem almost a pettiness to recall, after she speaks of one creature in particular as "too wise / to mourn—a life prisoner but reconciled." Again, how different are these in turn from the many celebrated passages of "straight" description, in which animal traits, refigured as man-mores, are esteemed as tokens of character and then of virtue?

> Make hay; keep
> the shop; I have one sheep; were a less
> limber animal's mottoes. This one
> finds sticks for the swan's-down-dress
> of his child to rest upon and would
> not know Gretel from Hänsel.
> As impassioned Handel—
>
> meant for a lawyer and a masculine German domestic
> career—clandestinely studied the harpsichord
> and never was known to have fallen in love,
> the unconfiding frigate-bird hides
> in the height and in the majestic
> display of his art. He glides
> a hundred feet or quivers about
> as charred paper behaves—full
> of feints; and an eagle
>
> of vigilance.

The final phrase, tucked into a new stanza, nicely conceals its satisfaction at having found a witty way of obliging man to serve as a middle man—nothing but a German domestic could translate the eagle into a language the pelican understands: this done, the poem is done with Germany, Handel, and harpsichords. The perception starts from and returns to its formative sayings. In the meantime it has made havoc of our pedagogic aids, which read, in a march of progress, "From Abstract to Concrete" or "From General to Particular. "

As a composer of words Moore's greatest affinities are with Francis Bacon, and the Baconian essay or prose-amble may be the least misleading analogy for one of her poems. To be curt, undeviating, end-stopped wherever a thought might enter, but at the same time vivid, striking, inventive in the highest degree conscionable, is the ideal of both writers. Like Bacon a despiser of ornament, Moore rejects with equal vehemence the aims of bringing conceit for a matter or matter for a conceit. She will frame no description that has any hint of the superlative, unless she can first set in the middle of it a skeptical gargoyle at least six syllables long:

> Rare unscent-
> ed, provident-
> ly hot, too sweet, inconsistent flower bed!

She refuses to claim the literary exemption from syllogisms, dependent clauses, subordinate conjunctions, and everything that smacks of the uncraftily sheltered: she will submit with the worst of us, and find her poetry there besides. Bacon's untheatrical rigor would have found nothing wanting in her resolve to be literal, and for range of style he leaves her plenty. "Nature is often hidden; sometimes overcome; seldom extinguished," is a sentence one can imagine her writing, or quoting, as easily as "It is good to commit the beginnings of all great actions to Argos with his hundred eyes, and the ends to Briareus with his hundred hands; first to watch, and then to speed."

But Bacon's essays sometimes trail off in QEDs, whereas Moore was born to the stroke they call in tennis *a concluder.* An extraordinary number of her endings are extraordinarily beautiful. In "The Student," "Sojourn in the Whale," "The Hero," the first section of "The Jerboa," she lifts the errant thing to its resting seat, with a parental touch so quick and encircling that we come to rely on her in every playground, including Eden. Nor does she ring a particle of pomp to occasions that need a different sort of authority: "Spenser's Ireland" and "To a Steam Roller" are famous because they close with famous jokes. Yet above all these are the endings carried out in perfect earnest. First, "Elephants," which has warned us hardship makes the soldier, teachableness the philosopher, and then turns to Socrates, who

> prudently testing the suspicious thing, knew
> the wisest is he who's not sure that he knows.
> Who rides on a tiger can never dismount;
> asleep on an elephant, that is repose.

These lines once had and still deserve for company, the last of another elephant-poem, "Melanchthon," with their less reconciled note: "Will / depth be depth, thick skin be thick, to one who can see no / beautiful element of unreason under it?" However, Moore never outdid the description of man in "The Pangolin"—bringing him by chance to the fore ("To explain grace requires a curious hand"), keeping him there till he changed everything—and this she left standing.

> Consistent with the
> formula—warm blood, no gills, two pairs of hands and a few
> hairs—that
> is a mammal; there he sits in his own habitat,
> serge-clad, strong-shod. The prey of fear, he, always
> curtailed, extinguished, thwarted by the dusk, work
> partly done,
> says to the alternating blaze,
> "Again the sun!
> anew each day; and new and new and new,
> that comes into and steadies my soul."

Felicities which here sound accidental the whole poem makes essential: man "curtailed," for instance, which takes us back to the pangolin "strongly intailed," a pun encouraging to all who if they pursue symbolic logic feel that they must do it on four legs.

In a memorable criticism Kenneth Burke conceived of Moore's "objectivist idiom" as fostering "an appraisal or judgment of many things in and for themselves. They would be encouraged to disclose their traits, not simply that they might exist through the vicarage of words, but that they might reveal their properties as workmanship (workmanship being a trait in which the ethical and the esthetic are one)." Only the first part of this seems to me false. It brings her too much into line with Williams, whose work vaguely resembles hers in matters of the surface, but whose brittler temperament had much to do with his interest in programs like objectivism. Pound, who usually comes next in the effort to triangulate her, is just as wrong for comparison, in spite of their mutual loyalty. Irony like Pound's, of the nervous modern sort, which regards its object from an unsteady point of view but with an advanced degree of scorn, was never part of her armor or weaponry, and she could have written "Mauberley" without the quotation marks. Her intellectual virtues came from the enlightenment and Protestantism; from the start, she had the concerns of a genuine moralist, as well as the ambition to be one; and she knew that the gesture of humility was to ask forgiveness from enemies rather than friends. These things helped to make "In Distrust of Merits" a better poem than "Pull Down Thy Vanity."

Of all her contemporaries, the Stevens of *Harmonium* and the early Eliot, who also called his work "observations," seem closest to the spirit of her poetry. In one appreciation of Eliot she mentions "certain qualities" that he shares with Steven—qualities she supposed would be sufficiently plain to her readers, though they were not so to the authors themselves—"reticent candor and emphasis by understatement" being the two she cares for most. Some lines from "La Figlia che Piange" and "Peter Quince at the Clavier" are quoted as proof: a juxtaposition both strange and right, which it took Moore to imagine. And with those poems in view, one can understand how far she does belong to her generation after all, the generation of "Prufrock," "Le Monocle de Mon Oncle," and "Marriage." Eliot was alluding to their shared enterprise when in a letter to Moore he thanked her for writing poems that forced him to consider each word. Revolutions in taste cannot give us better monuments; but they may force us to work at the new ones slowly. Moore knew what she had done and what she had made possible, and nothing could be more emphatic than the reticence with which she told us so: "Know that it will be there when it says, / 'I shall be there when the wave has gone by.' "

DIANE WOOD MIDDLEBROOK

The Problem of the Woman Artist:
Louise Bogan, "The Alchemist"

To tell the truth, there is very little that one can say about women poets, past, present, and (presumably) to come. One truth about them is an open secret: when they are bad they are very very bad, and when they are good, they are magnificent. . . . The problem of the woman artist remains unchanged. Henry James, in *The Tragic Muse*, spoke of "that oddest of animals, the artist who happens to be born a woman." (Louise Bogan, "What the Women Said," lecture at Bennington College, 1962)

Louise Bogan is one of a generation of distinguished American woman poets born between 1885–1900 whose art expresses a felt contradiction between writing and living a woman's life. The milieu of the early twentieth century—thanks to the recognized genius of Bogan's contemporaries Yeats, Eliot, Pound, Stevens, and Williams—saw a genuine cultural renaissance of poetry. But women writers remained marginal to this renaissance. The list of Bogan's female peers would include Elizabeth Madox Roberts, Elinor Wylie, H. D., Edna St. Vincent Millay, Genevieve Taggard, Babette Deutsch, Uonie Adams, and Marya Zaturenska, and among fiction writers, Katherine Anne Porter and Janet Lewis. Each is an impeccable stylist highly respected by fellow artists. Yet all worked in a climate of awareness that a woman must, as Uonie Adams said of Louise Bogan, "function not only as a poet of her own time but within the limits accorded a woman poet. . . . There could never be

From *Critical Essays on Louise Bogan*. © 1984 by Martha Collins. G. K. Hall & Co., 1984.

any confusion of the role of woman and the role of poet, or any exploitation of the role of woman. She knew, moreover, that she should not model herself upon the women she admired or who were closest to her in time."

Bogan rarely wrote directly about her mistrust of the origins of her poetry in a specifically female experience of the world: But her collected poems, *The Blue Estuaries: Poems, 1923 –1968,* contains a handful of poems on this theme which gives us what might be described as a private mythology constructed to account for her creativity. Bogan did not, in these poems, analyze her cultural situation; rather, she reflected its influence in a body of symbols that express the contradiction woman/artist in other bipolar metaphors: flesh/breath, low/high, earth/heaven, silence/voice. Central to the symbolisms of this mythology are, on the one hand, anxiety about aspects of the self which cannot be controlled; on the other hand, reverence for the mind and its powers. "The Alchemist," "Cassandra," and "Fifteenth Farewell" are among the poems which elaborate this myth. In them art is viewed as the product of both a freedom and a control hard to attain within the limits of a woman's mind, which Bogan viewed as sometimes helpless, often under domination by unconscious forces. Woman, in this mythology, is carefully distinguished from artist.

"The Alchemist"—written by the time Louise Bogan was twenty-five—displays her characteristic strength: a skilled formalism in which the syntax is simple and straightforward ("I broke my life, to seek relief"; "I had found unmysterious flesh"). And in it she addresses symbolically the problem of "that oddest of animals, the artist who happens to be born a woman."

In "The Alchemist" the contradiction between woman and artist is an implication latent within the explicit subject of the poem: the desire to attain self-transcendence through brutal self-control.

> I burned my life, that I might find
> A passion wholly of the mind,
> Thought divorced from eye and bone,
> Ecstasy come to breath alone.
> I broke my life, to seek relief
> From the flawed light of love and grief.
>
> With mounting beat the utter fire
> Charred existence and desire.
> It died low, ceased its sudden thresh.
> I had found unmysterious flesh—
> Not the mind's avid substance—still
> Passionate beyond the will.

Alchemy—one of the earliest efforts to develop an exact science that would combine philosophy and technology—regarded gold as the most spiritual metal. Bogan's poem is about an analogous quasi-scientific quest for purity. Her alchemist is a metaphor for the human type, frequently regarded as heroic, who seeks spiritual transcendence through esoteric study requiring rejection of the common life. Poetry is full of esoteric study requiring rejection of the common life. Poetry is full of such heroes: Shelley's Alastor, Byron's Manfred, Arnold's Scholar Gypsy. The narrator in Yeats's "Sailing to Byzantium" offers a close analogy to the speaker in "The Alchemist," for he too is a being "sick with desire" seeking the relief of a wisdom that can only be secure when he has attained a condition wholly of the mind. "Consume my heart away," he appeals, embracing like Bogan's alchemist a refining, intellectual fire. He too desires a form of existence divorced from eye and bone: "Once out of nature I shall never take / My bodily form in any natural thing." Bogan's poem, however, rejects the idea affirmed in "Sailing to Byzantium" that a world of pure spirit exists beyond the sphere of physical existence, to be attained by deserting or destroying the physical. The alchemist does indeed find in the crucible something in a pure form, but it is not "the mind's avid substance." It is "unmysterious flesh—still / Passionate." The creative mind may only deny, it may never escape, its dependence on tormented sensuous existence.

"The Alchemist," then, can be interpreted as a critique of a romantic theory of art. The meaning of the poem changes, however, if we view the alchemist not as a symbol for the romantic poet heroically bent on defying nature—Shelley, Bryon, Yeats—but as a *woman* poet hopelessly defying the social significance of her femininity.

From this perspective, the will to deny the body expressed in "The Alchemist" grows poignantly comprehensible. For the metaphorical gold she seeks—"passion wholly of the mind," "Thought," "Ecstasy come to breath"—are attainments essential to creativity: but in Western culture they have always been regarded as "masculine" attainments. Throughout her long career, Bogan's poetry reflects ambivalent acquiescence to the stereotype that makes aspiration to intellectual power a contradiction of the "feminine." This contradiction is rarely expressed in direct statement; rather, it infuses most of the poems that, like "The Alchemist," deal with a conflict between mental power and sexual passion. It is expressed in metaphors where "flesh" and "breath" form fateful polarities. "Flesh" is mortal, dumb, blind, hopelessly instinctual; it is low, associated with darkness and the earth, and it is feminine. "Breath," by contrast, is the medium of inspiration, speech, music—high achievements, not associated with the feminine sphere. This polarity is the explicit theme of a powerful poem, "Cassandra," in which

Bogan imagines Cassandra's clairvoyance as a consequence of liberation from feminine roles:

> To me, one silly task is like another.
> I bare the shambling tricks of lust and pride.
> This flesh will never give a child its mother,—
> Song, like a wing, tears through my breast, my side,
>
> And madness chooses out my voice again,
> Again. I am the chosen no hand saves:
> The shrieking heaven lifted over men,
> Not the dumb earth, wherein they set their graves.

Cassandra's fate as seer tragically ignored by the princes of Troy was the punishment Apollo ordained when she withheld promised sexual favors. She paid a high price for her ascent from femininity. In this respect, "Cassandra" is typical, for in Bogan's vision woman is frighteningly bound to and by her sexuality. It brings her low. In "The Crows," for example, Bogan likens an old woman who is still full of sexual passion to a harvested field, in which "there is only bitter / Winter-burning." The girl in "Chanson un Peu Naïve" is a "body . . . ploughed, / Sown, and broken yearly". Another, in "Girl's Song," lies with her lover in a field as on a grave: "And, since she loves [him], and she must, / Puts her young cheek against the dust."

Identification of the feminine with fields, seasonal cycles, and mortality has other implications in Bogan's poetry. The field is not only a fertile space, it is space enclosed for others' use. The gate to its enclosures is the awakening of sexuality. Before love, the girl in "Betrothed" has roamed freely with other maidens "In air traversed of birds"—"But there is only evening here, / And the sound of willows / Now and again dipping their long oval leaves in the water." The feminine personae in Bogan's early poems are as fatally determined as heroines in Hardy—and by the same rural and sexual cultural conventions. As Bogan writes in "Women":

> They cannot think of so many crops to a field
> Or of clean wood cleft by an axe.
> Their love is an eager meaninglessness
> Too tense, or too lax.
>
> They hear in every whisper that speaks to them
> A shout and a cry.
> As like as not, when they take life over their door-sills
> They should let it go by.

In these lyrics, Bogan is working with stereotypes of the feminine from which she, as author, maintains a knowing distance. These are *some* women, *other* women. Yet the same conflicting opposites—low/high, flesh/breath, feminine/masculine—furnish the imagery in which Bogan speaks as "I" describing her own creative powers. In these poems, as in "The Alchemist," the speaker seeks to purify herself of personal history, to become "thought divorced from eye and bone."

"Fifteenth Farewell" is a pair of sonnets in which the speaker wills a commitment to "breath"—identified with both life and art—as an escape from an unmanageable and painful sexual passion:

I

> You may have all things from me, save my breath,
> The slight life in my throat will not give pause
> For your love, nor your loss, nor any cause.
> Shall I be made a panderer to death,
> Dig the green ground for darkness underneath,
> Let the dust serve me, covering all that was
> With all that will be? Better, from time's claws,
> The hardened face under the subtle wreath.
>
> Cooler than stones in wells, sweeter, more kind
> Than hot, perfidious words, my breathing moves
> Close to my plunging blood. Be strong, and hang
> Unriven mist over my breast and mind,
> My breath! we shall forget the heart that loves,
> Though in my body beat its blade, and its fang.

II

> I erred, when I thought loneliness the wide
> Scent of mown grass over forsaken fields,
> Or any shadow isolation yields.
> Loneliness was the heart within your side.
> Your thought, beyond my touch, was tilted air
> Ringed with as many borders as the wind.
> How could I judge you gentle or unkind
> When all bright flying space was in your care?
>
> Now that I leave you, I shall be made lonely
> By simple empty days,—never that chill

> Resonant heart to strike between my arms
> Again, as though distraught for distance,—only
> Levels of evening, now, behind a hill,
> Or a late cock-crow from the darkening farms.

In the first sonnet, "You" is unmistakably a lover. But "you" also denotes in both sonnets the power of the masculine over the feminine as these two abstractions are consistently rendered in Bogan's poems, where "he" is nearly always either a voice or a pair of censorious and faithless eyes. This man, Bogan says, has always been in some sense beyond her, or at least beyond what she could gain by touching him physically. She could not apply ordinary value judgments ("gentle," "unkind") to one whose thought and ambition appeared boundless. Nor could she approach his mind by holding the man in her arms. Rather, his heart delivered blows and taught her by example to be definitively alone. "Fifteenth Farewell," part II, also makes use of the polarities described above, which place the feminine in the context of "forsaken fields" rather than "bright flying space," of "levels" rather than "tilted air," of a loneliness which is willed rather than sought. The masculine is above and beyond the imperiousness of flesh and seeks a noble though desperate distance from it.

Yet, if the masculine is identified with "air" in this elevated, authoritative sense, air is not exclusively the domain of men. This is the theme of "Fifteenth Farewell," part I, explicitly a rejection of suicide. The tone of triumph is almost militant and comes, significantly, from the speaker's recognition that she possesses "breath." Not merely ongoing life, "breath" is a creative power, like the "air" of thought in the second sonnet. It flows coolly in the throat, above as well as "close to" that source of "hot, perfidious words," the plunging blood; it appears to be the breath which shapes from active pain a formal art, "The hardened face under the subtle wreath." This is the kind of transformation which may be won by denial of the feminine, the body in which beat "love's blade and its fang."

All these poems may be seen to bear upon the project undertaken in "The Alchemist" to separate flesh from breath, to break one's life in order to attain a mental ecstasy, to transmute base metal into gold. At the opening of the poem the alchemist seems to think that if she could purge her passionate thought of any trace of its origins in a (female) body, she might ascend to that high plane occupied by the greatest spirits. But at the end of the poem, the "utter fire" of acute intelligence illuminates the absurdity, even the unworthiness, of such a goal. Hence, failure of the alchemist may be interpreted as a liberation of the woman as artist. The poem ends on a note of self-mocking relief, wry rather than bitter: "I had found unmysterious flesh." Explicitly, she denies a distinction between matter and spirit. Implicitly, she accepts her sex as a fundamental basis of her art. Implicitly, too, she challenges the long tradition in which the woman artist seems, in James's phrase, "that oddest of animals." While in her life Bogan never conquered the ambivalence toward the woman artist that colored her cultural milieu, "The Alchemist" in its technical and spiritual confidence testifies eloquently to the power of the female imagination. Further, it foreshadows the project of contemporary literary criticism to expose the cultural biases of the ahistorical ideologies of the early modern poets, as well as the project of contemporary women poets to transform art by asserting the validity of their subjectivity. In retrospect, Louise Bogan emerges as an unknowing precursor of those women poets who write today liberated from many constraints of that old contradiction—liberated, that is, from all but the inescapable constraints of poetry itself.

SANDRA COOKSON

"The Repressed Becomes the Poem": Landscape and Quest in Two Poems by Louise Bogan

Louise Bogan was an intensely personal poet whose poems were made from the most intimate material of her life: love, death, the mysteries of the unconscious, the terrors of mental illness, the ponderings of a subtle and analytical mind on the nature of life and art. But she was a personal poet who rejected direct autobiographical statement in her poems, except rarely and in the earlier work, and employed instead the obliquity of image used as symbol; who relied upon a symbolic language and the combined power of sound and rhythm and rhyme—form, in short—to convey meaning and emotion.

Although her poems are formal and symbolic structures, they cannot be separated from the most intimate psychological events of her life. For instance, in her poems that explore the unconscious in dream or vision and in her poems about sexual passion, images of a ravaged or hellish landscape symbolize the devastation of the psyche from assaults upon it by violently disruptive feelings which Bogan identifies as rooted deeply in her childhood. Archetypal images of the Medusa and the Furies, as well as a small gallery of more private myth figures, personify the poet's deepest fears and impulses. Thus, contrary to what one might expect from a poet who relies upon generalizing images such as these archetypal ones, and upon formal and traditional poetic structures, the urge toward the personal is always

From *Critical Essays on Louise Bogan*. © 1984 by Martha Collins. G. K. Hall & Co., 1984.

powerfully felt in Bogan's work. Her own brief remarks from a journal entry written late in life are of interest as the poet's view of the uses she made of her experience: "The poet represses the outright narrative of his life. He absorbs it, along with life itself. The repressed becomes the poem. Actually, I have written down my experience in the closest detail. But the rough and vulgar facts of it are not there." The poet's conviction of absolute fidelity to her experience, although she has transformed "the rough and vulgar facts" of it, is a traditional aesthetic position, with moral overtones, of formalist lyric poets. Bogan's notion that "the repressed becomes the poem" is a kind of twentieth-century commentary on Wordsworth's idea of the poem as experience "recollected in tranquillity."

The remark further illuminates the unique power of Bogan's poetry by providing an insight into her belief that the repressed material of her life was her true poetic raw material, that therefore true poetry comes from the unconscious, a belief she stated many times in reference to her poems. Bogan spent many years of her life in psychotherapy, but her greatest poems bear out the implication that her true access to "repressed" material remained largely a mystery of the poetic process.

Bogan's life and her poems are marked by two obsessions. The first is her preoccupation with a childhood full of half-remembered scenes of violence between her parents, which she focuses upon her mother. The second is her marriage to the poet and novelist Raymond Holden. Bogan left Holden in 1934 and divorced him in 1937, but his presence persisted in her poems. Both the poems and journal entries written late in life suggest that while Bogan probably succeeded in freeing herself from the Holden obsession, the terrors of her childhood remained with her to her death.

From her earliest poems to her latest, Bogan's landscapes and seascapes represent the poet's mental universe. Often they are the settings for journeys into the darkest regions of the self, undertaken in order to achieve peace through understanding. Understanding, Bogan hoped, would allow her to exorcise her personal demons, which she identified as hatred and sexual jealousy. Two of Bogan's most distinguished poems, "Putting to Sea" (1936) and "Psychiatrist's Song" (1967), complement each other as poems of quest and reconciliation. "Putting to Sea" concerns liberation from the violence of sexual jealousy and the rage which were exacerbated by the last years of the Holden relationship. "Psychiatrist's Song," looking back on that struggle from a distance of thirty years, celebrates the achievement of psychic equilibrium. Yet it still contains the haunting image of the damaged child, the victim of experiences too painful ever to fully come to light.

The sea voyage is the mode of these psychological and spiritual journeys, and Bogan signaled its importance in her work when she chose "A

Tale" (1921) as the opening poem in her collected poems, *The Blue Estuaries* (1968). "A Tale," though it is not chronologically the book's earliest, is Bogan's prototypical voyage poem. In it, a "youth" prepares to relinquish the everyday world of time and flux ("the break / Of waters in a land of change") in search of something enduring, "a light that waits / Still as a lamp upon a shelf." The ideal country which he seeks will be an austere place "where no sea leaps upon itself."

The poet, however, tells us that the youth's journey will not bring him wisdom attended by peace and steadiness of spirit. If, indeed, he does journey far enough to find the truth, it will be just the opposite of what he has hoped for:

> But he will find that nothing dares
> To be enduring, save where, south
> Of hidden deserts, torn fire glares
> On beauty with a rusted mouth,—
>
> Where something dreadful and another
> Look quietly upon each other.

At the center of his universe, the youthful voyager will find nameless terror, corrupted love, and presences monstrous beyond his comprehension. This hellish landscape, populated by demons, will recur throughout Bogan's poetry as the terrain of the unconscious.

In "Medusa," written at about the same time as a "A Tale," the speaker, paralyzed by the monster's gaze, finds herself suspended in a vast surreal landscape where she is condemned for eternity to watch "the yellow dust" rising in the wind. Another version of this hell is depicted in "M., Singing," written about fifteen years later, in which the song of a young girl releases the demons of the unconscious, "Those beings without heart or name," permitting them to "Leave the long harvest which they reap / In the sunk land of dust and flame."

Bogan was remarkably consistent in her use of a particular landscape with its cluster of images to signify an emotion or state of feeling. In the poems of her first book, *Body of This Death* (1923), passion is the "breeze of flame" ("Ad Castitatem") that consumes the field set afire and burned back to stubble after harvest. The image may originate in the agricultural practice of slash-and-burn, common in some tropical countries. The youthful Bogan lived in Panama for about a year with her first husband, and must have seen on many occasions whole fields set alight, the flames racing over the dry stalks. "Feuernacht" (1927) is a remarkably faithful depiction of such an event, while at the same time it clearly suggests the all-consuming power of sexual passion.

The blackened stubble which remains after the fire has burned itself out is a recurring image in these early poems, and signifies the woman's sexuality depleted by the fires of passion. The image belongs to Bogan's youth, and it disappears from her poems after the beautiful lyric of 1930, entitled "Song," in which the speaker attempts to renounce an impulse to sexual passion, claiming that she has long since paid her dues to it.

> Years back I paid my tithe
> And earned my salt in kind,
> And watched the long slow scythe
> Move where the grain is lined,
> And saw the stubble burn
> Under the darker sheaves.

Though it appears to have been Bogan's unhappy first marriage that gave expression to the pain of passion, the image of the young woman's sexuality as a "ravaged country" ("Ad Castitatem") carries over into the Holden years, where it is transformed into another tortured sexual landscape, the obscene and sterile tropical country of "Putting to Sea." Thirty years later in "Psychiatrist's Song," the same landscape recurs, but it is merely a dim shape on the horizon to the voyager now freed of the torments which it represents in the earlier poem.

In "Putting to Sea," the sea-voyage metaphor symbolizes the undertaking of a journey into the deepest self ("the gulf, the vast, the deep"), with the specific purpose of freeing the voyager from the obscenity of hatred. To accomplish this, she must confront it, and rejects its temptations, which take shape in the poem's unnatural tropical landscape. "With so much hated still so close behind / The sterile shores before us must be faced. . . ."

The voyager, first of the poem's two speakers, is the conscious self and controls the narrative. "Who, in the dark, has cast the harbor chain?" she asks, as if the journey were compelled by a force beyond her will. The land she is leaving is the everyday world described in natural, cyclical images, which connect it to sensual experience, as these lines suggest: "Sodden with summer, stupid with its loves, / The country which we leave. . . ." Its counterpart in the unconscious is the tropical land, described by the poem's second speaker, the voice of the treacherous unconscious. The voyager, shunning all inducements toward the tropical shore, must journey into an awesome moral proving ground, the "bare circle of ocean," which is deep as heaven's height and "barren with despair." Later in the poem, the landscape of the quotidian, the sea, and the tropical shore will be joined by a fourth psychological country, which suggests the tender promise of childhood left unfulfilled.

The voyager understands that the second speaker's tantalizing descriptions of a gaudy and exotically flamboyant artificial land where "love fountains from its deeps" are meant to seduce her with false promises of love and fulfillment. The sly tone of this voice is supposed to conceal from her the true hideousness of the landscape:

> "O, but you should rejoice! The course we steer
> Points to a beach bright to the rocks with love,
> Where, in hot calms, blades clatter on the ear;
>
> And spiny fruits up through the earth are fed
> With fire; the palm trees clatter; the wave leaps.
>
> Fleeing a shore where heart-loathed love lies dead
> We point lands where love fountains from its deeps.
>
> Through every season the coarse fruits are set
> In earth not fed by streams."

The voyager is not taken in. She knows that this is really the landscape of madness. It is fiend's country, far more dangerous than the everyday world she has fled "where heart-loathed love lies dead." Bogan's specific reference is to the failure of her second marriage, to Raymond Holden, for which she was later to blame herself as a "demon of jealousy." In 1936, she wrote her friend and editor at Scribner's, John Hall Wheelock, that this poem would "sum up the Holden suffering, endured so long, but now, at last, completely over."

With the resumption of the narrative by the first speaker, following the passage just quoted, a new landscape enters the poem.

> Soft into time
> Once broke the flower: pear and violet,
> The cinquefoil. The tall elm tree and the lime
>
> Once held out fruitless boughs, and fluid green
> Once rained about us, pulse of earth indeed.

The "birth" of flowers, emblematic for Bogan of New England where she was born and raised, suggests her own "early time." These limpid and tender lines also contrast with the harshness of the preceding images. Moreover, "fluid green" and "pulse of earth" suggest a primordial condition that is full of promise, teeming with life, but unformed.

The potential of this tender land is not to be realized, however. With the contrasting landscapes as her psychological terrain, the first speaker traces the seeds of her destructive impulses back to her childhood: "There, out of metal, and to light obscene, / The flamy blooms burn backward to their seed." Childhood is a land of promise, but within its tender depths anything can take root. In her view, the compulsion from which the voyager now seeks catharsis stems from this time of unformed life, from her childhood.

The poet-voyager has set herself a hard task. Lacking even the celestial guides of the mariner, she wonders at the necessity of this dark and perilous journey:

> The Way should mark our course within the night,
> The streaming System, turned without a sound.
> What choice is this—profundity and flight—
> Great sea? Our lives through we have trod the ground.
>
> Motion beneath us, fixity above.

"Putting to Sea" derives its power from the depiction of this moral/psychological deep. The descriptions of the great mythic sea and the stars have a silent and formidable grandeur, evoked equally by the bare, grand simplicity of the adjectives and the vibrations of a long tradition they set in motion. A line like "The streaming System, turned without a sound" is so suggestive that, while it is describing the absence of stars in the heavens, it evokes their presence by the infusion of light "streaming" produces. At the same time, the void and utter silence of these disturbed heavens must recall, in "turned without a sound," the ancient music of the spheres, so out of place in this poem where the heavens themselves conspire in the voyager's bafflement.

In the same letter to Wheelock, Bogan remarks on the poem's provenance. "I know what it's about, with my upper reason, just a little; it came from pretty far down, thank God." Bogan's comment states her conviction of the poem's origin in her subconscious, but it also suggests why "Putting to Sea" has such power; for in it resound echoes of the great mythic voyages which preceded it. The most reverberant of all is the quest of Odysseus. Dante provided Tennyson with the model for his Ulysses, and the opening lines of Bogan's last stanza suggest the spirit and tone of Tennyson's version of Ulysses' speech to his mariners:

> There lies the port; the vessel puffs her sail:
> There gloom the dark broad seas. My mariners,
> Souls that have toil'd, and wrought, and thought with me—

Bogan addresses her "mariners" with similar gravity: "Bend to the chart, in the extinguished night / Mariners! Make way slowly; stay from sleep."

Bogan may also be indebted to Baudelaire, if not for the actual sea-voyage metaphor, at least for certain aspects of its treatment in "Putting to Sea." Bogan's voyager has a specific moral purpose for her journey into the unknown, while Baudelaire's persona is a restless seeker after experience. Yet both poets share the belief that truth may be found in the search for the self. Bogan's final line, "And learn, with joy, the gulf, the vast, the deep," is almost an imitation of the last two lines of Baudeliare's "Le voyage": "Plonger au fond du gouffre, Enfer ou Ciel, qu'importe? / Au fond de l'Inconnu pour trouver du *nouveau!*" While Baudelaire exhorts his voyager to experience for its own sake, Bogan urges the striving for understanding. Her final line reaffirms her conviction that suffering can be surmounted as well as endured.

The most contemporary voyage which "Putting to Sea" recalls is the brief echo of "Sailing to Byzantium" heard in the second line. The voyager wonders at the extraordinary journey she is about to undertake. "This is no journey to a land we know," she says, echoing Yeats, who also rejects the everyday world, remarking of it, "That is no country for old men." Each of these poems partakes of the common impulse to represent the human journey as a sea voyage. In "Putting to Sea," Bogan both epitomizes that tradition and creates a poem uniquely her own.

Early in 1967, thirty years after the publication of "Putting to Sea" and just three years before her death, Bogan sent three "songs" to *New Yorker* poetry editor Howard Moss, with the note that they "seem to go together . . . [as poems] of dream and aberration." A way to read the shifting and merging voices in "Psychiatrist's Song" is in the light of dream logic, in which identities are often fluid and interchangeable. Moreover, in the course of the long journey which psychotherapy was for Bogan, perhaps psychiatrist and patient each take on attributes of the other.

In a typescript of the poem, the only draft extant, the title reads "Psychiatrist's Recitative and Aria." The published version retains the same stanzaic divisions. In the poem's opening section, which would be the recitative, the psychiatrist begins his monologue, musing in a general way upon the persons who have played crucial roles in the lives of his patients, but of whom "they" (the patients) cannot speak directly: "Those / Concerning whom they have never spoken and thought never to speak . . . ." In spite of the psychiatrist's hint that patients deliberately conceal things, we may infer that the reason they do not have access to the whole narrative of their lives is that much of what is crucial has been repressed, and remains hidden in the unconscious:

> That place
> Hidden, preserved,
> That even the exquisite eye of the soul
> Cannot completely see.

From that generalized and somewhat rambling diagnostic beginning, the psychiatrist's attention soon settles upon particulars, and we realize that he must now be thinking of one patient:

> But they are there:
> Those people, and that house, and that evening, seen
> Newly above the dividing window sash

At this point the narrative intensifies. Another voice enters, and from this moment to the end of the poem, the voice of the psychiatrist contains the voice of the patient. The sudden shift from generalities to particular details—"that house . . . that evening . . . the dividing window sash"—and the personal cry of anguish in the lines that follow, indicate that the point of view has shifted to that of the patient; yet there is no break in the narrative:

> The young will broken
> And all time to endure.

> Those hours when murderous wounds are made,
> Often in joy.

The images of the damaged child and the treacheries of passion recall major themes in Bogan's poems. As the recitative, providing exposition or background for the rest of the poem, this opening section, with its merging voices of psychiatrist and patient, is a poetic statement of the psychological traumas for which the journey of the next section was undertaken.

The second section, the aria of the typescript, begins with the line "I hear." The merging voices of psychiatrist and patient acknowledge the warning contained in the last line of the preceding section about the treachery of passion. The narration of the journey is taken over by the patient, whose voice dominates from now on, though the guiding presence of the psychiatrist is felt in the poem until the final stanzas. Since the patient is also the poet-voyager of "Putting to Sea," thirty years after, this "I" stands for the several selves of the poet. That she has absorbed the psychiatrist persona completely by the end of the poem suggests, perhaps, the health of the psyche achieved.

Although the old temptations to the evils of fiend's country are recalled in the opening lines, this tropical landscape is "far away" and no longer threatens the voyager. The old motif of sexual jealousy echoes mockingly in the three repetitions of "man"-words, probably a play on the free-associative technique often used in psychotherapy: "the *mango* trees (the *mang*rove swamps, the *man*drake root . . .)." The reminder of the "clattering" palms from "Putting to Sea" fixes the identity of this receding landscape, hazy now, having lost its clear sense of evil. The voyager "watches" the thicket of palms—not even sure anymore that they are palm trees, "as though at the edge of sleep." Indeed, the narration of this section has the dream character of a perfectly sequential and straightforward presentation of fantastic events.

The voyager has now achieved such control and certainty that she can journey toward the once disastrous landscape represented by the palms "in a boat without oars, / Trusting to rudder and sail." The idea that the voyager is in control of the journey contrasts with the formidable voyage of "Putting to Sea." Moreover, the whole landscape has been scaled down from the enormous and overpowering sea and sky of the earlier poem to a size more manageably human. She now leaves the boat and walks "fearlessly" to shore. Previously, even the ripples of the shallows might have been full of peril, for the sea has, until now, been an awesome and uncharted place. The lines that suggest control over a sea which will bring the speaker to a place of repose are reminiscent of Eliot's "*Damyata*," The Boat responded / Gaily, to the hand expert with sail and oar," from part 5 of *The Waste Land*, in which the rain brings with it the possibility of the renewal of life and hope.

The dangerous landscapes of ocean and palm trees recede, and the voyager finds herself "on firm dry land," with the solidity of earth all around her. The last stanza banishes the old terrors of "flesh and of ocean" that were given full expression in "Putting to Sea." If the last stanzas also evoke death in images of imminence, darkening, and silence, it is death welcomed, celebrated even, as the final healing. We need not be troubled by the implication that the cure for human suffering is death. Bogan was sixty-nine years old and in failing health when she wrote "Psychiatrist's Song." It is nearly her last poem, and marks the very last time she would use the voyage metaphor to set down in a poem the long struggle with her private demons. The truce between them was always, at best, a "troubled peace."

Bogan places a great deal of the burden for making the poem intelligible upon the reader. In "Putting to Sea" the poem's two voices were clearly separated. The voice out of fiend's country spoke a different language from that of the voyager or conscious self in the poem, and her speeches were set off from the voyager's narration by quotation marks. Bogan's decision to remove the recitative and aria directions from "Psychiatrist's Song" suggests a lightening of the poet's hand, a willingness to let the narrative take its own way.

Bogan takes more chances with language and form than she has done previously, and can risk beginning the poem with the halting awkwardness of a slightly pedantic and visually ungainly line. The play on "man" in "mango," "mangrove," and "mandrake," and the many irregularities in the free-verse line indicate greater flexibility and the freedom to experiment with the line and with the rhythms of common speech. The third line of the second section, with its truncated thought, "And the thickets of—are they palms?" is an illustration. And in the simple but strung-together statements of the line, "Coming to the shore, I step out of the boat; I leave it to its anchor," Bogan risks a kind of austere prosiness. In addition to its echoes of *The Waste Land*, "Psychiatrist's Song," is reminiscent throughout of Eliot's later poems of the 1930s, in particular "Marina" and "Coriolan."

The classical and formal Bogan still dominates in "Psychiatrist's Song," but her willingness to chance being prosaic places in relief the more poetically gorgeous phrases, such as "the exquisite eye of the soul," and the line with which she bridges the poem's two major sections, "Those hours when murderous wounds are made, / Often in joy." The elevated simplicity of the penultimate stanza is due in part to the extreme economy of the spare, predominantly one-syllable words. The luminosity of another late major poem, "After the Persian" (1951–53), glows for a moment in the final stanza. In the hortatory tone that is reminiscent of part 5, the "farewell" section of that poem, Bogan sounds again the note of sage or prophet, which is the final expression of her lifelong consciousness of herself as poet. Like "Putting to Sea," "Psychiatrist's Song" closes with an exhortation. But Bogan lowers the tone, and the moving prayer to earth, "Heal and receive me," ends the poem in an affecting combination of dignity and vulnerability.

Biographical Notes

ANNE BRADSTREET was born in 1612 or 1613, probably in or around Northamptonshire, England. Her father, Thomas Dudley, was steward to an earl. According to Cotton Mather, her mother, Dorothy Yorke, was "a Gentlewoman whose Extract and Estate were Considerable." After recovering from smallpox, the sixteen-year-old Anne married Simon Bradstreet, the Cambridge-educated son of a Nonconformist minister.

On March 29, 1630, the Bradstreets, the Dudleys, and other members of the Massachusetts Company set sail for the New World. They arrived in a poverty-stricken Salem on June 12. By December, the Company had settled in a place they called Newtown, site of present-day Cambridge, Massachusetts. In 1634, Anne and Simon Bradstreet and the Dudleys moved to Ipswich, where Anne Bradstreet's first child, Simon, was born and where she did most of her writing. After another move in 1640, the poet spent the remainder of her life in Andover.

Unbeknownst to her, John Woodbridge, the Minister of Andover, sailed back to England in 1647 with a copy of some of Bradstreet's poems. He arranged to have them published in London in 1650 under the title *The Tenth Muse, Lately Sprung Up in America*, making her the first published American poet. She spent the remainder of her life raising children and writing and revising her poetry. She died in Andover in September 1672.

EMILY DICKINSON was born in Amherst, Massachusetts, on December 10, 1830. From 1847 to 1848 she attended Mount Holyoke Female Seminary in South Hadley, Massachusetts. Her first known poem, "Awake ye muses nine, sing me a strain divine," a valentine to George Gould, was published in a February 1850 Amherst College *Indicator.*

Unmarried and reticent, Dickinson traveled very infrequently and remained in her parents' house all her life. She was certainly not unaware of her literary contemporaries, however. An avid reader of British and American authors, she heard Emerson speak at Amherst in 1857. In 1862, she wrote to Thomas Wentworth Higginson, a noted poet and critic, asking for literary advice. He responded, and although he thought that her poetry was a little strange, their correspondence turned into a lifelong friendship.

In March of 1883, Thomas Nash asked Dickinson to submit a volume of poems for publication. She never filled this request, and when she died in 1886, only seven of her poems had been published. While sorting through her sister's effects, Lavinia Dickinson discovered over nine hundred poems, divided and sewn into sixty little packets or "volumes." T. W. Higginson and Mabel Loomis Todd edited, considerably altered, and published some of these poems in 1890 and 1891. For the next sixty years variously edited volumes of Dickinson's poetry were published, and the complete variorum edition, *The Poems of Emily Dickinson,* edited by Thomas H. Johnson, appeared in 1955.

GERTRUDE STEIN was born in Allegheny, Pennsylvania, in 1874, the youngest of five children. Before she was grown up, both of her parents died, and Gertrude and her brother Leo were placed under the guardianship of their older brother, Michael, who continued to manage their father's estate and to provide for them throughout their lives.

Gertrude and Leo were very close; when he went to study at Harvard, she followed and began taking courses at Radcliffe. At the suggestion of William James, she undertook a series of experiments on automatic writing. She published her results in *The Harvard Psychological Review* in 1896 and 1898. Interested in pursuing a career in psychology, she began medical school at The Johns Hopkins University in the fall of 1898. By the end of her third year, however, she was no longer devoted to completing medical school. Searching for something to do, she joined Leo in the autumn of 1903 in Paris at 27 rue de Fleurus, the studio that became famous in the next several years for their extensive and daring collection of modem art.

Gertrude Stein began to write seriously in Paris: she completed her first novella, *Quod Erat Demonstrandum (Q. E. D.* or *Things As They Are)* in 1903; a year later, she finished *Fernhurst,* and the subsequent two years were spent translating Flaubert's *Trois Contes (Three Stories)* and writing *Three Lives.* She met Alice B. Toklas, her lifelong companion, in 1907. As her writing became more prolific and more experimental, Stein's circle of friends widened to include Matisse, Picasso, Hemingway, F. Scott Fitzgerald, Appollinaire, Gris, Marie Laurencin, Sherwood Anderson, and many other influential twentieth-century artists. Stein's early and middle works include *Tender Buttons* (1914), *The Making of Americans* (1925), *Composition as Explanation* (published posthumously), *Lucy Church Amiably* (1930), and How *to Write* (1931). Following the great success of *The Autobiography of Alice B. Toklas,* published in 1933, Stein returned to the United States on a speaking tour. Her lectures are collected in *Lectures in America* and *Narration.* Upon her return to Paris, she wrote *The Geographical History of America* (1936) and *Everybody's Autobiography* (1937). She continued to write throughout World War II and up until her death, of cancer, in 1946. Much of her work was published posthumously by Yale University Press in the 1950s.

H. D. (HILDA DOOLITTLE) was born on September 10, 1886, in Bethlehem, Pennsylvania. She entered Bryn Mawr College in 1904, but within two years withdrew because of poor health. For the next five years she wrote and lived with her family. In 1911, she traveled abroad and remained in England. Two years later she married Richard Aldington, a British Imagist poet.

H. D.'s first book, Sea *Garden,* was published in 1916, along with *Choruses from Iphigenia in Aulis,* a translation. She also became assistant editor of *The Egoist,* a post she later relinquished to T. S. Eliot. In 1918, she met Winifred Ellerman, a historical novelist who wrote under the name Bryher. Bryher remained a lifelong friend, benefactor, and companion. H. D.'s daughter, Perdita, was born in 1919; she also separated from her husband that year. For the next several years, she traveled extensively with Bryher— to Greece, the United States, then Egypt and Switzerland. From the mid-1920s to the early 1930s, H. D. wrote and published at a furious pace. *Heliodora and Other Poems* appeared in 1924, her *Collected Poems* in 1925, *Palimpsest,* a novel, in 1926, *Hippolytus Temporizes,* a verse drama, in 1927, *Hedylus,* a novel, in 1928, and *Red Roses for Bronze* in 1931.

From 1933 through 1934, H. D. was under analysis by Freud; she wrote about this experience in *Tribute to Freud,* published in 1956. Between the late 1930s and her death on September 28, 1961, H. D. wrote ten more books, including *The Hedgehog* (1936), a children's story, *The Walls Do Not Fall* (1944), the first of her *War Trilogy, Bid Me To Live* (1960), a novel, and *Helen in Egypt* (1961). In 1959 she received the Brandeis University Creative Arts

Award for Poetry and in 1960 she was the first woman to receive the Award of Merit Medal for Poetry from the American Academy of Arts and Letters.

MARIANNE MOORE was born on November 15, 1887, in Kirkwood, Missouri. She graduated from Bryn Mawr College in 1909 and from Carlisle Commercial College a year later. In 1911, she began to teach business classes at the United States Industrial Indian School. Her first poems appeared in 1915, in *The Egoist, Poetry,* and *Others.* Moore and her mother moved to New York City in 1918, and three years later *Poems* was published by Egoist Press. That same year, she began part-time work as a librarian in the Hudson Park branch of the New York Public Library. *Observations* was published by Dial Press in 1924; the publisher also gave Moore a $2,000 award for "unusual literary value." The following year she became editor of *The Dial* magazine, a post she retained until the magazine ceased publication in 1929. *Selected Poems* was published in 1935, and ten years later Moore received a Guggenheim Fellowship. In 1947 she was elected to The National Institute of Arts and Letters, and in 1949 she received an honorary degree from Wilson College, the first of sixteen such degrees that she'received from American institutions.

Collected Poems, published in 1951, won the Pulitzer Prize, a National Book Award, and a Bollingen Prize. Moore was a visiting lecturer at Bryn Mawr College in 1953, and the following year her translation of *The Fables of La Fontaine* appeared, winning the Croix de Chevalier des Arts et Lettres. *Predilections,* a collection of essays and reviews, was published in 1955, and six years later *A Marianne Moore Reader* became available. As Marianne Moore aged, various festivities were held in her honor: The National Institute of Arts and Letters celebrated her seventy-fifth birthday, and in 1964 *Festschrift for Marianne Moore's Seventy-Seventh Birthday* and *Omaggio a Marianne Moore* were published. Her *Complete Poems* appeared in 1967, winning the Edward McDowell Medal and the Poetry Society of America's Gold Medal. The year 1968 brought Moore a National Medal for Literature and the opportunity for the long-time baseball fan to pitch the first ball of the season at Yankee Stadium. Named Senior Citizen of the Year by the New York Conference on Aging in 1969, Marianne Moore also received her last honorary degree, from Harvard University, in that year. She died on February 5, 1972, and the second edition of *The Complete Poems of Marianne Moore,* with her final revisions, was published in 1981.

LOUISE BOGAN was born on August 11, 1897, in Livermore Falls, Maine. She grew up in New England and entered Boston University in 1915. A year later, however, she left school and married Curt Alexander, an Army career man. In 1917, they moved to the Panama Canal Zone, where their daughter was born. Two of Bogan's poems, "Betrothed," and "The Young Wife," were published that year in the magazine *Others*. In 1918, she returned to the United States with her daughter; her marriage broke up soon afterward.

Bogan continued to write and she held a number of jobs, including work at various branches of the New York Public Library. Her first book, *Body of This Death*, was published in 1923. A year later she began writing book reviews and accepted the managing editorship of *The Measure*. Her second book, *Dark Summer*, was published in 1929, and in 1930 she received the John Reed Memorial Prize from *Poetry*. A year later, close to a nervous breakdown, she entered the New York Neurological Institute. Her recovery was speedy, and a month later she resumed her normal life.

In 1933, Bogan received a Guggenheim Fellowship for writing abroad, went to Europe, and, upon her return, had another brief breakdown. Her third book, *The Sleeping Fury*, was published in 1937, and *Poems and New Poems* appeared in 1941.

From 1948 through 1968, Bogan taught at seven different universities ranging from the University of Washington to New York University. She continued to write poetry and criticism, which was collected and published in 1955 as *Selected Criticism: Poetry and Prose*, and she made several collaborative translations: Goethe's *Elective Affinities* with Elizabeth Mayer, poems by Paul Valéry with May Sarton, and *The Journals of Jules Renard* with Elizabeth Roget. Bogan also continued to receive awards: she won the Bollingen Prize in 1955, a $5,000 prize from The American Academy of Poets in 1959, the Senior Creative Arts Award from Brandeis in 1962, and a $10,000 prize from the National Endowment for the Arts. Her last book of poetry, *The Blue Estuaries: Poems 1923–1968*, was published in 1969. A year later, on February 4, 1970, Louise Bogan died. *A Poet's Alphabet: Reflections on the Literary Art and Vocation* was published posthumously.

Contributors

HAROLD BLOOM is Sterling Professor of the Humanities at Yale University and Henry W. and Albert A. Berg Professor of English at the New York University Graduate School. He is the author of over 20 books, including *Shelley's Mythmaking* (1959), *The Visionary Company* (1961), *Blake's Apocalypse* (1963), *Yeats* (1970), *A Map of Misreading* (1975), *Kabbalah and Criticism* (1975), *Agon: Toward a Theory of Revisionism* (1982), *The American Religion* (1992), *The Western Canon* (1994), and *Omens of Millennium: The Gnosis of Angels, Dreams, and Resurrection* (1996). *The Anxiety of Influence* (1973) sets forth Professor Bloom's provocative theory of the literary relationships between the great writers and their predecessors. His most recent books include *Shakespeare: The Invention of the Human*, a 1998 National Book Award finalist, and *How to Read and Why*, which was published in 2000. In 1999, Professor Bloom received the prestigious American Academy of Arts and Letters Gold Medal for Criticism.

JANE DONAHUE EBERWEIN is a professor of English at Oakland University in Rochester, Michigan.

SHIRA WOLOSKY teaches English at Yale University. She is the author of *Emily Dickinson: A Voice of War.*

JOANNE FEIT DIEHL teaches English at the University of California at Davis. She is the author of *Dickinson and the Romantic Imagination.*

SHARON CAMERON is a professor of English at The Johns Hopkins University. Her most recent book is *The Corporeal Self. Allegories of the Body in Melville and Hawthorne.*

RANDA K. DUBNICK teaches English at the University of Kansas.

ADALAIDE MORRIS teaches English at the University of Iowa. She has written many articles on American women poets, is the author of *Wallace Stevens: Imagination and Faith,* and coeditor of *Extended Outlooks: The Iowa Review Collection of Contemporary Women Writers.*

BONNIE COSTELLO is an assistant professor of English at Boston University. She is the author of *Marianne Moore: Imaginary Possessions.*

DAVID BROMWICH is a professor of English at Princeton University.

DIANE WOOD MIDDLEBROOK is a professor of English at Stanford University.

SANDRA COOKSON is a poet and critic. She has taught at the University of Connecticut, Storrs.

Bibliography

Abel, Elizabeth, ed. *Writing and Sexual Difference*. Chicago: The University of Chicago Press, 1982.

Evans, Mari, ed. *Black Women Writers (1950–1980): A Critical Evaluation*. New York: Anchor Press/Doubleday, 1984.

Gilbert, Sandra M., and Susan Gubar, eds. *Shakespeare's Sisters: Feminist Essays on Women Poets*. Bloomington: Indiana University Press, 1979.

Jacobus, Mary, ed. *Women Writing and Writing About Women*. London: Croom Helm in association with The Oxford Women's Studies Committee, 1979.

McConnell-Ginet, Sally, Ruth Barker, and Nelly Furman, eds. *Women and Language in Literature and Society*. New York: Praeger Publishers, 1980.

Moers, Ellen. *Literary Women*. Garden City, NY: Doubleday and Company, 1979.

Rich, Adrienne. *On Lies, Secrets and Silence*. New York: W. W. Norton and Company, 1979.

Vendler, Helen. *Part of Nature, Part of Us*. Cambridge: Harvard University Press, 1980.

ANNE BRADSTREET

Ball, Kenneth R. "Puritan Humility in Anne Bradstreet's Poetry." *Cithera* 13 (November 1973): 29–41.

McCay, Mary A. "Anne Hutchinson and Anne Bradstreet: Two New England Women." *Dutch Quarterly Review* 11, no. 1 (1981): 2–21.

Mawer, Randall R. " 'Farewel Dear Babe': Bradstreet's Elegy for Elizabeth." *Early American Literature* 15, no. 1 (Spring 1980): 29–41.

Rosenmeier, Rosamund. "Divine Translation: A Contribution to the Study of Anne Bradstreet's Method in the Marriage Poems." *Early American Literature* 12, no. 2 (Fall 1977): 121–34.

Salska, Agnieszka. "Puritan Poetry: Its Public and Private Strain." *Early American Literature* 19, no. 2 (Fall 1984): 167–21.

Stanford, Ann. *Anne Bradstreet: The Wordly Puritan: An Introduction to Her Poetry*. New York: Burt Franklin and Company, 1974.

EMILY DICKINSON

Beauchamp, William. "Riffaterre's *Semiotics of Poetry* with an Illustration in the Poetry of Emily Dickinson." *CENTRUM* 1, no. 1 (Spring 1981): 36–47.

Blake, Caesar R., and Carlton F. Wells, eds. *The Recognition of Emily Dickinson*. Ann Arbor: University of Michigan Press, 1968.

Burbick, Joan. "Emily Dickinson and the Revenge of the Nerves." *Women's Studies* 7, nos. 1 and 2 (1980): 95–110.

Cameron, Sharon. *Lyric Time: Dickinson and the Limits of Genre*. Baltimore: The Johns Hopkins University Press, 1979.

Diehl, Joanne Feit. "Dickinson and Bloom: An Antithetical Reading of Romanticism." *Texas Studies in Literature and Language* 23 (1981): 418–41.

Frye, Northrop. "Emily Dickinson." In *Major Writers of America*, edited by Perry Miller. New York: Harcourt, Brace and World, Inc., 1962.

Gilbert, Sandra M., and Susan Gubar. "A Woman-White: Emily Dickinson's Yarn of Pearl." In *The Madwoman in the Attic*. New Haven: Yale University Press, 1979.

Homans, Margaret. *Women Writers and Poetic Identity*. Princeton: Princeton University Press, 1980.

Juhasz, Suzanne, ed. *Feminist Critics Read Emily Dickinson*. Bloomington: Indiana University Press, 1983.

Keller, Karl. *The Only Kangaroo among the Beauty: Emily Dickinson's America*. Baltimore: The Johns Hopkins University Press, 1979.

Knox, Helene. "Metaphor and Metonymy in Emily Dickinson's Figurative Thinking." *Massachusetts Studies in English* 7/8 (1981): 49–56.

Wolosky, Shira. *Emily Dickinson: A Voice of War*. New Haven: Yale University Press, 1984.

GERTRUDE STEIN

Bridgeman, Richard. *Gertrude Stein in Pieces*. New York: Oxford University Press, 1970.

DeKoven, Marianne. "Gertrude Stein and Modern Painting: Beyond Literary Cubism." *Contemporary Literature* 22, no. 1 (Winter 1981): 81–95.

Delta, a review of the Centre d'Etude et de Recherches sur les écrivains du sud aux Etats-Unis (Center of Studies and Research on Writers of the Southern United States). Special issue on Gertrude Stein, no. 10 (May 1980).

Dubnick, Randa. *The Structure of Obscurity: Gertrude Stein, Language and Cubism*. Bloomington: Indiana University Press, 1984.

Liston, Maureen R. *Gertrude Stein: An Annotated Critical Bibliography*. Kent: Kent State University Press, 1979.

Perloff, Marjorie. "Poetry As Word System: The Art of Gertrude Stein." *American Poetry Review* 10 (1979): 33–43.

Steiner, Wendy. *Exact Resemblance to Exact Resemblance: The Literary Portraiture of Gertrude Stein*. New Haven: Yale University Press, 1978.

Sutherland, Donald. *Gertrude Stein: A Biography of Her Work*. New Haven: Yale University Press, 1951.

Walker, Jayne L. *The Making of a Modernist: Gertrude Stein from* Three Lives *to* Tender Buttons. Amherst: University of Massachusetts Press, 1984.

Weinstein, Norman. *Gertrude Stein and the Literature of Modern Consciousness*. New York: Frederick Ungar Publishing Company, 1970.

H. D. (HILDA DOOLITTLE)

DuPlessis, Rachel Blau. "Romantic Thralldom in H. D." *Contemporary Literature* 20, no. 2 (Spring 1979): 178–203.

DuPlessis, Rachel Blau, and Susan Stanford. "Woman is Perfect: H. D.'s Debate With Freud." *Feminist Studies* 7, no. 3 (Fall 1981): 417–30.

Friedman, Susan. "Creating a Woman's Mythology: H. D.'s *Helen in Egypt.*" *Women's Studies* 5, no. 2 (1977): 163–97.

Gelpi, Albert. "Hilda in Egypt." *The Southern Review* 18, no. 2 (Summer 1982): 233–50.

Gilbert, Sandra M. "H. D.? Who Was She?" *Contemporary Literature* 24, no. 4 (Winter 1983): 496–511.

Gubar, Susan. "The Echoing Spell of H. D.'s *Trilogy.*" *Contemporary Literature* 19, no. 2 (Spring 1978): 196–218.

————. "Sapphistries." *Signs 10*, no. 1 (Autumn 1984): 43–62.

Morris, Adalaide. "Reading H. D.'s 'Helios and Athene.' " *Iowa Review* 12, no. 2/3 (Spring/Summer 1981): 155–63.

MARIANNE MOORE

Abbott, Craig S. *Marianne Moore: A Descriptive Bibliography*. Pittsburgh: University of Pittsburgh Press, 1977.

Boroff, Marie. *Language and the Poet: Verbal Artistry in Frost, Stevens and Moore*. Chicago: The University of Chicago Press, 1979.

Costello, Bonnie. "Marianne Moore and Elizabeth Bishop: Friendship and Influence." *Twentieth Century Literature* (Marianne Moore issue) 30, no. 2/3 (Summer/Fall 1984): 130–49.

_____. *Marianne Moore: Imaginary Possessions*. Cambridge: Harvard University Press, 1981.

Glatstein, Jacob. "Marianne Moore." Translated by Doris Vidaver. *Yiddish* 6, no. 1 (Spring 1985): 67–73.

Newlin, Margaret. " 'Unhelpful Hymen!': Marianne Moore and Hilda Doolittle." *Essays in Criticism* 27, no. 3 (July 1977): 216–30.

Phillips, Elizabeth. *Marianne Moore*. New York: Frederick Ungar Publishing Company, 1982.

LOUISE BOGAN

Bowles, Gloria. "Louise Bogan: To be (or not to be?) a Woman Poet." *Women's Studies* 5, no. 2 (1977): 131–35.

Collins, Martha, ed. *Critical Essays on Louise Bogan*. Boston: G. K. Hall and Company, 1984.

Moore, Patrick. "Symbol, Mask and Meter in the Poetry of Louise Bogan." In *Gender and Literary Voice*. New York: Holmes and Meier Publishers, Inc., 1980.

Ridgeway, Jacqueline. "The Necessity of Form to the Poetry of Louise Bogan." *Women's Studies* 5, no. 2 (1977): 137–49.

Acknowledgments

"'No rhet'ric we expect': Argumentation in Bradstreet's 'The Prologue'" by Jane Donahue Eberwein from *Early American Literature* 16, no. 1 (Spring 1981), © 1981 by University of North Carolina Press. Reprinted by permission of the University of North Carolina Press.

"Emily Dickinson: A Voice of War" (originally entitled "Introduction") by Shira Wolosky from *Emily Dickinson: A Voice of War* by Shira Wolosky, © 1984 by Yale University. Reprinted by permission of Yale University Press.

"Ransom in a Voice': Language as Defense in Dickinson's Poetry" by Joanne Feit Diehl from *Feminist Critics Read Emily Dickinson*, edited by Suzanne Juhasz, © 1983 by Indiana University Press. Reprinted by permission.

"*Et in Arcadia Ego:* Representation, Death, and the Problem of Boundary in Emily Dickinson" (originally entitled "*Et in Arcadia Ego:* Representation, Death, and the Problem of Boundary") by Sharon Cameron from *Lyric Time: Dickinson and the Limits of Genre* by Sharon Cameron, © 1979 by The Johns Hopkins University Press. Reprinted by permission.

"Two Types of Obscurity in the Writings of Gertrude Stein" by Randa K. Dubnick from *The Emporia State Research Studies* 24, no. 3 (Winter 1976), © 1976 by Emporia Kansas State College. Reprinted by permission of the author.

"The Concept of Projection: H. D.'s Visionary Powers" by Adalaide Morris from *Contemporary Literature* 25, no. 4 (Winter 1984), © 1984 by the Board of Regents of the University of Wisconsin System. Reprinted by permission of the University of Wisconsin Press.

"The 'Feminine' Language of Marianne Moore" by Bonnie Costello adapted from *Women and Language in Literature and Society*, edited by Sally McConnell-Ginet, Ruth Borker, and Nelly Furman, © 1980 by Praeger Publishers. Reprinted by permission of Greenwood Publishing Group, Inc.

"Emphatic Reticence in Marianne Moore's Poems" (originally entitled "Marianne Moore's Poems") by David Bromwich from *Poetry* 139, no. 6 (March 1982), © 1982 by the Modern Poetry Association. Reprinted by permission of the author.

"The Problem of the Woman Artist: Louise Bogan, 'The Alchemist' " by Diane Wood Middlebrook from *Critical Essays on Louise Bogan*, edited by Martha Collins, © 1984 by Martha Collins. Reprinted by permission of Twayne Publishers, Gale Group.

"'The Repressed Becomes the Poem': Landscape and Quest in Two Poems by Louise Bogan" by Sandra Cookson from *Critical Essays on Louise Bogan*, edited by Martha Collins, © 1984 by Martha Collins. Reprinted by permission of Twayne Publishers, Gale Group.

Index